WITHDR.

Robin to the Rescue

Robin to the RESCUE

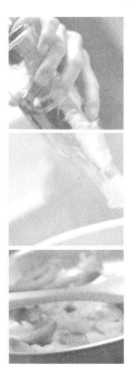

Quick & Simple Recipes
for Delicious Home Cooking

Robin Miller

The Taunton Press

This book (and my life) is dedicated to my precious little boys, Kyle and Luke,

and to my husband, Darrin. You provide the spirit and joy that make each

new day better than the last.

Text © 2008 by Robin Miller
Photographs © 2008 by Judd Pilossof (food photography) and Jeremy Frechette (photos of author)

The Taunton Press
Inspiration for hands-on living®

The Taunton Press, Inc., 63 South Main Street, PO Box 5506, Newtown, CT 06470-5506
e-mail: tp@taunton.com

Editor: Pam Hoenig
Copy editor: Valerie Cimino
Proofreader: Li Agen
Indexer: Heidi Blough
Jacket/Cover design: Carol Singer and Kimberly Adis
Interior design & layout: Richard Oriolo
Photographers: Jeremy Frechette (photos of Robin); Judd Pilossof (food photography)
Food stylist for food photography: Liz Duffy

Library of Congress Cataloging-in-Publication Data
Miller, Robin, 1964-
  Robin to the rescue : quick & simple recipes for delicious home cooking / Robin Miller.
      p. cm.
  Includes bibliographical references and index.
  ISBN 978-1-60085-004-2 (alk. paper)
  1. Quick and easy cookery. I. Title.

TX833.5.M5455 2008
641.5'55--dc22

                              2007042719

Printed in the United States of America
10 9 8 7 6 5 4 3 2 1

The following names/manufacturers appearing in *Robin to the Rescue* are trademarks: Bazooka®,
Bisquick®, Clamato®, Cuisinart®, Del Monte®, McCormick®, Nutella®, SpaghettiOs®, Tabasco®

Acknowledgments

I have several people to thank for this book, an accomplishment that wouldn't have been possible without some key players. First and foremost, *Robin to the Rescue* is the perfect extension of my Food Network show, *Quick Fix Meals*, because the strategies from the show are used throughout the book. Suffice it to say, if it weren't for Food Network, you might not know my strategies! First, Brooke Johnson, President of Food Network, thanks for another amazing year; I feel your overwhelming support every day, whether we communicate or not. Bob Tuschman, thanks for giving me the chance to share my recipes and ideas with the folks at home watching Food Network; if it weren't for you, I wouldn't be where I am today. Ronnie Weinstock, thanks for grabbing the show by the "horns" and turning it into something amazing; your vision and gumption took my show to the next level and beyond.

As for my show's production, Mark Dissin, you've made *Quick Fix Meals* the best it can be (until we make it better!). I love your "shoot from the hip" style and I believe you get the most from me on set. Jimmy Zankel, I cherish your never-ending words of encouragement; with your input, you turn my words on paper into mouth-watering delicacies on air. Mike Schear, thanks for directing each show with ease and for your incredible attention to detail. Ashley Archer and Charlie Granquist, what can I say? Your culinary direction on set is seamless and you make every act run smoothly. You are not only true professionals, but also a joy to be around. Jen Messina, I adore the way you dance around the set trying to show me the time cards! Your smiling face is there to greet me every morning and I truly look forward to it. Jenna Zimmerman, you're always ready with the slate! Thanks for bringing your great spirit to the set every day. Eddie Ruotolo, my audio man, thanks for making me sound great and for taking care of my little boys when they came to the studio—you made them feel like little rock stars. Curt Lachowin, my audio from "upstairs," thanks for starting every day with "Have a good show!" Jay, Hugh, Tori, and Claus, the extraordinary camera team, thanks for following me around the kitchen; you don't miss a beat! Dustin Drury, thanks for making sure I'm "all set." Wendy Waxman, your prop design is lovely and you've made my studio kitchen feel like my home. Santos Loo and Mariana Black, although I don't see you much during the day, please know that I appreciate the behind-the-scenes work you do for every act (Mariana, thanks for the adorable "Kyle's Yogurt" and "Luke's Cherry Pie" labels!). Meredith Carlin, thanks for handling every detail (from the largest to the minutiae). You work tirelessly on the show and I truly appreciate it. Keira Karlin, somehow you manage to make me look better than I could ever look in "real life," even in HD! Rita Botelho, thank you for making me feel comfortable and stylish at the same time. You've also become a true friend. Victor Lorenzo, thanks for your boundless energy and willingness to help me whenever I need anything. You're an amazing individual and I appreciate your caring nature.

In the publicity department, Carrie Welch, thanks not only for your amazing PR work, but also for that energetic smile you bring to every venue. Lauren Mueller, I can't imagine being at Food Network without you. Your public relations efforts aside (which are both brilliant and boundless), you've been there for me, night and day, since my first day at the network. You've become a dear friend and I am lucky to know you.

Now for the folks responsible for this book. Pam Hoenig, my editor, our second book together was a breeze! Your great words of wisdom have made the book the best it can be. Also at Taunton, Melissa Possick, thanks for your tireless publicity efforts and words of encouragement when I needed them. Allison Hollett, thanks for joining me on the book tour. You were a breath of fresh air in cities nationwide! Valerie Cimino, thanks for running a fine-toothed comb through this manuscript; you did a wonderful job. Katie Benoit, you should get worker's compensation for handling my crazy schedule! Thank you Wendi Mijal for managing and editing the photography (just gorgeous!) and Carol Singer for the fantastic book design. Kristin, the props for the book cover were amazing. Ilona Gollinger at Conair, thanks for donating the Cuisinart® slow cooker and food processor that appear on the dazzling pages of this book. Thank you, Kevin Hamric at Taunton for your vigorous sales efforts and John Baciagalupi for getting my books into the right stores for folks who need Quick Fix Meals every week.

At Food Network, Susan Stockton, thanks for your creativity and forethought and for making our second book together downright awesome! You are an absolute dream to work with. Seth McGinnis, your creative ideas on paper reveal what a true talent you are. In the Food Network kitchens, thank you Jay Brooks, Charlie Granquist, Bob Hoebee, and Santos Loo for the incredible food styling. Your outstanding vision and creativity turn my simple recipes into works-of-art on paper.

Alberto Machuca, thank you for making me look beautiful for the book cover—I don't know how you do it! Must be something in your big bag of tricks! Jeremy Frechette, once again, thanks for turning a photo shoot into a dance party! You have amazing talent and I am fortunate to get to work with you. And thanks to Judd Pilossof for his beautiful food photography inside the book.

A *huge* thanks goes out to my literary agent, Debra Goldstein. I sincerely appreciate the countless hours you spent making sure *everything* regarding this book was in place. I slept soundly at night knowing you had the controls.

Lastly, and most importantly, my family. Darrin, thanks for keeping the family strong, safe, and sound while I travel for my shows and book events. Nothing makes me feel safer than knowing you're at the helm. To my boys, Kyle and Luke, having you on set was one of the happiest moments of my life. You finally got to see where "mommy works" and you were fantastic little chefs on camera. I was proud and honored to have you with me. Thank you for *being you* and for making my life complete.

Contents

Robin to the Rescue:
The Quick Fix Way

The goal behind *Robin to the Rescue* is simple: to give you a variety of strategies for getting weeknight meals to the table without fussing, stressing, or spending a lot of time doing it. The recipes in this book are easy and fast, using everyday ingredients in delicious, nutritious, and time-efficient ways. I also realize that for busy home cooks every day is busy in a different way. For that reason, I've taken the recipes in this book one step further, giving you alternative prep options for every single one. Take Italian Braised Beef over Egg Noodles (page 170), which is ready in about 35 minutes. But what if you're going to be out all day, either at work or running errands, and want dinner on the table as soon as you get home? Well, you can also make this delicious dish in the slow cooker, in 4 hours on HIGH or 6 to 8 hours on LOW, whatever best suits your schedule. You can also make a Meal Kit of it, so, with just a little pre-prep, you can have a dinner on the table in 5 minutes. *Robin to the Rescue* is all about helping you get good food on the table with the least amount of effort in the way that makes the most sense to you and your family.

Here's a rundown on the mealtime strategies and meal-planning features you'll find in *Robin to the Rescue*:

@ **MAKE IT MEAL KIT:** Meal Kits are partially prepped and assembled meals that you start in advance and finish later. The beauty of a Meal Kit is that you prepare it when you've got a little extra time (say, when you're making dinner on the weekend). When you're ready to finish the meal (say, Monday at 6 p.m. when everyone's starved and cranky!), you simply pick up where you left off, without having to spend any extra time dicing, slicing, sautéing, waiting for water to boil, and so on. Items in a Meal Kit typically include:

- **pre-chopped vegetables (in some cases, pre-roasted or pre-sautéed vegetables)**
- **coated or crusted chicken breasts or turkey tenderloin**
- **marinated beef or pork**
- **pre-cooked rice or pasta**
- **prepared sauces, vinaigrettes, glazes, or dips**

I will show you how to start the meal and then package it so that it lasts until you're ready to complete it (either in the fridge or freezer or on the countertop). Thanks to the Meal Kit strategy, by starting a recipe in advance, you can finish it later in about 20 minutes or less—sometimes in just 5 minutes! Imagine this: you can race home after work on Tuesday and enjoy Seared Almond-Crusted Chicken with Baby Corn & Tomatoes (page 84) in just minutes because it's ready and waiting in your refrigerator. Or how about Beef & Mushroom Tart (page 161) on Wednesday? Or Clams Rockefeller (page 203) for your Friday night guests? With a Meal Kit, a little bit of pre-planning will reap delicious, quick results.

@ **BANK A BATCH:** My philosophy of "do it once, enjoy it twice" plays out in my Bank a Batch strategy. When you're making a dish, double the recipe and pop the extra meal in the fridge or freezer to be pulled out when you've got to get dinner on the table immediately. Banked meals are ideal for those days when you clearly have *no* time to make dinner, even if you have a Meal Kit stashed in the refrigerator. When you're time-starved (and the rest of the family is plain-old "starved"), you can just pull a banked meal from the freezer, defrost it in the microwave, and serve up a fabulous, homemade meal in no time. Yes, lasagna is an outstanding freezer staple, but imagine stocking your ice box with Thai Chicken & Noodles (page 94), Orange-Garlic Shrimp (page 213), and Chipotle Pork Soft Tacos (page 144). Nothing's better than money (or meals!) in the bank!

@ SLOW COOK IT: There's no doubt about it—the slow cooker is a Quick Fix cook's ally in the kitchen. In this book, I will show you how to take a stovetop meal and transform it into a slow-cooked one for those days when you know you're going to be out of the house for most of the day. Simply load up the slow cooker in the morning, turn it on, and get on with your day. When you're finished working and/or running errands, you'll come home to a family-friendly, mouthwatering meal, hot out of the slow cooker.

@ MORPH IT: *Morphing* means to take a recipe (or part of the recipe) that you're already making, double it, and transform the extras into an entirely different meal. My attitude is, if I'm going to cook a dish, I'd like to get more than one night out of it! That doesn't mean I want to make turkey melts with my leftover turkey (although those are yummy too). Instead, I can turn my Cereal-Crusted Chicken with Curry Cream (page 92) into Warm Chicken–Cherry Waldorf in Romaine (page 90), or Filet Mignon with Spicy Rémoulade (page 178) into Warm Steak & Penne Salad with Tomato Soup French Dressing (page 194). Cook once, enjoy the payoff for many meals to come.

@ HAVE IT YOUR WAY: Have it Your Way allows you to take a recipe you love and enjoy it a different way by switching up the ingredients. For example, swap broccoli for green beans in Roasted Green Beans with Grape Tomatoes & Olives (page 242) or turn the roasted tomato-olive mixture from the same recipe into a delicious pasta sauce. Or substitute chicken for beef in the Moroccan Beef Stew (page 172). You can also create vegetarian meals, such as replacing chicken with tofu in Chicken with Eggplant, Capers & Black Olives (page 86). There are no hard and fast rules with my recipes; I just want you to have fun and enjoy every minute and every bite.

@ 5 INGREDIENTS OR LESS: In *Robin to the Rescue* you're going to find a lot of recipes that call for 5 ingredients or less. (Remember, when counting the number of ingredients, salt, pepper, olive oil, and water don't count. I assume you have those on hand.) For a full list of them, check out pages 305–306. Fewer ingredients means less prep but *not* less flavor—enjoy Baked Chicken with Green Spinach–Horseradish Sauce (page 112), Roasted Garlic–Artichoke Dip (page 28), and Pork Tenderloin with Strawberry Glaze (page 142).

@ **THE QUICK FIX RECIPE INDEX:** Starting on page 302 you'll find a recipe index organized so you see at a glance which recipes require 5 ingredients or less and which you can Meal Kit, Bank a Batch of, Slow Cook, or Morph. In addition, to give you even more options, I've indexed all the sauces, glazes, marinades, vinaigrettes, dressings, and dips used in my recipes so you can access them fast if you're looking for a new way to prepare chicken, or fish, or beef, or whatever it is you have taste for. So, for example, by checking the index, you'll find out that the Honey–Sesame Dressing in Turkey–Spinach Salad with Strawberries, Kiwi & Cashews (page 128) makes an excellent marinade for grilled shrimp, salmon, or roasted chicken breasts. Or that instead of topping pan-seared chicken with Artichoke–Basil Pesto (page 114), you can fold the pesto into cooked pasta or spoon it over roasted salmon. One sauce, multiple uses—that's the key to the Quick Fix way of cooking.

Basically, I've tried to make this book as versatile, flexible, and useful as possible for people who want to enjoy wonderful, fresh food in a new way every day.

. . . getting weeknight meals

to the table without fussing,

stressing, or spending a lot

of time doing it.

Your Quick Fix Stash

Stock your pantry the right way and you'll be able to put most of my recipes together in minutes with little or no pre-planning. In this chart, I'm going to give you the Quick Fix Stash lowdown—the ingredients you want to make sure you always have on hand in your fridge, freezer, and cupboard. I am going to assume that you have a decent selection of dried herbs and spices, and salt and pepper.

I am the queen of buying in bulk. I buy chicken, turkey (whole tenderloins and ground), pork (tenderloins and chops), and beef (steaks and ground sirloin) in large portions, and then (as you'll see in the chart) I prep everything *before* it goes into the freezer. That way, I am ready to throw the meat into a hot pan or thread it onto a skewer after a quick thaw in the microwave—though for some of my recipes you don't even need to do that! The same goes for vegetables.

YOUR PANTRY STASH

STORAGE TIME: **Unopened items, 6 months to 1 year; opened items, 3 months**

Oils: olive, toasted sesame, canola, peanut, flavored olive oils	Canned tuna (white and light in water)	Bread crumbs: plain and seasoned
Vinegar: balsamic, red wine, white wine, mirin (rice wine)	Canned clams (chopped and whole baby clams)	Crackers, oats, and cereals (all three can be transformed into crunchy coatings for chicken and fish)
Canned beans: white, black, pink, navy, kidney, chickpeas	Canned salmon	
Canned tomatoes (whole, diced, pureed)	Reduced-sodium broths: chicken, vegetable, beef	Rice: white, brown, basmati, jasmine (instant and regular)
Canned tomato sauce	Fruit preserves and marmalades	Couscous
Canned tomato paste	Oil-packed sun-dried tomatoes	Quinoa
Canned and jarred artichoke hearts (in marinade and water-packed)	Roasted red peppers	Pasta: a variety of shapes and sizes
	Nuts: peanuts, cashews, almonds, pistachios, pine nuts, walnuts	Cornstarch (for instant gravies)
	Seeds: sunflower, sesame	

YOUR FRIDGE & FREEZER STASH

The Refrigerator Door

STORAGE TIME: **6 months for bottled sauces, condiments, olives, and capers; 5 days for pestos and tapenades**

Olives (pitted, stuffed): kalamata, niçoise, oil-cured	Hot sauce	Prepared horseradish
Asian sauces: hoisin, reduced-sodium soy sauce, black bean, tamari	Worcestershire sauce	Ketchup
	Liquid smoke	Mayonnaise
	Mustard (honey, spicy, country-style)	Capers

Dairy and Eggs

STORAGE TIME: Hard cheeses, 2 weeks in the fridge, 3 months in the freezer; soft cheeses, 1 week in the fridge, 3 months in the freezer; other products, 1 week in the fridge

Cheese (cheddar, mozzarella, Monterey Jack, Swiss, blue, feta, goat): cubed, shredded, sliced, crumbled

Parmesan cheese: chunk, grated, shredded

Low-fat sour cream

Low-fat plain and flavored yogurt

Low-fat milk

Butter

Eggs

Frozen stuffed pasta (manicotti, ravioli, tortellini)

Vegetables & Fruit

STORAGE TIME: 5 days in the refrigerator, 3 months in the freezer (package in sealable plastic containers or bags in 1-cup measures)

Onions: chopped or sliced

Carrots: chopped or shredded

Celery: chopped or cut into sticks

Bell peppers: chopped or sliced into thin strips

Garlic: minced or chopped

Packages of frozen vegetables: peas, corn, carrots, succotash, green beans, wax beans, snap peas, snow peas, broccoli, cauliflower

Packages of frozen fruit: strawberries, blackberries, raspberries, blueberries, sliced peaches

Meat/Fish/Poultry

STORAGE TIME: 3 days in the refrigerator, 3 months in the freezer (store in sealable plastic containers or bags or tightly wrapped in plastic, followed by heavy-duty aluminum foil)

CHICKEN Whole breasts (with bone or without), the breast halves separated into recipe-size portions (4 halves for 4 servings); they can then be further prepped by pounding them thin, cutting them into cubes, or cutting them into slices crosswise

TURKEY TENDERLOIN Store it whole (with or without a marinade; one tenderloin is enough for a meal), or prep it further by cutting it into cubes or 1-inch-thick medallions

GROUND TURKEY Working with 1 pound at a time, shape it into meatballs or patties

PORK TENDERLOIN Store it whole (with or without a marinade; one 1¼-pound tenderloin is enough for a meal), or prep it further by cutting it into cubes or 1-inch-thick medallions

PORK CHOPS Bone-in or boneless, trimmed of fat, packaged in meal portions

GROUND BEEF Working with 1 pound at a time, shape into meatballs or patties

STEAK Flank (with or without a marinade), sirloin, rib-eye, packaged in meal portions

SHRIMP Buy them frozen in 1-pound bags

SCALLOPS Sea or bay

FISH FILLETS & FISH STEAKS Tilapia, halibut, flounder, cod, bass, salmon, and/or tuna steaks or fillets in meal portions

Soups and Starters

WHY WRITE A CHAPTER THAT COMBINES starters with soups? Because you can enjoy either one before a meal, or you can combine the two to make a complete meal. Mix and match the recipes in this chapter and you'll be eating a variety of fun meals all week long, without spending lots of time in the kitchen.

Many of my soups can be served warm or chilled and all can be made ahead or right before eating. Soups work well with Quick Fix strategies, and all my soups take well to refrigeration for at least three days and freezing for at least three months. For frozen soup, you can thaw and reheat right in the same pot or container, whether it's stovetop or in the microwave.

When I serve soup before a meal, I typically serve smaller portions (around 1 cup). When I serve it as a main course, I ladle out at least 2 cups and round out the meal with rolls or bread. Add a mixed green salad and you can call it a day—and a good day, that's for sure!

Starters are fun to make *and* fun to serve. Plus, let's face it, kids love eating with their hands, so starters and little bites are perfect for smaller mouths. The same is true of my pizzas, calzones, and breads—they're fantastic to munch on either at a party, before dinner, or as dinner with a salad served alongside. Pizzas, calzones, and quiches can be complete meals by themselves, but I put them with starters because, when served in smaller portions, they're an excellent way to begin a meal.

. . . you'll be eating a variety of fun meals

all week long, without spending lots

of time in the kitchen.

Tomato Gazpacho with Pineapple & Jícama

No cooking required! If you want, add crab, shrimp, lobster, or any cooked firm white fish (such as halibut, cod, or monkfish). Serve this up with Onion Knots (page 264).

Total Time: 10–15 minutes

Prep time: 10–15 minutes

Serves 4

Two 28-ounce cans diced tomatoes, drained

1 cup Clamato® or tomato juice

1 cup diced fresh or canned pineapple

1 medium green bell pepper, seeded and diced

½ cup peeled and finely diced jícama

¼ cup finely chopped scallions (white and green parts)

2 tablespoons chopped fresh parsley

¼ teaspoon hot sauce

Salt and freshly ground black pepper to taste

1. Place the tomatoes in a food processor and process until finely chopped (but not pureed).

2. Transfer to a large bowl and stir in the Clamato juice, pineapple, bell pepper, jícama, scallions, parsley, and hot sauce. Season with salt and pepper. Serve immediately or chill for 30 minutes before serving.

bank a batch Make a double batch and store the extra for up to 3 months in the freezer. Thaw overnight in the refrigerator before serving (I don't recommend thawing in the microwave because the heat will "cook" the vegetables).

morph it This also makes an excellent sauce for pasta or a marinade and/or sauce for chicken, shrimp, scallops, or baked white fish (such as cod, flounder, halibut, trout, or tilapia).

Wild Mushroom Soup with Arugula & Walnuts

This is an earthy, rich, and wonderful meal that's full of color, flavor, and crunch! Serve warm dinner rolls on the side and you'll please every palate at the table.

Total Time: 22–23 minutes
Prep time: 10 minutes
Active cooking time:
12–13 minutes

Serves 4

1 tablespoon unsalted butter

18 ounces wild mushrooms (any combination of chanterelle, oyster, shiitake, cremini, portabella, etc.), stems removed and caps sliced

½ cup chopped yellow onion

3 cloves garlic, minced

1 teaspoon dried thyme

1 cup dry white wine

6 cups reduced-sodium chicken broth

2 bay leaves

1 cup milk (preferably 1% milk fat or higher)

1 cup chopped arugula

¼ cup chopped walnuts

1. Melt the butter in a large saucepan over medium heat. Add the mushrooms, onion, and garlic and cook, stirring, until softened, about 5 minutes. Add the thyme and cook for 1 minute, until fragrant. Add the wine and simmer for 1 minute. Add the broth and bay leaves, bring to a simmer, and let simmer for 5 minutes. Remove the bay leaves and, using an immersion blender, puree until smooth (or use a regular blender and work in batches; return the soup to the pan). Add the milk and simmer for 1 minute to heat through.

2. Ladle the soup into bowls and top with a sprinkling of the arugula and walnuts.

make it a meal kit/bank a batch **Make the soup and store in a sealable container for up to 3 days in the refrigerator or 3 months in the freezer. Thaw overnight in the refrigerator or in the microwave for a few minutes on LOW. Reheat in a medium saucepan over medium heat or in the microwave for a few minutes on HIGH before topping with the arugula and walnuts.**

morph it **Make the soup with extra mushrooms from Wild Mushroom Turnovers with Romano Cheese (page 34), or make a double batch of mushrooms in this recipe (just don't double the onions, garlic, and thyme) and make the turnovers with the extras!**

. . . a wonderful meal that's full

of color, flavor, and crunch!

Cream of Asparagus Soup

I love fresh asparagus, and it's amazing in this belly-warmer. Serve with warm rolls or a loaf of Italian bread. I also like this with 5-Ingredient Watercress Salad with Pears, Goat Cheese & Pine Nuts (page 283).

Total Time: 18–20 minutes

Prep time: 10 minutes

Active cooking time: 8–10 minutes

Serves 4

2 teaspoons olive oil

2 teaspoons unsalted butter

1 cup chopped leeks (white part only)

1 pound asparagus, woody bottoms trimmed and stalks cut into 1-inch pieces

4 cups reduced-sodium vegetable or chicken broth

2 cups milk (preferably 1% milk fat or higher)

½ cup light sour cream, plus extra for garnish

1 tablespoon chopped fresh dill

1. Heat the oil and butter together in a large saucepan over medium-high heat. Add the leeks and cook, stirring, until softened, about 3 minutes. Add the asparagus and broth, bring to a simmer, and let simmer until the asparagus is knife-tender, 5 to 7 minutes.

2. Using an immersion blender, puree until smooth (or use a regular blender and work in batches; return the soup to the pan). Reduce the heat to low, stir in the milk and sour cream, and cook for 1 minute to heat through.

3. Ladle the soup into bowls and top with a dollop of sour cream and a sprinkling of dill.

make it a meal kit Chop the leeks and asparagus and store in a sealable container or plastic bag for up to 4 days in the refrigerator or 3 months in the freezer. When ready to finish the meal, cook the vegetables as directed (no need to thaw them first). The finished soup will also keep for up to 3 days in the refrigerator.

bank a batch Make a double batch of the soup and store the extra for up to 3 months in the freezer. Thaw overnight in the refrigerator or in the microwave for 4 to 6 minutes on LOW. Reheat in a large saucepan over medium heat or in the microwave for a few minutes on HIGH.

have it your way Jazz up the soup by topping it with a generous dollop of fresh lump crabmeat or steamed or grilled shrimp.

Instead of fresh asparagus, substitute 1 pound of frozen green peas and follow the recipe as instructed.

. . . jazz up the soup by topping

it with a generous dollop of fresh

lump crabmeat . . .

Sweet Potato Soup with Smoked Cheddar & Chives

The combination of sweet potatoes and smoky Cheddar is outstanding. You could also make the soup with an equal amount of Yukon Gold potatoes, as they're also slightly sweet. I like to serve this with 5-Ingredient Broccoli Ranch Slaw (page 269) on the side.

Total Time: 29 minutes

Prep time: 10 minutes

Active cooking time:
11 minutes

Walk-away time: 8 minutes

Serves 4

1¼ pounds sweet potatoes, peeled and cut into 2-inch pieces

2 teaspoons olive oil

2 leeks (white part only), rinsed well and chopped

2 cloves garlic, minced

1 tablespoon sugar

4 cups reduced-sodium vegetable broth

One 12-ounce can evaporated milk

Salt and freshly ground black pepper to taste

½ cup shredded smoked Cheddar cheese (or any smoked cheese)

¼ cup minced fresh chives

1. Place the potatoes in a large saucepan and pour over enough water to cover. Set the pan over high heat, bring to a boil, and let boil until the potatoes are fork-tender, about 8 minutes. Drain and set aside.

2. Heat the oil in a large saucepan over medium heat. Add the leeks, garlic, and sugar and cook, stirring, until the leeks soften, about 5 minutes. Add the sweet potatoes and broth, bring to a simmer, and let simmer for 5 minutes.

3. Using an immersion blender, puree until smooth (or use a regular blender and work in batches; return the soup to the pan). Add the evaporated milk and simmer for 1 minute to heat through. Season with salt and pepper.

4. Ladle the soup into bowls and top with a sprinkling of the smoked Cheddar and chives.

make it a meal kit Cut the potatoes and store them in the saucepan covered with cool water at room temperature or in the refrigerator for up to 8 hours. Chop the leeks and garlic and store in a sealable container or plastic bag for up to 3 days in the refrigerator. When ready to finish the dish, place the saucepan over the heat and cook as directed. Also, the finished soup will keep for up to 3 days in the refrigerator.

bank a batch Make a double batch and store the extra in a sealable container for up to 3 months in the freezer. Thaw overnight in the refrigerator or in the micro-wave for 4 to 6 minutes on LOW. Reheat in a large saucepan or in the microwave for 3 to 5 minutes on HIGH.

have it your way Instead of Cheddar cheese and chives, try Havarti and parsley, or Parmesan and basil!

. . . sweet potatoes and smoky

Cheddar—outstanding!

Vichyssoise with Sour Cream & Chives

Vichyssoise on the table in 22 minutes—your friends won't believe it! I serve the soup warm or chilled with a mixed green salad on the side or Baby Spinach Salad with Strawberry–Sherry Vinaigrette (page 279).

Total Time: 22 minutes

Prep time: 10 minutes

Active cooking time: 12 minutes

Serves 4

2 teaspoons unsalted butter

2 leeks (white part only), rinsed well and chopped

2 cloves garlic, minced

1 teaspoon dried thyme

1 teaspoon dried marjoram

1½ pounds Yukon Gold potatoes, peeled and cut into 2-inch chunks

6 cups reduced-sodium vegetable or chicken broth

1 cup sour cream

Salt and freshly ground black pepper to taste

1 tablespoon chopped fresh chives

1. Melt the butter in a large saucepan or Dutch oven over medium heat. Add the leeks and garlic and cook, stirring, until softened, about 3 minutes. Add the thyme and marjoram and cook for 1 minute, until fragrant. Add the potatoes and broth, increase the heat to high, and bring to a boil. Reduce the heat to medium-low, partially cover, and simmer until the potatoes are fork-tender, about 8 minutes.

2. Using an immersion blender, puree until smooth (or use a regular blender and work in batches; return the soup to the pan). Remove from the heat and whisk in the sour cream. Season with salt and pepper. Ladle the soup into bowls and top with a sprinkling of chives.

have it your way Instead of thyme and marjoram, try 1 teaspoon dried tarragon or, instead of sour cream, use plain yogurt and top with chopped fresh basil or parsley.

slow cook it Cook the leeks and garlic as directed with the thyme and marjoram (in the butter in a saucepan or skillet). Transfer the softened vegetables to a large slow cooker and add the potatoes and broth. Cover and cook on LOW for 6 to 8 hours or on HIGH for 3 to 4 hours. Puree and finish as directed.

Garlicky Cream of Broccoli Soup

What a warm and wonderful addition to any meal—and so simple to prepare. I like to serve sourdough rolls dunked in basil-infused olive oil on the side or Bruschetta with Chipotle–Cilantro Butter (page 265).

Total Time: 20 minutes
Prep time: 10 minutes
Walk-away time: 10 minutes

Serves 4

4 cups fresh or thawed frozen broccoli florets

½ cup chopped onion

1 stalk celery, chopped

1 medium carrot, peeled and chopped

4 cloves garlic, minced

3 cups reduced-sodium vegetable or chicken broth

2 cups milk (preferably 1% milk fat or higher)

Salt and freshly ground black pepper to taste

1. In a large saucepan, combine the broccoli, onion, celery, carrot, and garlic. Pour in the broth and set the pan over high heat. Bring to a boil, reduce the heat to medium, and simmer until the vegetables are knife-tender, about 10 minutes.

2. Using an immersion blender, puree until smooth (or use a regular blender and work in batches; return the soup to the pan). Add the milk and simmer for 1 minute to heat through. Season with salt and pepper and serve.

make it a meal kit Chop the vegetables and store in a sealable container or plastic bag for up to 4 days in the refrigerator or 3 months in the freezer. When ready to finish the meal, cook the vegetables as directed (no need to thaw them first). The finished soup will also keep for up to 3 days in the refrigerator.

bank a batch Make a double batch of the soup and store the extra for up to 3 months in the freezer. Thaw overnight in the refrigerator or in the microwave for 4 to 6 minutes on LOW. Reheat in a large saucepan over medium heat or in the microwave for a few minutes on HIGH.

have it your way Asparagus snapped into small pieces, cauliflower florets, or seeded and coarsely chopped red bell pepper may be substituted for the broccoli so you can enjoy a completely different soup any time you desire!

Three-Onion Soup with Cheese-Smothered Toast

Onion soup was one of my childhood favorites, and I still crave it! For a vegetarian version, substitute vegetable broth for the beef broth. I like to serve this with a red lettuce salad topped with cherry tomatoes and ranch dressing or Cucumber Salad with Oranges & Mint (page 272).

Total Time: 31–32 minutes

Prep time: 10 minutes

Active cooking time:
11–12 minutes

Walk-away time: 10 minutes

Serves 4

2 teaspoons olive oil

1 cup yellow onion, thinly sliced into half-moons

1 cup red onion, thinly sliced into half-moons

2 leeks (white part only), rinsed well and chopped

2 cloves garlic, minced

4 cups reduced-sodium beef broth

2 bay leaves

1 teaspoon dried thyme

½ teaspoon salt

¼ teaspoon freshly ground black pepper

4 slices French or Italian bread (about 1 inch thick)

1 cup shredded Swiss cheese

1. Heat the oil in a large saucepan or Dutch oven over medium heat. Add the onions, leeks, and garlic and cook, stirring, until soft, about 10 minutes.

2. Add the broth, bay leaves, thyme, salt, and pepper, increase the heat to high, and bring to a boil. Reduce the heat to medium, partially cover, and simmer for 10 minutes.

3. Remove the bay leaves and season to taste with salt and pepper.

4. Preheat the broiler.

5. Top each bread slice with an equal amount of the shredded cheese. Ladle the soup into individual ovenproof bowls and place a cheese-topped bread slice in the center of each bowl. Place the bowls on a baking sheet and broil until the cheese melts, 1 to 2 minutes. Serve immediately.

bank a batch Make a double batch of the soup and store the extra in a sealable container for up to 3 days in the refrigerator or 3 months in the freezer. Thaw overnight in the refrigerator or in the microwave for 4 to 6 minutes on LOW. Reheat in a large saucepan or in the microwave for a few minutes on HIGH before ladling into bowls and adding the bread.

have it your way If you don't have Swiss cheese handy, shredded mozzarella cheese works great too!

White Bean Soup with Andouille & Collard Greens

This soup is a complete meal! Just add a warm French baguette and you're golden. Feel free to experiment with different types of sausage, including the wonderful variety of flavored chicken sausages sold with the other poultry products at the supermarket.

Total Time: 25 minutes

Prep time: 10 minutes

Active cooking time: 15 minutes

Serves 4

1 tablespoon olive oil

1 cup chopped yellow onion

12 ounces andouille or chorizo sausage, diced

4 cups reduced-sodium chicken broth

Two 15-ounce cans cannellini or other white beans, drained

1 bunch fresh collard greens, washed well, tough stems removed, and chopped, or two 10-ounce packages frozen chopped collard greens, thawed

1 tablespoon sherry vinegar or red wine vinegar

Salt and freshly ground black pepper to taste

1. Heat the oil in large saucepan over medium-high heat. Add the onion and cook, stirring, until softened, about 3 minutes. Add the sausage and cook, stirring, for 2 minutes. Add the broth and bring to a simmer.

2. Using a fork, slightly mash most of the white beans and add to the pan. Simmer for 5 minutes, then add the collard greens and simmer until wilted, about 3 minutes. Stir in the vinegar, season with salt and pepper, and serve.

make it a meal kit Chop the onion, sausage, and collard greens and store each separately in sealable containers or plastic bags for up to 4 days in the refrigerator or 3 months in the freezer. When ready to finish the meal, cook as directed (no need to thaw anything first). The finished soup will also keep for up to 3 days in the refrigerator.

bank a batch **Make a double batch of the soup and store the extra for up to 3 months in the freezer. Thaw overnight in the refrigerator or in the microwave for 4 to 6 minutes on LOW. Reheat in a large saucepan over medium heat or in the microwave for a few minutes on HIGH.**

have it your way **Bank a Batch without the sausage so that you have a soup base that you can flavor later with any sausage you want.**

Instead of sausage, substitute soy bacon, soy sausage, or crumbled tempeh.

For a great party soup, add ¾ pound cooked medium shrimp or fresh lump crabmeat when you add the vinegar.

. . . add a warm French baguette

and you're golden.

Chicken Gumbo

If your spice rack is fully stocked, you can throw this together with ease. One ingredient you might not have is okra; it helps to thicken the gumbo. It's increasingly available in supermarkets fresh, but frozen works just fine. I like to serve my gumbo over rice to soak up the delicious broth.

Total Time: 29 minutes

Prep time: 10 minutes

Active cooking time: 9 minutes

Walk-away time: 10 minutes

Serves: 4 to 6

2 teaspoons olive oil

1 cup chopped onion

2 stalks celery, chopped

1 medium green bell pepper, seeded and chopped

1¼ pounds boneless, skinless chicken breasts, cut into 2-inch pieces

1 teaspoon dried thyme

1 teaspoon dried oregano

½ teaspoon salt

2 bay leaves

½ teaspoon onion powder

½ teaspoon garlic powder

½ teaspoon dry mustard

¼ teaspoon cayenne

¼ teaspoon freshly ground black pepper

One 10-ounce package frozen sliced okra, thawed (about 1½ cups sliced)

2 links andouille sausage or any seasoned cooked sausage, such as chorizo (2 to 3 ounces), diced

4 cups reduced-sodium chicken broth

2 cups tomato juice

Heat the oil in a large saucepan over medium-high heat. Add the onion, celery, and bell pepper and cook, stirring, until softened, about 3 minutes. Add the chicken and cook until browned on all sides, about 5 minutes. Add the thyme, oregano, salt, bay leaves, onion powder, garlic powder, mustard, cayenne, and black pepper and stir to coat. Cook for 1 minute, until the spices are fragrant. Add the okra, sausage, broth, and tomato juice and bring to a simmer. Reduce the heat to medium and simmer until the chicken is cooked through, about 10 minutes. Remove the bay leaves before serving.

make it a meal kit Mix together the dried spices, dice the sausage, and chop the vegetables. Store each of the components in sealable containers or plastic bags, the spices for up to 2 weeks at room temperature and the sausage and chopped vegetables for up to 4 days in the refrigerator or 3 months in the freezer. When ready to finish the meal, cook the vegetables (no need to thaw them first) and proceed as directed.

bank a batch Make a double batch of the soup and store in a sealable container for up to 3 days in the refrigerator or 3 months in the freezer. Thaw overnight in the refrigerator or in the microwave for 4 to 6 minutes on LOW. Reheat in a large saucepan over medium heat or in the microwave for a few minutes on HIGH.

have it your way For a New Orleans–style shrimp gumbo, substitute 1¼ pounds peeled, deveined, and cooked medium shrimp for the chicken.

slow cook it Combine all the ingredients in a medium to large slow cooker and mix well to combine. Cover and cook on LOW for 6 to 8 hours or HIGH for 3 to 4 hours.

For a New Orleans–style gumbo,

substitute shrimp for the chicken.

Southwestern Pork Soup

I like to serve this with tortilla chips crumbled over the top. Or try it with Sun-Dried Tomato Cheese Crackers: In a small bowl, combine ½ cup minced oil-packed sun-dried tomatoes, ⅓ cup cream cheese, and 1 tablespoon chopped fresh basil. Spread the mixture on whole-grain or water crackers.

Total Time: 28–33 minutes

Prep time: 10–15 minutes

Active cooking time: 8 minutes

Walk-away time: 10 minutes

Serves 4 to 6

2 teaspoons olive oil

1 cup chopped onion

1 medium green bell pepper, seeded and chopped

1 fresh jalapeño chile pepper, seeded and minced

3 cloves garlic, minced

One 1¼-pound pork tenderloin, trimmed of silverskin and cut into 1-inch pieces

1 teaspoon chili powder

1 teaspoon ground cumin

½ teaspoon salt

¼ teaspoon freshly ground black pepper

6 cups reduced-sodium chicken broth

One 14-ounce can diced tomatoes

One 15-ounce can pink beans, rinsed and drained

1 cup diced avocado

2 tablespoons chopped fresh cilantro

Lime wedges

1. Heat the oil in a large saucepan over medium-high heat. Add the onion, bell pepper, jalapeño, and garlic and cook, stirring, until softened, about 3 minutes. Add the pork and cook until browned on all sides, about 5 minutes total. Add the chili powder, cumin, salt, and pepper and stir to coat. Add the broth, tomatoes, and beans and bring to a simmer. Reduce the heat to medium and simmer until the pork is cooked through, about 10 minutes.

2. Ladle the soup into bowls, top with the avocado and cilantro, and serve with lime wedges on the side for squeezing.

make it a meal kit Mix together the dried spices and chop the vegetables. Store each separately in sealable containers or plastic bags, the spices for up to 2 weeks at room temperature and the vegetables for up to 4 days in the refrigerator or 3 months in the freezer. When ready to finish the meal, cook the vegetables (no need to thaw them first) and finish as directed. The finished soup, without the avocado, cilantro, and lime, will also keep for up to 3 days in the refrigerator.

bank a batch Make a double batch (without the avocado, cilantro, and lime wedges) and store the extra for up to 3 months in the freezer. Thaw overnight in the refrigerator or in the microwave for 4 to 6 minutes on LOW. Reheat in a large saucepan or in the microwave for 3 to 5 minutes on HIGH. Finish as directed.

slow cook it Combine the pork, onion, bell pepper, jalapeño, garlic, chili powder, cumin, salt, and pepper in a medium to large slow cooker and stir to combine. Stir in the broth, tomatoes, and beans, cover, and cook on LOW for 6 to 8 hours or HIGH for 3 to 4 hours. Finish as directed.

Roasted Garlic–Artichoke Dip

This is the perfect starter for any meal. Serve it with wedges of whole-grain pita and a variety of fresh vegetables, such as sliced zucchini and yellow squash, baby carrots, cherry or grape tomatoes, celery sticks, and broccoli and cauliflower florets.

Total Time: 20 minutes
Prep time: 5 minutes
Walk-away time: 15 minutes

Serves 4

½ cup garlic cloves, peeled

One 15-ounce can white beans, rinsed and drained

One 14-ounce can artichoke hearts, drained

2 tablespoons tahini (sesame paste)

1 tablespoon fresh lemon juice

Salt and freshly ground black pepper to taste

1. Preheat the oven to 400°F.

2. Wrap the garlic cloves in aluminum foil and roast until tender, about 15 minutes. Transfer to a blender or food processor, add the beans, artichoke hearts, tahini, and lemon juice, and process until smooth. Season with salt and pepper.

bank a batch Make a double batch of the dip and store the extra in a sealable container or plastic bag for up to 3 months in the freezer. Thaw overnight in the refrigerator (I don't recommend thawing in the microwave).

Make a double batch of the dip; it makes a great topping for grilled or rotisserie chicken. Store for up to 2 weeks in the refrigerator.

morph it Make a double batch of the roasted garlic and use the extra in Herb-Crusted Flounder Fillets in Roasted Garlic Sauce (page 222), Coconut Shrimp with Curried Tomato, Lime & Roasted Garlic Coulis (page 214), or Rotelle with Braised Zucchini, Roasted Garlic, Oregano & Feta (page 52). Store for up to 5 days in the refrigerator or 3 months in the freezer. Thaw overnight in the refrigerator or in the microwave for a few minutes on LOW.

Veggie Pot Stickers

I like to keep dozens of these in my freezer, so I can pull them out and have dinner on the table in minutes. Serve them with soy sauce, duck sauce, sweet and sour sauce, or hoisin sauce on the side for dipping. Add Cucumber Salad with Oranges & Mint (page 272) for a complete meal.

Total Time: 25 minutes
Prep time: 15 minutes
Active cooking time: 10 minutes

Makes 16 pot stickers;
serves 6 to 8

2 teaspoons toasted sesame oil

½ cup shredded carrots

½ cup shredded red or green cabbage

¼ cup chopped scallions (white and green parts)

1 tablespoon reduced-sodium soy sauce

16 wonton wrappers

1 tablespoon peanut or canola oil

1. Heat the sesame oil in a large skillet over medium heat. Add the carrots, cabbage, and scallions and cook, stirring, until the cabbage softens, about 3 minutes. Add the soy sauce and cook until the liquid evaporates, about 1 minute.

2. Arrange the wonton wrappers on a flat work surface. Spoon 1 heaping teaspoon of the vegetable mixture onto the center of each wrapper. Fold over the wrapper, making a triangle, and, using wet fingers (dip your fingers in a small bowl of water), press the edges together to seal.

3. Heat the peanut oil in a large skillet over medium heat. Add the wontons, in batches if necessary to prevent crowding, and cook until golden brown, about 3 minutes per side. Serve warm.

make it a meal kit Assemble the pot stickers and store, covered with plastic wrap, for up to 3 days in the refrigerator before cooking.

bank a batch Make a double batch and, before cooking, arrange the extras on a baking sheet and freeze until firm. Transfer them to a sealable container or plastic bag (to free up freezer space) and store for up to 3 months in the freezer. There's no need to thaw the pot stickers; cook them as directed above, then cover the pan and cook for 1 to 2 more minutes, until the filling is hot.

Red Pepper Hummus with Toasted Pita Triangles

I could easily eat a gallon of this stuff in one sitting. It's *that* good. Plus, it's colorful and fresh tasting, making it ideal for an appetizer, light snack, or savory treat for guests.

Total Time: 11–16 minutes

Prep time: 5–10 minutes

Active cooking time:
6 minutes

Serves 4

TOASTED PITA TRIANGLES

4 whole-wheat pita pockets, cut into triangles

Cooking spray

Garlic salt to taste

RED PEPPER HUMMUS

One 15-ounce can chickpeas, rinsed and drained

1 cup roasted red peppers (from a water-packed jar)

¼ cup tahini (sesame paste)

2 tablespoons fresh lemon juice

3 cloves garlic

1 teaspoon ground cumin

Salt and freshly ground black pepper to taste

2 tablespoons chopped fresh parsley

1. Preheat the oven to 400°F.

2. Place the pita triangles on a large baking sheet and spray the tops with cooking spray. Sprinkle them with garlic salt. Bake until golden brown and crisp, about 6 minutes.

3. Meanwhile, in a blender or food processor, combine the chickpeas, red peppers, tahini, lemon juice, garlic, and cumin. Process until smooth. Season with salt and pepper. Transfer to a serving bowl and top with the parsley. Serve the hummus with the toasted pita triangles arranged on the side.

bank a batch Make a double batch of the hummus and store the extra in a sealable container or plastic bag for up to 3 months in the freezer. Thaw overnight in the refrigerator or in the microwave for a few minutes on LOW.

Make a double batch of the pita triangles and store for up to 5 days at room temperature or 3 months in the freezer. Reheat (directly from the freezer) on a large baking sheet for 10 minutes at 350°F.

morph it Make a double batch of the hummus and use the extra as a topping for grilled or roasted chicken, fish (such as halibut, tilapia, or flounder) or lean steak (such as flank or skirt). It will keep for up to 5 days in the refrigerator.

have it your way Instead of roasted red peppers, try oil-packed (and drained) sun-dried tomatoes.

I could easily eat a gallon

of this stuff in one sitting.

Quick Spanakopita

Talk about impressive party food. Just don't tell everyone how incredibly simple it is to prepare! This also makes a nice meal when you add a side salad.

Total Time: 55 minutes

Prep time: 20 minutes

Walk-away time: 25 minutes

Resting time: 10 minutes

Makes 8 spanakopita;
serves 8

Cooking spray

One 10-ounce package frozen chopped spinach, thawed and drained well (squeeze the spinach in paper towels to remove all excess water)

1½ cups crumbled feta cheese (about 6 ounces)

¾ cup cottage cheese

½ cup chopped onion

2 large eggs, lightly beaten

2 tablespoons chopped fresh parsley

1 tablespoon chopped fresh dill or 1 teaspoon dried

1 teaspoon fresh lemon juice

¼ teaspoon ground nutmeg

½ teaspoon salt

¼ teaspoon freshly ground black pepper

Twenty-four 9x14-inch sheets frozen phyllo dough, thawed

1. Preheat the oven to 400°F. Coat a 12-cup (full-size) muffin tin with cooking spray.

2. In a large bowl, combine the spinach, feta, cottage cheese, onion, eggs, parsley, dill, lemon juice, nutmeg, salt, and pepper. Mix well to combine.

3. Unroll the phyllo dough sheets on a flat surface. Cut the sheets in half vertically (crosswise), making 48 sheets. Press 2 sheets of dough into 8 of the muffin cups (leave the remaining 4 muffin cups empty), allowing the pastry to hang over the sides. Spray the phyllo with cooking spray. Fill the cups with 1 to 2 tablespoons of the spinach mixture. Top with 2 more sheets of phyllo. Repeat the layers (spinach mixture, phyllo) until each cup has 3 layers of phyllo and 3 layers of spinach mixture, ending with the spinach mixture. Fold the overhanging phyllo back over the muffin cup to cover the filling; spray the surface with cooking spray.

4. Bake until the edges of the phyllo are golden brown, about 25 minutes. Let stand for 10 minutes before serving.

bank a batch Bake a double batch and keep the extras on hand to satisfy a sudden attack of the munchies or for when you have last-minute guests. When cool, wrap the entire pan in plastic wrap and store for up to 3 days in the refrigerator or for 3 months in the freezer (when freezing, cover the plastic with aluminum foil). Reheat (directly from the freezer) in a 300°F oven until hot, about 30 minutes.

have it your way Instead of feta, try goat cheese or shredded Swiss cheese; instead of parsley try basil, and instead of dill, try chives.

. . . don't tell everyone

how incredibly simple this is . . .

5-Ingredient Wild Mushroom Turnovers with Romano Cheese

Turnovers in a Quick Fix cookbook? You betcha! And when you swap the fillings and use leftover ingredients from another meal, the prep time is slashed to almost nil. That's Quick Fix heaven.

Total Time: 29–31 minutes

Prep time: 15 minutes

Active cooking time: 4 minutes

Walk-away time: 10–12 minutes

Makes 12 turnovers; serves 6

2 teaspoons olive oil

2 cups sliced fresh wild mushrooms (any variety, any combination)

1 teaspoon dried thyme

1 sheet frozen puff pastry, thawed according to package directions

¼ cup freshly grated pecorino romano or Parmesan cheese

1. Preheat the oven to 400°F.

2. Heat the oil in a large skillet over medium-high heat. Add the mushrooms and cook until softened, about 3 minutes. Add the thyme and cook for 1 minute, until fragrant. Remove from the heat and set aside.

3. Unroll the puff pastry on a flat work surface and roll into a 14-inch square. Using a sharp knife, cut the pastry into 12 squares. Top each with the mushroom mixture (about 1 heaping teaspoon) and 1 teaspoon of the grated cheese. Dip your fingers into a small dish of water and wet the edges of each pastry square. Fold over one corner of the square, making a triangle and pressing the edges to seal.

4. Place the turnovers on a baking sheet about 2 inches apart. Bake until puffed up and golden brown, 10 to 12 minutes. Serve warm.

bank a batch Make a double (or triple) batch of the turnovers and, before baking, arrange the extras in a single layer on a baking sheet. Freeze until firm, then transfer to sealable containers or plastic bags (to free up freezer space) and store for up to 3 months in the freezer. Bake as directed, directly from the freezer (without thawing), adding 5 to 8 minutes to the baking time if necessary.

have it your way No mushrooms in the house? Not to worry: top each square with 1 teaspoon of prepared sun-dried tomato pesto, basil pesto, or leftover chili before folding over and baking. Let your imagination run wild!

5-Ingredient Pesto–Vegetable Strudel Bites

Thanks to the prepared puff pastry, you can simply assemble, bake, and serve these turnovers. The most difficult thing about the recipe is being patient—the aroma from the oven is truly tempting!

Total Time: 18–20 minutes

Prep time: 10 minutes

Walk-away time: 8–10 minutes

Makes 12 bites; serves 6

1 frozen sheet puff pasty, thawed according to package directions

1 cup prepared basil pesto

1½ cups finely chopped mixed vegetables (use fresh or thawed frozen)

1 large egg, slightly beaten

⅓ cup freshly grated Parmesan cheese

1. Preheat the oven to 400°F.

2. Unroll the puff pastry on a flat work surface and roll into a 12x16-inch rectangle. Spread the pesto all over the pastry, to within ½ inch of the edges. Top evenly with the chopped vegetables. Starting from the shorter end, roll up the pastry jellyroll style. Place the roll, seam side down, on a baking sheet. Using a sharp knife, cut the roll crosswise into 12 equal pieces. Separate the pieces slightly to allow the heat to circulate during baking. Brush the beaten egg over the pastry, then sprinkle with the Parmesan.

3. Bake until the pastry is puffed up and golden brown, 8 to 10 minutes. Serve warm.

make it a meal kit Assemble the roll, brush with the egg, and sprinkle with the Parmesan. Cover and store for up to 3 days in the refrigerator before baking as directed.

bank a batch Assemble two rolls and, before baking, also cut the extra roll as directed. Place the slices in a single layer on a baking sheet and freeze until firm, then transfer to a sealable container or plastic bag (to free up freezer space) and store for up to 3 months in the freezer. When ready to enjoy, bake as directed right from the freezer (without thawing), adding 5 to 8 minutes to the baking time if necessary. Perfect for your next party!

have it your way Next time you make a salad at the deli, grab extras to make this winner. Great choices include broccoli florets, carrots, red onions, scallions, celery, zucchini, yellow squash, asparagus, olives, and bell peppers.

Spinach–Cheese Calzone

Thanks to store-bought pizza dough, you can create calzones with an unlimited amount of filling combinations. I like to serve a tomato salad on the side (sliced beefsteak tomatoes with balsamic vinegar and fresh basil leaves) or Mixed Cherry Tomato Salad (page 281).

Total Time: 35 minutes
Prep time: 15 minutes
Walk-away time: 15 minutes
Resting time: 5 minutes

Makes 1 calzone; serves 4 to 6 as an appetizer, 2 to 3 as a main course

One 15-ounce container ricotta cheese

8 ounces mozzarella cheese, shredded

One 10-ounce package frozen chopped spinach, thawed, drained well, and squeezed dry

$\frac{1}{2}$ teaspoon salt

$\frac{1}{2}$ teaspoon freshly ground black pepper

1 pound fresh or frozen bread or pizza dough, thawed according to package directions

2 tablespoons freshly grated Parmesan cheese

1. Preheat oven to 400°F.

2. In a medium bowl, combine the ricotta, mozzarella, spinach, salt, and pepper.

3. On a lightly floured work surface, roll the dough out into a 15-inch circle. Spread the cheese mixture over one half of the circle, to within 1 inch of the edge. Lift the other side of the dough and fold it over, forming a half-moon. Pinch the edges together to seal.

4. Transfer to a large baking sheet and sprinkle the top with the Parmesan. Bake until puffed up and golden brown, about 15 minutes. Let stand for 5 minutes before slicing crosswise into thick slices.

make it a meal kit Assemble the calzone and, before baking, wrap with plastic wrap and store for up to 2 days in the refrigerator before baking.

bank a batch Make two calzones and, before baking, wrap the extra one in plastic, then wrap in aluminum foil, and store for up to 3 months in the freezer. Bake as directed right from the freezer (without thawing), adding 10 minutes to the baking time if necessary.

have it your way Excellent substitutions for the spinach include thawed frozen broccoli, roasted red peppers, pepperoni, and/or sweet or hot Italian sausage (pork or turkey, cooked and crumbled).

Excellent with broccoli, roasted red peppers,

pepperoni, and/or Italian sausage . . .

Provençal-Style Pizza

This is my version of the anchovy and onion pizza from Provence (also known as pissaladière). If serving for dinner, to round out the meal, accompany the pizza with a mixed green salad or Romaine Salad with Roasted Cherry Tomatoes & Blue Cheese (page 273).

Total Time: 27–29 minutes

Prep time: 10 minutes

Active cooking time:
5 minutes

Walk-away time:
12–14 minutes

Serves 4 as a main course,
6 to 8 as an appetizer

1 tablespoon olive oil

2 cups yellow onions thinly sliced into half-moons

1 tablespoon light brown sugar

1 pound fresh or frozen bread or pizza dough, thawed according to package directions

1 cup pitted and chopped niçoise olives

8 anchovy fillets, chopped

2 teaspoons chopped fresh thyme

Salt and freshly ground black pepper to taste

2 tablespoons freshly grated Parmesan cheese

1. Preheat the oven to 450°F.

2. Heat the oil in a large skillet over medium-high heat. Add the onion and sugar and cook, stirring, until golden brown and caramelized, about 5 minutes. Remove from the heat.

3. On a lightly floured work surface, roll the dough out into an 8x14-inch oval. Transfer the oval to a large baking sheet and top with the caramelized onions to within ½ inch of the edges of dough. Top the onions with the olives, anchovies, and thyme. Season with salt and pepper and sprinkle with the Parmesan. Bake until puffed up and golden brown, 12 to 14 minutes. Cut into wedges and serve warm or at room temperature.

make it a meal kit Caramelize the onions and store in a sealable container for up to 4 days in the refrigerator. When ready to finish, roll out the dough and top with the prepped onions. Finish as directed.

have it your way To turn this into a hearty, complete meal, top the pizza with shredded cooked chicken, scallops, or shrimp before baking.

Rosemary-Rubbed Flatbread

A big *thank you* goes out to the makers of refrigerated and frozen pizza and bread dough. Serve this instead of plain dinner rolls for a dinnertime surprise.

Total Time: 15–17 minutes
Prep time: 5 minutes
Walk-away time: 10–12 minutes

Serves 4 to 6

Cooking spray

1 pound fresh or frozen bread or pizza dough, thawed according to package directions

1 tablespoon olive oil

4 cloves garlic, minced

2 tablespoons chopped fresh rosemary

Salt and freshly ground black pepper to taste

1. Preheat the oven to 450°F. Coat a large baking sheet with cooking spray.

2. On a lightly floured work surface, roll the dough out into a 9x15-inch rectangle. Brush the oil all over the top of the dough and sprinkle with the garlic and rosemary. Season the top with salt and pepper. Bake until puffed up and golden brown, 10 to 12 minutes. Cut into wedges or squares and serve warm or at room temperature.

have it your way Swap other herbs for the rosemary. Excellent choices would be fresh thyme, fresh oregano, fresh basil, or fresh tarragon.

Salad Bar Quiche with Cheddar & Parmesan

This quiche makes a great brunch, lunch, or light dinner meal. I like to serve a side salad of mixed greens topped with mandarin oranges or grapes, tossed in a light vinaigrette, or Red Lettuce with Honey–Maple Vinaigrette (page 282).

Total Time: 30 minutes
Prep time: 10 minutes
Walk-away time: 20 minutes

Serves 4 to 6

One 9-inch refrigerated pie crust

One 10-ounce package frozen chopped spinach, thawed, drained well, and squeezed dry

2 cups chopped mixed fresh or thawed frozen vegetables

1 cup ricotta cheese

¾ cup shredded mild or sharp Cheddar cheese

¼ cup milk

2 large eggs, lightly beaten

2 teaspoons Dijon mustard

1 teaspoon dried oregano

½ teaspoon salt

¼ teaspoon freshly ground black pepper

2 tablespoons freshly grated Parmesan cheese

1. Preheat the oven to 375°F.

2. Press the pie crust into the bottom and up the sides of a 9-inch tart pan with a removable bottom or a 9-inch pie pan. Set aside.

3. In a large bowl, combine the spinach, vegetables, ricotta, Cheddar, milk, eggs, mustard, oregano, salt, and pepper. Spoon the filling into the pie crust and sprinkle the Parmesan evenly over the top.

4. Bake until a knife inserted near the center comes out clean and the crust is golden brown, about 20 minutes.

make it a meal kit Assemble the quiche, cover with plastic wrap, and store for up to 3 days in the refrigerator before baking as directed.

bank a batch Make two quiches and, before baking, cover the extra one with plastic wrap, then aluminum foil, and store for up to 3 months in the freezer. Bake as directed right from the freezer (without thawing), adding 10 minutes to the baking time if necessary.

have it your way Use any variety and combination of vegetables—from leftover sautéed vegetables to chopped-up salad bar selections to thawed frozen vegetables from your very own freezer. My personal favorites for this quiche include bell peppers, cauliflower, and asparagus.

. . . makes a great brunch, lunch,

or light dinner meal.

Pasta and Risotto

A T LEAST THREE MORNINGS A WEEK (usually before dawn, when my son Kyle gets up), you'll find me in the kitchen cooking pasta.

Why? Because I'm prepping ahead! On a busy weeknight, I find that there's nothing worse than waiting for water to boil; it seems to boil faster when I'm busy doing something else. I know, I know, a watched pot—but having a pound or two of cooked pasta in my refrigerator gives me that same comfortable feeling I get when I'm on the road and know that I have a full tank of gas.

Pasta is a Quick Fix staple because it's crowd- and kid-pleasing, it's inexpensive, and you can prep in advance because it lasts a week in the refrigerator when stored in sealable containers or plastic bags. Pasta is also a morphing wonder. I often make double or triple batches of plain pasta so I can create a variety of meals at whim. There's no question cooked pasta works with any type of sauce (vegetable, meat, poultry, fish), plus the flavors can easily go global—Italian, Asian, Mexican, Indian, take your pick. Fully prepared pasta dishes will also last for several days in the refrigerator or for up to three months in the freezer.

Baked pasta dishes like lasagne and macaroni and cheese are incredibly freezer-friendly, making them ideal for my "Bank a Batch" strategy. They'll freeze for up to three months, so you can know you've got one "in the bank," which is especially nice for a week when time is at a minimum. Since I have little ones (and an occasional babysitter), I also freeze pasta and casseroles in individual portions. Come mealtime, my sitter can pull the servings from the freezer and reheat just what she needs. This not only saves her time and effort, but also, no food is wasted!

. . . you can prep pasta in advance

because it lasts a week in the

refrigerator . . .

Rigatoni Caprese

In this dish, I combine my dad's two favorite things—rigatoni and Caprese salad, a simple combination of good-quality mozzarella, vine-ripened tomatoes, fresh basil, and fruity extra-virgin olive oil.

To cut the basil leaves into chiffonade, pile 8 to 10 leaves on top of one another, roll them up widthwise, then slice the roll into thin strips. Repeat until you have cut them all.

Total Time: 15 minutes

Prep time: 15 minutes

Serves 4

1 pound rigatoni or penne pasta

¼ cup extra-virgin olive oil

2 large ripe tomatoes, diced

½ pound fresh mozzarella cheese, diced

1 cup fresh basil leaves, cut into chiffonade (thin strips)

2 tablespoons drained capers

Salt and freshly ground black pepper to taste

1. Cook the pasta according to the package directions. Drain and transfer to a large bowl. (If desired, you can transfer the pasta to a pre-warmed bowl that's been warmed under hot running water; dry it out before adding the pasta!)

2. Fold in the oil and tomatoes until the pasta is coated with the oil. Fold in the mozzarella, basil, and capers, season with salt and pepper, and serve.

make it a meal kit Cook and drain the pasta. Toss together the oil, tomatoes, and diced cheese. Store each separately in sealable containers or plastic bags for up to 3 days in the refrigerator. When ready to finish the meal, reheat the pasta in the microwave for a few minutes on HIGH. Toss the warm pasta with the tomato-cheese mixture. Fold in the basil and capers and season with salt and pepper just before serving.

Citrus Olive–Pasta Salad

This dish is super-easy to throw together if you've got a well-stocked pantry; you should always have mandarin oranges on hand because they spruce up all kinds of salads. It's an excellent choice for a picnic or tailgate party. I like to serve Onion Knots (page 264) with this.

Total Time: 10–15 minutes

Prep time: 10–15 minutes

Serves 4

1 pound rotelle, fusilli, or farfalle (bowtie) pasta

1 cup pitted cured olives, drained and cut in half

One 11-ounce can mandarin orange segments, drained

½ cup orange juice

2 tablespoons olive oil

1 tablespoon chopped fresh rosemary

2 teaspoons Dijon mustard

2 teaspoons fresh lemon juice

1 teaspoon finely grated lemon zest

1 teaspoon finely grated orange zest

Salt and freshly ground black pepper to taste

1. Cook the pasta according to the package directions. Drain and transfer to a large bowl. Fold in the olives and mandarin segments.

2. In a small bowl, whisk together the orange juice, oil, rosemary, mustard, lemon juice, lemon zest, and orange zest. Pour the mixture the pasta and stir to combine. Season with salt and pepper.

make it a meal kit Cook and drain the pasta; make the dressing (from the orange juice to the orange zest); and cut the olives in half. Store each component separately in sealable containers or plastic bags; the dressing and the olives will keep for up to 1 week in the refrigerator, the pasta for up to 3 days. When ready to finish the meal, toss the pasta with the dressing and fold in the olives and orange segments. Season with salt and pepper. For a warm salad, reheat the pasta in the microwave for a few minutes on HIGH before tossing with the remaining ingredients.

morph it Make a double batch of the orange juice mixture and use it as a marinade and/or sauce for chicken, shrimp, or pork. Use half of the mixture as a marinade and the other half as a sauce to drizzle over the top of the finished dish.

Orzo with Spicy Edamame

How spicy is this dish? As hot as you want it, since you control the amount of chile pepper and hot sauce you add. Serve it with Green Beans with Pineapple Vinaigrette (page 243).

Total Time: 15–20 minutes

Prep time: 10–15 minutes

Active cooking time: 5 minutes

Serves 4

1 pound orzo pasta

1 tablespoon olive oil, or more as needed

2 cloves garlic, minced

1 fresh serrano chile pepper, seeded and minced

One 10-ounce package fresh or thawed frozen shelled edamame

1 teaspoon chili powder

1/2 teaspoon hot sauce, or more to taste

1/4 cup chopped scallions (white and green parts)

2 tablespoons chopped fresh cilantro

Salt and freshly ground black pepper to taste

1. Cook the orzo according to the package directions. Drain and transfer to a large bowl.

2. Meanwhile, heat 1 tablespoon of the oil in large skillet over medium-high heat. Add the garlic and chile and cook for 1 minute. Add the edamame and cook, stirring, until golden brown, about 3 minutes. Add the chili powder and hot sauce and cook for 1 minute to heat through.

3. Pour the contents of the skillet over the orzo and stir to combine, adding more oil if necessary to prevent the pasta from sticking together. Fold in the scallions and cilantro, season with salt and pepper, and serve.

make it a meal kit Cook and drain the orzo; sauté the edamame mixture (the olive oil through the hot sauce). Store each separately in sealable containers or plastic bags for up to 3 days in the refrigerator. When ready to finish the meal, toss the orzo with the edamame mixture and reheat in the microwave for a few minutes on HIGH. Fold in the scallions and cilantro and season with salt and pepper just before serving.

have it your way Add 2 cups diced cooked chicken, turkey, or steak or 1/2 pound cooked small shrimp when you toss the edamame with the orzo.

Penne–Artichoke Caponata

Caponata is a Sicilian dish whose main ingredient is eggplant. I've substituted artichoke hearts and added capers. Partner this with Red Lettuce with Honey–Maple Vinaigrette (page 282).

Total Time: 18–23 minutes

Prep time: 10–15 minutes

Active cooking time: 8 minutes

Serves 4

1 pound penne pasta

1 tablespoon olive oil

1 cup chopped onion

2 stalks celery, chopped

1 cup diced fennel bulb

2 cloves garlic, chopped

One 15-ounce can tomato sauce

One 14-ounce can artichoke hearts (not marinated), drained and chopped

½ cup golden or dark raisins

¼ cup white wine vinegar

2 tablespoons sugar

2 tablespoons drained capers

1 teaspoon dried thyme

2 tablespoons chopped fresh parsley

Salt and freshly ground black pepper to taste

1. Cook the pasta according to the package directions. Drain; transfer to a large bowl.

2. Meanwhile, heat the oil in a large skillet over medium-high heat. Add the onion, celery, fennel, and garlic and cook, stirring, until softened, about 3 minutes. Add the tomato sauce, artichokes, raisins, vinegar, sugar, capers, and thyme, bring to a simmer, and let simmer for 5 minutes.

3. Pour the contents of the skillet over the penne and stir to combine. Fold in the parsley, season with salt and pepper, and serve.

make it a meal kit Cook and drain the pasta; cook the artichoke mixture (the olive oil through the thyme). Store each separately in sealable containers or plastic bags for up to 3 days in the refrigerator. When ready to finish the meal, toss the pasta with the caponata mixture and reheat in a medium saucepan over medium heat or in the microwave for a few minutes on HIGH. Fold in the parsley and season with salt and pepper just before serving.

Rotelle with Roasted Fennel, Baby Carrots & Shaved Pecorino Romano

Roasting fennel caramelizes this anise-flavored vegetable, and roasting carrots further brings out their inherent sweetness. Toss the two together with round pasta, fresh basil, and shaved sharp cheese and you've got a real winner. I like to serve Parmesan-Crusted Rolls (page 263) on the side.

Total Time: 20–25 minutes

Prep time: 20–25 minutes

Serves 4

Cooking spray

2 fennel bulbs, thinly sliced

2 cups baby carrots

1 tablespoon chopped fresh thyme

1 tablespoon olive oil, or more if desired

Salt and freshly ground black pepper to taste

1 pound rotelle or a spiral-shaped pasta

2 tablespoons balsamic vinegar

¼ cup chopped fresh basil

One 2- to 4-ounce chunk pecorino romano or Parmesan cheese

1. Preheat the oven to 400°F. Coat a large baking sheet with cooking spray.

2. In a large bowl, combine the fennel, carrots, thyme, and oil. Season with salt and pepper and toss to combine. Arrange the vegetables in a single layer on the prepared sheet and roast until they are golden brown and tender, about 20 minutes.

3. Meanwhile, cook the pasta according to the package directions. Drain, transfer to a large bowl, add the roasted vegetables and vinegar, and toss to combine, adding more oil if desired. Fold in the basil and season with salt and pepper. Transfer the mixture to a serving platter and, using a vegetable peeler, shave the cheese over the pasta and vegetables just before serving.

make it a meal kit Cook and drain the pasta and roast the vegetables. Store each separately in sealable containers or plastic bags for up to 3 days in the refrigerator. When ready to finish the meal, toss the pasta with the roasted vegetables, vinegar, and oil (plus more oil if necessary) and reheat in a medium saucepan over medium heat or in the microwave for a few minutes on HIGH. Finish as directed.

Pasta Shells with Roasted Artichoke Hearts & Broccoli

In this dish, I toss roasted vegetables with shell-shaped pasta, fresh rosemary, and heavy cream—divine! I like to serve Mixed Cherry Tomato Salad (page 281) on the side.

Total Time: 20 minutes

Prep time: 20 minutes

Serves 4

Cooking spray

One 14-ounce can artichoke hearts (not marinated), drained and quartered

2 cups broccoli florets

1 tablespoon chopped fresh rosemary

1 tablespoon olive oil

Salt and freshly ground black pepper to taste

1 pound medium pasta shells or spiral-shaped pasta

1/2 cup heavy cream

1/4 cup chopped fresh parsley

1/2 cup freshly grated Parmesan cheese

1. Preheat the oven to 400°F. Coat a large baking sheet with cooking spray.

2. In a large bowl, combine the artichoke hearts, broccoli, rosemary, and oil until the vegetables are coated with the oil and rosemary. Season with salt and pepper and toss to combine. Arrange the vegetables on the prepared sheet and roast until they are golden brown and tender, about 20 minutes.

3. Meanwhile, cook the pasta according to the package directions. Drain, transfer to a large bowl, add the roasted vegetables and heavy cream, and toss to combine. Fold in the parsley and season again with salt and pepper. Top with the cheese just before serving.

make it a meal kit Cook and drain the pasta. Roast the vegetables. Store each separately in sealable containers or plastic bags for up to 3 days in the refrigerator. When ready to finish the meal, combine the pasta, roasted vegetables, and heavy cream and reheat in a large saucepan over medium heat or in the microwave for a few minutes on HIGH. Finish as directed above.

Tricolor Pasta with Creamy Parmesan Sauce

Any pasta shape will work with this—just select one with nooks and crannies to soak up the sauce. And you can add chicken or shrimp for a protein. I like to serve Warm Spinach Salad with Pancetta, Gorgonzola & Pine Nuts (page 275) on the side.

Total Time: 21–26 minutes
Prep time: 15–20 minutes
Active cooking time: 6 minutes

Serves 4

1 pound tricolor rotelle or farfalle (bowtie) pasta

2 teaspoons olive oil

¼ cup diced shallots

3 cloves garlic, minced

½ cup dry white wine or vermouth

1 cup heavy cream

¼ cup sour cream

1 cup freshly grated Parmesan cheese

¼ cup chopped fresh basil

Salt and freshly ground black pepper to taste

1. Cook the pasta according to the package directions. Drain and set aside.

2. While the pasta is cooking, heat the oil in a large saucepan over medium-high heat. Add the shallots and garlic and cook, stirring, until softened, about 3 minutes. Add the wine and cook for 1 minute. Reduce the heat to low, add the heavy cream and sour cream, and cook for 1 minute. Add the Parmesan and cook until it melts, about 1 minute, stirring constantly.

3. Remove from the heat, fold in the pasta and basil, season with salt and pepper, and serve.

make it a meal kit Cook and drain the pasta. Make the sauce (the oil through the Parmesan). Store each separately in sealable containers or plastic bags for up to 3 days in the refrigerator. When ready to finish the meal, combine the pasta and sauce and reheat in a medium saucepan over medium heat or in the microwave for a few minutes on HIGH. Stir in the basil and season with salt and pepper just before serving.

Rotelle with Braised Zucchini, Roasted Garlic, Oregano & Feta

Zucchini comes alive when paired with roasted garlic and salty feta cheese. Keep it simple and serve a mixed green salad with prepared dressing on the side.

Total Time: 24 minutes

Prep time: 15 minutes

Active cooking time: 9 minutes

Serves 4

½ cup garlic cloves, peeled

1 pound rotelle or other spiral-shaped pasta

2 teaspoons olive oil

2 medium zucchini, chopped

½ cup diced red onion

1 teaspoon dried oregano

1 cup reduced-sodium chicken broth

2 tablespoons chopped fresh parsley

Salt and freshly ground black pepper to taste

½ cup crumbled feta cheese

1. Preheat the oven to 400°F.

2. Wrap the garlic cloves in aluminum foil and roast until golden brown and tender, about 15 minutes. Set aside.

3. Cook the rotelle according to the package directions. Drain, reserving 1 cup of the cooking water. Transfer the pasta to a large bowl.

4. Meanwhile, heat the oil in a large skillet over medium heat. Add the zucchini and onion and cook, stirring, until golden brown, about 3 minutes. Add the oregano and cook for 1 minute. Add the broth and roasted garlic, bring to a simmer, and let simmer for 5 minutes.

5. Pour the mixture over the pasta and toss to combine, adding the pasta cooking water if necessary to moisten it. Fold in the parsley and season with salt and pepper. Transfer to a serving platter, top with the feta, and serve.

make it a meal kit Roast the garlic. Cook and drain the pasta. Prep the zucchini and onion and combine. Crumble the feta. Store each of the components separately in sealable containers or plastic bags for up to 3 days in the refrigerator. When ready to finish the meal, cook the zucchini and onion as directed, adding the broth and pre-roasted garlic when instructed. Reheat the pasta in the microwave for 2 minutes on HIGH. Pour the broth mixture over pasta as directed and add the parsley, salt, and pepper. Top with the feta and serve.

morph it Make a double batch of the roasted garlic and use the extra in Herb-Crusted Flounder Fillets in Roasted Garlic Sauce (page 222), Roasted Garlic–Artichoke Dip (page 28), or Coconut Shrimp with Curried Tomato, Lime & Roasted Garlic Coulis (page 214).

Linguine with Porcini–Vermouth Sauce

Using dried porcini mushrooms in a recipe does double duty. You get the woodsy mushrooms to chew on and you can use the soaking liquid (for rehydrating the 'shrooms) as a base for the sauce. I like to serve Beet–Arugula Salad with Buttermilk–Blue Cheese Dressing (page 270) on the side.

Total Time: 26 minutes

Prep time: 20 minutes

Active cooking time: 6 minutes

Serves 4

1 ounce dried porcini mushrooms

1/2 cup hot water

1 pound linguine or spaghetti

2 teaspoons olive oil

1/4 cup diced pancetta or bacon

2 cloves garlic, minced

1/2 cup dry vermouth

1/2 cup heavy cream

2 tablespoons chopped fresh parsley

Salt and freshly ground black pepper to taste

1/4 cup freshly grated Parmesan cheese

1. Soak the mushrooms in the hot water for 15 minutes, then strain through a paper towel–lined sieve, reserving the soaking liquid. Set the mushrooms and soaking liquid aside.

2. Meanwhile, cook the pasta according to the package directions and drain.

3. While the pasta is cooking, heat the oil in a large skillet over medium-high heat. Add the pancetta and cook until crisp, about 3 minutes. Add the garlic and cook for 1 minute. Add the mushrooms and vermouth and cook for 1 minute. Add the mushroom soaking liquid and bring to a simmer. Reduce the heat to low and add the heavy cream. Simmer for 1 minute to heat through. Add the linguine and toss to combine. Remove from the heat, fold in the parsley, and season with salt and pepper. Sprinkle with the Parmesan just before serving.

make it a meal kit Soak the mushrooms in the hot water as directed, then transfer the mushrooms (in the soaking liquid) to a sealable container. Cook and drain the pasta and store in a plastic bag. Both will keep for up to 3 days in the refrigerator. When ready to finish the meal, make the mushroom sauce as directed, stir in the cooked pasta, and reheat for 2 to 3 minutes. (If desired, before adding the pasta to the sauce, reheat it in the microwave for 1 minute on HIGH; this will speed up the heating process.) Finish as directed.

have it your way Substitute dried shiitake or Chinese black mushrooms for the porcini if desired.

Cavatappi with Caramelized Zucchini & Warm Blue Cheese Sauce

Cavatappi is a fun, corkscrew-shaped pasta that delivers a nice change from traditional pasta shapes. In this dish, it's swimming in a creamy, rich sauce that boasts sharp, blue-veined cheese. I like to serve this with Onion Knots (page 264) and Cucumber Salad with Oranges & Mint (page 272).

Total Time: 25 minutes

Prep time: 15 minutes

Active cooking time: 10 minutes

Serves 4

1 pound cavatappi or fusilli pasta

2 teaspoons olive oil

1 medium onion, sliced into half-moons (about 1 cup)

1 large (or 2 medium) zucchini, halved lengthwise and thinly sliced into half-moons

1 teaspoon dried thyme

$\frac{1}{2}$ teaspoon salt

$\frac{1}{4}$ teaspoon freshly ground black pepper

$1\frac{1}{2}$ cups milk (preferably 1% milk fat or higher)

$\frac{2}{3}$ cup crumbled blue cheese

2 tablespoons chopped fresh parsley

1. Cook the cavatappi according to the package directions. Drain and set aside.

2. While the pasta is cooking, heat the oil in a large skillet over medium-high heat. Add onions and zucchini and cook, stirring, until tender, about 5 minutes. Add the thyme, salt, and pepper and cook for 1 minute, until the thyme is fragrant. Add the pasta and toss to combine. Remove from the heat.

3. Place the milk in a medium saucepan and set the pan over medium heat. When tiny bubbles appear around the edges of the pan, reduce the heat to low and stir in the blue cheese until it melts. Add the sauce to the pasta mixture and toss to combine. Cook for 1 minute to heat through. Remove from the heat, stir in the parsley, season with more salt and pepper, and serve.

make it a meal kit Cook and drain the pasta. Slice the onion and zucchini. Make the blue cheese sauce (combining and heating the milk and blue cheese). Store each of the components separately in sealable containers or plastic bags for up to 3 days in the refrigerator. When ready to finish the meal, cook the onion and zucchini as directed and add the pasta when instructed. Reheat the blue cheese sauce in a medium saucepan over medium heat or in the microwave for a few minutes on HIGH. Add the warm sauce to the pasta mixture and heat through. Stir in the parsley and season with salt and pepper just before serving.

have it your way If you don't have zucchini, or want to try the dish with something different, broccoli florets, broccoli rabe, yellow squash, and snow peas also work great.

. . . this is a nice change from

traditional pasta shapes.

Linguine with Peas, Shiitake Mushrooms & Sage

The distinct taste of wild mushrooms, both porcini and shiitake, lends an earthiness to all kinds of sauces. In this dish I use linguine, and the tender noodles wrap their arms around the mushrooms, sweet leeks, green peas, and sharp cheese. I often serve Pear–Cucumber Salad with Balsamic & Shaved Romano Cheese (page 274) on the side.

Total Time: 30–32 minutes

Prep time: 20 minutes

Active cooking time: 10–12 minutes

Serves 4

1 ounce dried porcini mushrooms

½ cup hot water

1 pound linguine

2 teaspoons olive oil

2 leeks (white part only), washed well and chopped

2 cups sliced fresh shiitake mushroom caps

1 tablespoon chopped fresh sage or 1 teaspoon dried

1 cup frozen green peas

1 cup reduced-sodium vegetable broth

2 tablespoons chopped fresh parsley

Salt and freshly ground black pepper to taste

One 4-ounce chunk aged Asiago or Romano cheese

1. Soak the porcini mushrooms in the hot water for 15 minutes, then strain through a paper towel–lined sieve, reserving the soaking liquid. Set the mushrooms and soaking liquid aside.

2. Cook the linguine according to the package directions. Drain and set aside.

3. While the pasta is cooking, heat the oil in a large skillet over medium heat. Add the leeks and cook, stirring, until softened, about 2 minutes. Add the drained porcinis and the shiitakes and cook, stirring a few times, until softened, 3 to 5 minutes. Add the sage and stir to coat. Add the peas, broth, and reserved porcini soaking liquid, bring to a simmer, and let simmer for 5 minutes. Add the linguine and toss to combine.

4. Remove from the heat, stir in the parsley, and season with salt and pepper. Transfer to a warm serving platter and, using a vegetable peeler, shave the cheese over the top right before serving.

make it a meal kit Cook and drain the pasta, then transfer to a plastic bag. Soak the mushrooms as directed and store the mushrooms (in the soaking liquid) in a sealable container. Both will keep for up to 3 days in the refrigerator. When ready to finish the meal, make the mushroom sauce as directed, then stir in the cooked pasta and cook until reheated. Finish as directed.

. . . tender noodles wrap their arms

around the mushrooms, sweet leeks,

green peas, and sharp cheese.

Mexican Spaghetti

This recipe was given to me by a friend born in Mexico whose mom made it for him. It's a super-easy blender sauce that's great cold, at room temperature, and hot. I love to serve Parmesan-Crusted Rolls (page 263) with this.

Total Time: 20–25 minutes

Prep time: 15–20 minutes

Active cooking time:
5 minutes

Serves 4

1 pound spaghetti

One 28-ounce can diced tomatoes, undrained

1 teaspoon onion flakes

1/2 teaspoon garlic powder

1 low-sodium vegetable bouillon cube, broken up

2 pickled jalapeño chile peppers, seeded and chopped

Salt and freshly ground black pepper to taste

1/4 cup freshly grated Parmesan cheese

1. Cook the spaghetti according to the package directions. Drain and set aside.

2. While the pasta is cooking, combine the tomatoes, onion flakes, garlic powder, bouillon cube, and jalapeños in a blender and process until smooth. Transfer the mixture to a medium saucepan, set the pan over medium-high heat, bring to a simmer, and let simmer for 5 minutes. Season with salt and pepper.

3. Transfer the spaghetti to a warm serving platter and top with the sauce. Sprinkle with the Parmesan and serve.

make it a meal kit Cook and drain the spaghetti. Make the sauce (the tomatoes through the salt and pepper). Store each separately in sealable containers or plastic bags for up to 3 days in the refrigerator for the pasta and up to 4 days for the sauce. When ready to finish the meal, combine the spaghetti and sauce and reheat in a large saucepan over medium heat or in the microwave for a few minutes on HIGH. Sprinkle the Parmesan over the top just before serving.

bank a batch Make a double batch of the sauce and store the extra for up to 3 months in the freezer. Thaw overnight in the refrigerator or in the microwave for 5 minutes on LOW. Reheat in a saucepan over medium heat or in the microwave for a few minutes on HIGH. While you're reheating it, cook your pasta.

morph it Make a double batch of the sauce. Spoon it over grilled chicken, roasted fish, or steamed vegetables, or use it as a simmer sauce for shrimp, scallops, or cubed chicken or pork.

Orzo with Broiled Feta, Tomatoes & Olives

Broiling firm cheeses like feta and goat cheese creates a golden brown, caramelized crust that softens the sharp tang of the cheese. Served with olives, herbs, and tomatoes, this dish is like a Greek salad with pasta!

Total Time: 16–17 minutes

Prep time: 15 minutes

Active cooking time:
1–2 minutes

Serves 4

1 pound orzo or any small pasta

Cooking spray

2 medium ripe beefsteak tomatoes, thinly sliced into rounds

1 cup crumbled feta cheese

1 cup sliced pitted Greek olives

3 tablespoons chopped fresh parsley

3 tablespoons chopped fresh basil

2 tablespoons olive oil

2 tablespoons red wine vinegar

Salt and freshly ground black pepper to taste

1. Cook the orzo according to the package directions. Drain and set aside.

2. While the pasta is cooking, preheat the broiler. Coat a large baking sheet with cooking spray. Arrange the tomato slices on the sheet in a single layer. Top the tomato slices with the feta and broil until the cheese is just golden, 1 to 2 minutes. Remove from the oven and, when cool enough to handle, chop the tomato and feta into ½-inch pieces. Set aside.

3. In a large bowl, combine the cooked orzo, olives, parsley, basil, oil, and vinegar. Fold in the chopped tomatoes and feta, season with salt and pepper, and serve hot or at room temperature.

make it a meal kit Cook and drain the orzo. Roast the tomatoes with the feta. Store each separately for up to 3 days in the refrigerator. When ready to finish the meal, reheat the orzo in the microwave for a few minutes on HIGH. Reheat the tomatoes in the microwave for 1 minute on HIGH. Finish as directed (from combining the orzo with the olives, parsley, etc.).

have it your way Add 2 cups diced cooked chicken or ham or cooked medium shrimp. Or substitute a firm goat cheese or crumbled blue cheese for the feta if desired.

Three-Mushroom Spinach Fettuccine

Have fun mushroom shopping for this recipe! I love to serve Mixed Cherry Tomato Salad (page 281) and Parmesan-Crusted Rolls (page 263) with this.

Total Time: 23–25 minutes

Prep time: 15 minutes

Active cooking time:
8–10 minutes

Serves 4

1 pound spinach or regular fettuccine

2 teaspoons olive oil

1 cup chopped yellow onion

4 cloves garlic, minced

1 cup sliced portabella mushroom caps (2 to 3 caps)

1 cup sliced oyster or cremini mushrooms

1 cup sliced shiitake mushroom caps

1 teaspoon dried thyme

1 teaspoon dried oregano

1/2 cup sweet or dry Marsala wine

1 cup reduced-sodium chicken broth

2 tablespoons chopped fresh parsley

Salt and freshly ground black pepper to taste

1/4 cup freshly grated pecorino romano or Parmesan cheese

1. Cook the fettuccine according to the package directions. Drain and set aside.

2. While the pasta is cooking, heat the oil in a large skillet over medium-high heat. Add the onion and garlic and cook, stirring, until softened, about 3 minutes. Add the mushrooms and cook until softened, 3 to 5 minutes. Add the thyme and oregano and cook 1 minute, until fragrant. Add the Marsala and cook 1 minute. Add the broth and bring to a simmer. Add the fettuccine and toss to combine.

3. Remove from the heat, stir in the parsley, and season with salt and pepper. Sprinkle with the Parmesan just before serving.

make it a meal kit Cook and drain the fettuccine. Make the mushroom sauce (the oil through the broth). Store each separately for up to 3 days in the refrigerator. When ready to finish the meal, combine the fettuccine and mushroom sauce and reheat in a medium saucepan over medium heat or in the microwave for a few minutes on HIGH. Finish as directed.

Beet Ravioli in Gorgonzola Broth

Thanks to cooked beets and wonton wrappers, this is really just an "assembly" job! Serve it with Braised Spinach with Pink Beans & Ham (page 254).

Total Time: 22–27 minutes
Prep time: 20–25 minutes
Active cooking time: 2 minutes

Serves 4

1 cup canned or jarred beets, drained

½ cup ricotta cheese

½ teaspoon dried sage

Pinch of salt

Pinch of freshly ground black pepper, or to taste

48 wonton wrappers (look for them in the refrigerated section)

2 cups reduced-sodium chicken broth

2 bay leaves

½ cup crumbled Gorgonzola or other crumbly blue cheese

2 tablespoons chopped fresh parsley

1. In a food processor, combine the beets, ricotta, sage, salt, and pepper and process until smooth.

2. Arrange 24 of the wonton wrappers on a flat surface. Place 1 heaping teaspoon of the beet mixture in the center of each wrapper. Dip one finger into water and wet the edges of the wrapper, then top with a second wrapper and press down the edges to seal. Repeat with the remaining wrappers and filling.

3. Combine the broth and bay leaves in a large saucepan over medium-high heat and bring to a simmer. Add the ravioli and simmer until the wrappers are cooked (opaque), about 2 minutes. Remove the bay leaves.

4. Transfer the ravioli and broth to shallow bowls, top with the Gorgonzola and parsley, and serve.

make it a meal kit Assemble the ravioli and store in a sealable container or plastic bags (in a single layer) for up to 1 week in the refrigerator or 3 months in the freezer. When ready to finish the meal, bring the broth to a simmer (with the bay leaves) and add the ravioli straight from the fridge or freezer (they'll take a few extra minutes if frozen). Finish as directed.

bank a batch Make a double batch of the ravioli and serve in Warm Blue Cheese Sauce from Cavatappi with Caramelized Zucchini & Warm Blue Cheese Sauce (page 56) or a store-bought Alfredo sauce, or with chopped parsley and grated romano or Parmesan over the top.

Tortellini with Sage–Walnut Sauce

Sage is an excellent addition to this dish, which boasts crunchy walnuts and a creamy, shallot-infused sauce. For added color, look for tricolor tortellini in your supermarket's refrigerated case. I like to serve Beet–Arugula Salad with Buttermilk–Blue Cheese Dressing (page 270) or Roasted Green Beans with Grape Tomatoes & Olives (page 242) on the side.

Total Time: 29 minutes

Prep time: 15 minutes

Active cooking time: 14 minutes

Serves 4

1 pound cheese tortellini

SAGE–WALNUT SAUCE

¹/₂ cup chopped walnuts

2 teaspoons olive oil

¹/₄ cup chopped shallots

1 teaspoon dried sage

1 cup reduced-sodium chicken broth

¹/₂ cup heavy cream

2 tablespoons chopped fresh parsley

Salt and freshly ground black pepper to taste

1. Cook the tortellini according to the package directions. Drain and set aside.

2. While the tortellini are cooking, place the walnuts in a large dry skillet over medium heat and cook until they are toasted and fragrant, about 3 minutes, shaking the pan frequently to prevent burning. Remove the walnuts from the pan and set aside.

3. In the same skillet, heat the oil over medium heat. Add the shallots and cook, stirring, until softened, about 3 minutes. Add the sage and cook for 1 minute, until fragrant. Add the broth, bring to a simmer, and let simmer for 5 minutes.

4. Reduce the heat to low, add the heavy cream, and let simmer for 1 minute to heat through. Return the walnuts to the pan, stir in the tortellini, and cook for 1 minute to heat through. Remove from the heat, stir in the parsley, season with salt and pepper, and serve.

make it a meal kit Cook and drain the tortellini. Make the sauce (up to the point of adding the walnuts back to the skillet). Store each separately in sealable containers or plastic bags for up to 3 days in the refrigerator. When ready to finish the meal, combine the tortellini, sauce, and walnuts and reheat in a medium saucepan over medium heat or in the microwave for a few minutes on HIGH. Stir in the parsley and season with salt and pepper just before serving.

have it your way For a terrific variation, substitute sliced or slivered blanched almonds for the walnuts and dried tarragon for the sage.

For added color, look for

tricolor tortellini . . .

White Lasagne with Béchamel Sauce

This casserole boasts three cheeses, shredded zucchini, creamy white sauce, and tender noodles. I use no-cook noodles, but regular lasagne noodles will work too (and there's no need to cook them first, I promise!). Radicchio Cups with Hearts of Palm, Yogurt & Dill (page 278) makes a beautiful accompaniment to this.

Total Time: 68 minutes
Prep time: 20 minutes
Active cooking time: 3 minutes
Walk-away time: 45 minutes

Serves 8

Cooking spray

BÉCHAMEL SAUCE
¼ cup (½ stick) unsalted butter
¼ cup all-purpose flour
4 cups milk (preferably 1% milk fat or higher)
½ teaspoon salt

One 15-ounce container ricotta cheese
8 ounces mozzarella cheese, shredded, divided
1 cup shredded zucchini
1 teaspoon garlic powder
Pinch of ground nutmeg
Pinch of salt
Pinch of ground white pepper
12 sheets no-cook lasagne noodles
¼ cup freshly grated Parmesan cheese

1. Preheat the oven to 425°F. Coat a 9x13-inch baking dish with cooking spray.

2. For the béchamel, melt the butter in a medium saucepan over medium heat. Add the flour and whisk until blended and smooth, about 1 minute (don't let the flour brown). Gradually whisk in the milk and increase the heat to medium high. Bring to a boil and cook for 2 minutes, stirring constantly. Stir in the salt and remove from the heat.

3. For the filling, in a medium bowl, combine the ricotta, half of the mozzarella, the zucchini, garlic powder, nutmeg, salt, and pepper.

4. Spoon ½ cup of the béchamel into the prepared pan and spread it over the bottom. Arrange 4 noodles on top of the sauce, allowing them to overlap slightly. Spread 1 cup of the béchamel over the noodles. Top with half of the ricotta-zucchini mixture. Arrange 4 more noodles over the ricotta filling and top with another cup of the béchamel. Top with the remaining filling, then the remaining noodles. Pour over the remaining béchamel and sprinkle the top with the remaining mozzarella. Sprinkle the Parmesan over the top.

5. Cover the pan with aluminum foil and bake for 30 minutes. Uncover and bake until bubbling and the top is golden brown, about another 15 minutes. If you end up with any leftovers, you can freeze in individual portions so that you can just pull single servings from the freezer and reheat as needed.

make it a meal kit Make the béchamel and the ricotta filling. Store each separately in sealable containers for up to 5 days in the refrigerator. When ready to finish the meal, assemble the lasagne as directed, then bake and serve.

bank a batch Make a double batch of the entire recipe and store the extra pan (before baking) for up to 5 days in the refrigerator or 3 months in the freezer. Thaw overnight in the refrigerator or in the microwave for 8 to 10 minutes on LOW. Bake as directed.

Artichoke Manicotti in Pesto Cream

As a kid, I always ordered manicotti from our favorite Italian restaurant. This spruced-up version contains tangy artichoke hearts in the filling, and I created a creamy pesto sauce as the topping, instead of a red sauce. I like to serve my light Cucumber Salad with Oranges & Mint (page 272) on the side.

Total Time: 48–53 minutes
Prep time: 20–25 minutes
Active cooking time: 3 minutes
Walk-away time: 25 minutes

Serves 4 to 6

Cooking spray

1 pound manicotti shells

One 14-ounce can artichoke hearts (not marinated), drained

½ cup ricotta cheese

½ cup shredded mozzarella cheese

1 teaspoon dried oregano

PESTO CREAM

2 tablespoons pine nuts

2 cups packed fresh basil leaves

1 cup heavy cream

2 tablespoons olive oil

2 tablespoons freshly grated Parmesan cheese, plus more as desired

2 cloves garlic, chopped

1. Preheat the oven to 375°F. Coat a 9x13-inch baking dish with cooking spray.

2. Cook the manicotti shells according to the package directions, then drain.

3. Meanwhile, in a food processor, combine the artichoke hearts, ricotta, mozzarella, and oregano and process until smooth. Spoon the mixture into the manicotti shells and place the shells side by side in the prepared pan. Set aside.

4. Place the pine nuts in a small dry skillet over medium heat and toast them until golden brown, about 3 minutes, shaking the pan frequently to prevent burning. Transfer the nuts to a food processor, add the basil, heavy cream, oil, Parmesan, and garlic, and process until smooth. Pour over the stuffed manicotti in the pan.

5. Bake the manicotti until the sauce is bubbly and the top is golden brown, about 25 minutes. Top with extra Parmesan before serving if desired.

make it a meal kit Cook and drain the shells. Make the manicotti filling and the pesto cream. Store each separately in sealable containers or plastic bags for up to 5 days in the refrigerator. When ready to finish the meal, stuff the artichoke filling into the manicotti shells and arrange in the pan as directed. Spoon the pesto cream over the shells and bake as directed.

bank a batch Make a double batch of the entire recipe and store for up to 5 days in the refrigerator or 3 months in the freezer. Thaw overnight in the refrigerator or in the microwave for 8 to 10 minutes on LOW. Bake as directed.

Caramelized Onions with Red Peppers & Balsamic Vinegar over Spinach Fettuccine

Sugary golden brown onions give depth to any dish. Add charred roasted red peppers and tangy balsamic vinegar, and you've got a sensational meal. I think this is a complete meal, but feel free to add a mixed green salad with a creamy dressing.

Total Time: 27–29 minutes

Prep time: 15 minutes

Active cooking time: 12–14 minutes

Serves 4

12 ounces spinach fettuccine

1 tablespoon olive oil

1 medium onion, sliced into half-moons (about 1 cup)

2 tablespoons sugar

1 cup sliced roasted red peppers (from a water-packed jar)

2 tablespoons balsamic vinegar

1 cup reduced-sodium vegetable broth

Salt and freshly ground black pepper to taste

1. Cook the pasta according to the package directions. Drain and set aside.

2. While the pasta is cooking, heat the oil in a large skillet over medium heat. Add the onions and sugar and cook, stirring a couple of times, until the onions are golden brown and caramelized, 8 to 10 minutes. Stir in the red peppers and vinegar and cook for 2 minutes. Add the broth and pasta and simmer for 2 minutes to heat through. Season with salt and pepper and serve.

make it a meal kit Cook and drain the fettuccine. Caramelize the onions. Store each separately in sealable containers or plastic bags for up to 3 days in the refrigerator. When ready to finish the meal, combine the fettuccine, caramelized onions, red peppers, vinegar, and broth and reheat in a large saucepan over medium heat or in the microwave for a few minutes on HIGH. Season with salt and pepper before serving.

Penne with Chorizo & Sweet Peppers in Garlic Cream Sauce

Chorizo is a garlicky pork sausage that lends tremendous flavor to all kinds of dishes. I like to serve this with Baby Spinach Salad with Strawberry–Sherry Vinaigrette (page 279).

Total Time: 19 minutes

Prep time: 15 minutes

Active cooking time: 4 minutes

Serves 4

1 pound penne pasta

2 teaspoons olive oil

4 cloves garlic, minced

2 cups diced chorizo or andouille sausage

2 cups chopped roasted red peppers (from a water-packed jar)

1 cup heavy cream

Salt and freshly ground black pepper to taste

1/4 cup freshly grated Parmesan cheese

1. Cook the pasta according to the package directions. Drain and set aside in a large serving bowl.

2. While the pasta is cooking, heat the oil in a large skillet over medium-high heat. Add the garlic and cook for 1 minute. Add the sausage and red peppers and cook for 2 minutes, until softened. Reduce the heat to low, add the heavy cream, bring to a simmer, and let simmer for 1 minute.

3. Remove from the heat and season with salt and pepper. Pour over the penne and sprinkle with the Parmesan just before serving.

make it a meal kit Cook and drain the pasta. Make the sauce (the oil through the heavy cream). Store each separately in sealable containers or plastic bags for up to 3 days in the refrigerator. When ready to finish the meal, combine the pasta and sauce and reheat in a medium saucepan over medium heat or in the microwave for a few minutes on HIGH. Season with salt and pepper and top with the Parmesan just before serving.

Ditalini with Turkey Sausage

This is a dish for kids and kids-at-heart! Ditalini is a fun shape, and the little pasta pieces take well to flavor-packed sausage slices. Partner this with steamed broccoli, Garlic-Roasted Asparagus with Almonds (page 241), or Red Lettuce with Honey–Maple Vinaigrette (page 282).

Total Time: 25–30 minutes
Prep time: 15–20 minutes
Active cooking time:
10 minutes

Serves 4

1 pound ditalini pasta

2 teaspoons olive oil

1 pound sweet turkey sausage, cut across into 1/4-inch-thick slices

One 15-ounce can tomato sauce

One 6-ounce can tomato paste

1 cup reduced-sodium chicken broth

1 teaspoon dried oregano

1/4 cup chopped fresh basil

1/4 cup freshly grated Parmesan cheese

1. Cook the pasta according to the package directions. Drain and set aside.

2. Heat the oil in a large skillet over medium heat. Add the sausage and cook until browned on both sides, about 5 minutes. Add the tomato sauce, tomato paste, broth, and oregano and bring to a simmer. Partially cover the pan and simmer until the sausage is cooked through, about 5 minutes. Add the pasta and stir to combine.

3. Remove from the heat and stir in the basil. Sprinkle with the Parmesan just before serving.

make it a meal kit Cook and drain the pasta. Slice the sausage. Combine the sauce ingredients (the tomato sauce through the oregano). Store each separately in sealable containers or plastic bags for up to 3 days in the refrigerator. When ready to finish the meal, cook the sausage as directed and add the pre-mixed sauce. Finish as directed.

bank a batch Prep a double batch of the sausage and store (before cooking) for up to 5 days in the refrigerator or 3 months in the freezer. Thaw overnight in the refrigerator or in the microwave for 8 to 10 minutes on LOW. Cook as directed and serve over mashed potatoes, alongside rice pilaf, or with dipping sauces, such as hoisin, black bean, or honey mustard. The sausage is also wonderful dunked in the Spicy Raisin Ketchup from Chicken Skewers with Spicy Raisin Ketchup (page 98).

morph it Make a double batch of the sausage and use the extras instead of the chicken meatballs in Spicy Chicken Meatballs in Tomato–Lime Dip (page 110).

. . . a dish for kids and

kids-at-heart!

Pasta Casino

This dish is always a winner, with smoky bacon, chewy clams, sweet green bell pepper, and refreshing parsley nestled into al dente linguine. I like to serve it with Rosemary-Roasted Vegetable Medley (page 259) or Seared Goat Cheese over Greens (page 276).

Total Time: 26 minutes

Prep time: 15 minutes

Active cooking time: 11 minutes

Serves 4

1 pound linguine

4 slices bacon, diced

1 medium green bell pepper, seeded and chopped

3 cloves garlic, minced

One 11-ounce can baby clams, undrained

1 cup reduced-sodium chicken broth

2 bay leaves

¼ cup chopped fresh parsley

Salt and freshly ground black pepper to taste

One 4-ounce chunk aged Asiago cheese

1. Cook the pasta according to the package directions. Drain and set aside.

2. While the pasta is cooking, cook the bacon in a large skillet over medium heat until crisp. Add the bell pepper and garlic and cook, stirring, until softened, about 3 minutes. Add the clams with their liquid from the can, the broth, and the bay leaves, bring to a simmer, and let simmer for 5 minutes. Remove the bay leaves, stir in the linguine, and toss to combine.

3. Remove from the heat, stir in the parsley, and season with salt and pepper. Transfer to a serving platter and, using a vegetable peeler, shave the cheese over the top of the pasta right before serving.

make it a meal kit Cook and drain the pasta. Make the clam sauce (the bacon through the bay leaves). Store each separately in sealable containers or plastic bags for up to 3 days in the refrigerator. When ready to finish the meal, remove the bay leaves from the clam sauce, combine the pasta and sauce, and reheat in a medium saucepan over medium heat or in the microwave for a few minutes on HIGH. Finish as directed.

Bowties with Pancetta & Tuna

Serve this warm or chilled. You can also substitute two 6-ounce cans of water-packed tuna or salmon for fresh (add the canned fish directly to the pasta, without heating it first).

Total Time: 25 minutes

Prep time: 15 minutes

Active cooking time: 10 minutes

Serves 4

1 pound farfalle (bowtie) pasta

2 teaspoons olive oil

$\frac{1}{2}$ cup diced pancetta, bacon, or ham

2 tuna steaks (5 to 6 ounces each)

Salt and freshly ground black pepper to taste

1 cup reduced-sodium vegetable or chicken broth

1 cup quartered oil-packed artichoke hearts

2 tablespoons chopped fresh parsley

1. Cook the pasta according to the package directions. Drain and transfer to a large bowl.

2. While the pasta is cooking, heat the oil in a large skillet over medium heat. Add the pancetta and cook, stirring, until golden and crisp, about 3 minutes. Season both sides of the tuna with salt and pepper; add to the hot pan and cook until browned, about 2 minutes per side. Add the broth and artichokes, bring to a simmer, and simmer until the fish is just cooked through and fork-tender, about 5 minutes.

3. Remove from the heat and stir the mixture into the pasta, breaking up the tuna into bite-size chunks. Stir in the parsley and season with salt and pepper.

make it a meal kit Cook and drain the pasta. Cook the pancetta. Store each separately in sealable containers or plastic bags for up to 3 days in the refrigerator. When ready to finish the meal, reheat the pasta the microwave for a few minutes on HIGH. Reheat the pancetta in a large skillet over medium heat. Finish as directed.

morph it Make with extra tuna from Grilled Tuna Steaks with Chipotle–Citrus Sauce (page 233).

have it your way Instead of tuna, substitute 2 diced boneless, skinless chicken breast halves or 1 pound medium shrimp, peeled and deveined. Simmer long enough to cook the chicken through, 5 to 7 minutes, or 3 to 4 minutes for the shrimp, until they're opaque and just cooked through.

Asparagus–Wild Mushroom Risotto with Parmesan

Risotto has a bad rap because of the constant stirring it requires. I have two thoughts on that: One, you can shorten the cooking time by using pre-cooked rice (see Morph It, right), or two, you can enjoy the time in the kitchen catching up with a loved one. Have a glass of wine, take turns stirring, chitchat for a bit, and the next thing you know, the risotto is creamy and wonderful! I like to serve this with a mixed green salad with a light vinaigrette or Mixed Cherry Tomato Salad (page 281).

Total Time: 38 minutes

Prep time: 10 minutes

Active cooking time: 28 minutes

Serves 4

2 teaspoons olive oil

2 shallots, chopped

2 cloves garlic, minced

6 cups sliced wild mushrooms (any combination of porcini, cremini, shiitake, chanterelle, oyster, etc.)

1 teaspoon dried thyme

1 cup Arborio (short-grain) rice

2$\frac{1}{2}$ to 3 cups reduced-sodium beef broth, or more if needed

2 cups chopped fresh or frozen (no need to thaw) asparagus spears (1-inch pieces)

$\frac{1}{2}$ cup freshly grated Parmesan cheese

Salt and freshly ground black pepper to taste

2 tablespoons chopped fresh parsley

1. Heat the oil in a large saucepan over medium heat. Add the shallots and garlic and cook for 1 minute. Add the mushrooms and cook, stirring a few times, until they soften, about 5 minutes. Add the thyme and cook for 1 minute, until fragrant. Add the rice and cook, stirring, until translucent and coated with the oil, about 1 minute. Add 1 cup of the broth and the asparagus and let simmer, stirring, until the liquid is almost entirely absorbed. Continue adding broth in $\frac{1}{2}$-cup measurements, waiting until the liquid is almost entirely absorbed before adding the next $\frac{1}{2}$ cup, until the rice is tender (about 20 minutes from start to finish).

2. Stir in the Parmesan and cook until the cheese melts. Season with salt and pepper. Ladle the risotto into warm bowls, top with the parsley, and serve immediately.

bank a batch Make a double batch of the entire meal and store the extra in a sealable container or plastic bag for up to 4 days in the refrigerator or 3 months in the freezer. Thaw overnight in the refrigerator or in the microwave for 5 minutes on LOW. Reheat in a large saucepan (with extra broth if needed) over medium heat or in the microwave for a few minutes on HIGH.

morph it To shorten the cooking time, make the dish with extra rice from Steak & Shiitake Fried Rice (page 184) and cut the cooking time down to 8 to 10 minutes. Add all of the broth (2½ cups) at once, instead of adding it in ½-cup measurements.

Make Quick Fix Risotto Cakes. Prepare a double batch of the risotto. When cool enough to handle, shape the risotto into cakes, each about 4 inches in diameter and 1 inch thick. Heat 1 tablespoon olive oil in a large skillet over medium-high heat until hot (1 to 2 minutes). Add the risotto cakes and cook for 2 minutes per side, until golden brown and heated through. Serve with a puree of roasted red peppers drizzled over the top (puree roasted red peppers in a blender with fresh basil and balsamic vinegar until smooth) or spoon over store-bought roasted red pepper sauce or tomato sauce.

have it your way Instead of Parmesan, substitute an equal amount of shredded sharp Cheddar or pecorino romano.

Zucchini Risotto with Gorgonzola

In this creamy concoction, I combine short-grain rice, zucchini, onion, garlic, oregano, and fresh chives, simmered in rich chicken broth. I like to serve it with Red Lettuce with Honey–Maple Vinaigrette (page 282) or Mixed Cherry Tomato Salad (page 281).

Total Time: 35 minutes

Prep time: 10 minutes

Active cooking time:
25 minutes

Serves 4

2 teaspoons olive oil

2 medium zucchini, cut into ¼-inch dice

½ cup chopped onion

3 cloves garlic, minced

1 teaspoon dried oregano

1 cup Arborio (short-grain) rice

2½ to 3 cups reduced-sodium chicken broth, or more if needed

½ cup crumbled Gorgonzola or other blue cheese

Salt and freshly ground black pepper to taste

2 tablespoons chopped fresh chives

1. Heat the oil in a large saucepan over medium heat. Add the zucchini, onion, and garlic and cook, stirring, until softened, about 3 minutes. Add the oregano and cook for 1 minute, until fragrant. Add the rice and cook, stirring, until translucent and coated with the oil, about 1 minute. Add 1 cup of the broth and cook until the liquid is almost entirely absorbed. Continue adding broth in ½-cup measurements, waiting until the liquid is almost entirely absorbed before adding the next ½ cup, until the rice is tender (about 20 minutes from start to finish).

2. Stir in the Gorgonzola and cook until the cheese melts. Season with salt and pepper. Ladle the risotto into warm bowls, top with the chives, and serve immediately.

bank a batch Make a double batch of the entire meal and store the extra in a sealable container or plastic bag for up to 4 days in the refrigerator or 3 months in the freezer. Thaw overnight in the refrigerator or in the microwave for 5 minutes on LOW. Reheat in a large saucepan (with extra broth if needed) over medium heat or in the microwave for a few minutes on HIGH.

morph it Make Quick Fix Risotto Cakes. See the Morph It for Asparagus–Wild Mushroom Risotto with Parmesan on page 77 for directions.

have it your way Swap crumbled feta or goat cheese for the Gorgonzola if desired.

. . . make Quick Fix Risotto Cakes

with the leftovers . . .

3

Chicken and Turkey

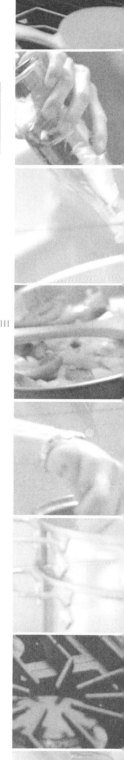

CHICKEN AND TURKEY ARE THE ULTIMATE Quick Fix foods because they can be prepped ahead, they cook quickly, both enjoy playing with other ingredients, and they can easily morph from one meal to the next with an entirely new set of ingredients. And, unless you're vegetarian, I bet a week doesn't go by at your house without chicken on the menu at least two times!

I always buy my chicken in big batches from the warehouse store. I typically buy boneless, skinless chicken breasts, ground turkey, and turkey tenderloin. When I get home, I freeze the poultry in *usable* portions, meaning about 1 pound for four servings. Sometimes, I freeze individual breasts of chicken so I can just pull one or two from the freezer with ease, depending on how many people I'm serving or whether I'm just adding a little protein to a soup, stew, or pasta dish. Finished dishes also freeze well, and my freezer is never complete without a container of turkey chili and a "banked batch" of a chicken dish of some sort.

Since protein-packed chicken and turkey are relatively mild in flavor, they work well with all kinds of global ingredients, from American Southwestern to Southeast Asian!

Chicken and turkey are ultimate Quick

Fix foods because they can be

prepped ahead . . .

Spanish Chicken

Chicken, broccoli, and two types of tomatoes (sun-dried and fresh) smothered in golden brown, gooey mozzarella cheese that's spiked with tangy Parmesan —got your taste buds going yet? The dish is fantastic with Onion Knots (page 264).

Total Time: 23–24 minutes

Prep time: 10 minutes

Active cooking time: 13–14 minutes

Serves 4

1 tablespoon olive oil

2 cloves garlic, minced

1¼ pounds boneless, skinless chicken breasts, cut into 1-inch pieces

2 cups fresh or thawed frozen broccoli florets

1 cup drained oil-packed sun-dried tomatoes, chopped

1 cup chopped Roma (plum) tomatoes

1 cup shredded mozzarella cheese

2 tablespoons freshly grated Parmesan cheese

1. Heat the oil in a large, ovenproof skillet over medium heat. Add the garlic and cook for 1 minute. Add the chicken and cook until golden brown on all sides, about 5 minutes. Add the broccoli, sun-dried tomatoes, and Roma tomatoes, partially cover the skillet, and simmer until the fresh tomatoes break down and the chicken is cooked through, about 5 minutes.

2. Meanwhile, preheat the broiler. Sprinkle the chicken mixture with the mozzarella and Parmesan. Place the pan under the broiler and broil until the cheese is golden and bubbly, 2 to 3 minutes.

bank a batch Make a double batch of the chicken mixture and transfer half to a casserole dish. Top with the cheese as directed, cover with plastic wrap, and store for up to 3 days in the refrigerator or up to 3 months in the freezer. When ready to eat, bake at 350°F until the cheese is melted and the casserole is heated through, about 45 minutes. If frozen, thaw the casserole overnight in the refrigerator or in the microwave for 8 to 10 minutes on LOW. To finish cooking in the microwave, cook for 5 minutes on HIGH.

Seared Almond-Crusted Chicken with Baby Corn & Tomatoes

Crusting chicken with crunchy almonds is an incredible way to spruce up an otherwise bland piece of meat. To make your life easier, pound the chicken between two pieces of plastic wrap or in a plastic bag for easier cleanup. This is perfect over rice.

Total Time: 20 minutes

Prep time: 10 minutes

Active cooking time: 10 minutes

Serves 4

2 tablespoons Dijon mustard

4 boneless, skinless chicken breast halves, pounded to a $\frac{1}{2}$-inch thickness

1 cup sliced blanched almonds

1 tablespoon olive oil

One 14-ounce can diced tomatoes, undrained

1 cup canned baby corn, drained and cut crosswise into 1-inch pieces

1 $\frac{1}{2}$ teaspoons curry powder

$\frac{1}{2}$ teaspoon salt

$\frac{1}{4}$ teaspoon freshly ground black pepper

2 tablespoons chopped fresh cilantro

1. Brush the mustard all over both sides of the chicken. Place the almonds in a shallow dish, add the chicken, and turn to coat both sides evenly.

2. Heat the oil in a large skillet over medium heat. Add the chicken and cook until golden brown (being careful not to burn the almonds), about 2 minutes per side. Add the tomatoes, corn, curry powder, salt, and pepper and bring to a simmer. Partially cover the skillet and simmer until the chicken is cooked through, about 5 minutes. Remove from the heat and top with the cilantro.

make it a meal kit Coat the chicken with the mustard and almonds; combine the tomatoes, corn, curry, salt, and pepper. Store each separately in sealable containers or plastic bags. Both will keep in the refrigerator for up to 3 days. When ready to finish the meal, brown the chicken, add the sauce ingredients, and finish as directed.

morph it Coat and brown a double batch of the chicken. Before adding the sauce ingredients, remove half of the chicken from the pan once it's cooked through, let cool, and store in a plastic bag in the refrigerator for up to 3 days or the freezer for up to 3 months. Use it in Warm Chicken–Cherry Waldorf in Romaine (page 90). Warm the chicken in the microwave for 1 minute on HIGH, or just serve it chilled in the salad.

. . . cook twice the amount of chicken

and morph it into Warm Chicken–Cherry

Waldorf in Romaine . . .

Chicken with Eggplant, Capers & Black Olives

Think of this as ratatouille with chicken. My version boasts olives and capers, which contribute both sweetness and saltiness to the dish. The eggplant mixture is also excellent served alongside cheese and crackers. A side of couscous completes this meal in just 5 minutes!

Total Time: 25–30 minutes

Prep time: 10–15 minutes

Active cooking time:
15 minutes

Serves 4

1 tablespoon olive oil

1¼ pounds boneless, skinless chicken breasts, cut into 1-inch pieces

1 medium eggplant, peeled and cut into 1-inch pieces

1 cup diced onion

2 cloves garlic, minced

One 14-ounce can diced tomatoes, undrained

1 cup canned pitted black olives, drained and thinly sliced

1 tablespoon drained capers

1 teaspoon dried thyme

1 teaspoon dried oregano

2 bay leaves

¼ cup chopped fresh basil

Salt and freshly ground black pepper to taste

1. Heat the oil in a large skillet over medium-high heat. Add the chicken and cook until browned on all sides, about 5 minutes. Remove from the pan and set aside. To the same skillet, add the eggplant, onion, and garlic and cook, stirring, until softened, about 3 minutes. Return the chicken to the pan and add the tomatoes, olives, capers, thyme, oregano, and bay leaves. Bring to a simmer, reduce the heat to low, then partially cover the skillet and simmer until the chicken is cooked through, about 5 minutes.

2. Remove from the heat, remove the bay leaves, stir in the basil, season with salt and pepper, and serve.

make it a meal kit Brown the chicken and remove it from the pan as directed. Make the eggplant-tomato mixture. Store each separately in sealable containers or plastic bags in the refrigerator for up to 3 days. When ready to finish the meal, combine the browned chicken and eggplant mixture and simmer as directed.

morph it Make a double batch of the eggplant-tomato mixture and remove half of it before returning the chicken to the pan. Use the sauce to simmer shrimp, scallops, or tofu chunks, or serve it as a topping for couscous. It will keep for up to 3 months in the freezer. Thaw overnight in the refrigerator. Reheat in a medium saucepan or in the microwave for a few minutes on HIGH.

have it your way For a vegetarian version, substitute 1 pound extra-firm tofu (cut into cubes) for the chicken and cook as directed.

Think of this as ratatouille

with chicken.

Mulligatawny Stew over Rice

Mulligatawny is a hearty dish, like a thick stew or soup, and almost always contains chicken and rice. My version boasts loads of vegetables, garlic, ginger, curry, sweet coconut, and fresh cilantro.

Total Time: 24–31 minutes

Prep time: 10–15 minutes

Active cooking time:
14–16 minutes

Serves 4

2 cups instant rice

1 tablespoon olive oil

1 cup chopped onion

2 medium carrots, chopped

2 stalks celery, chopped

2 cloves garlic, minced

2 teaspoons peeled and minced fresh ginger

1¼ pounds boneless, skinless chicken breasts, cut into 1-inch pieces

1 tablespoon curry powder

3½ cups (two 14.5-ounce cans) reduced-sodium chicken broth

One 14-ounce can unsweetened coconut milk

¼ cup chopped fresh cilantro

Salt and freshly ground black pepper to taste

1. Cook the rice according to the package directions.

2. Meanwhile, heat the oil in a large saucepan over medium-high heat. Add the onion, carrots, celery, garlic, and ginger and cook, stirring, until the vegetables soften, about 3 minutes. Add the chicken and cook until golden brown, 3 to 5 minutes. Add the curry powder, stir to coat, and cook for 1 minute. Add the broth, bring to a simmer, and continue to simmer until the chicken is cooked through, about 5 minutes. Add the coconut milk and simmer for another 2 minutes.

3. Remove from the heat, stir in the cilantro, and season with salt and pepper. Spoon the rice into bowls and top with the mulligatawny stew.

make it a meal kit Cook the rice and chop the vegetables and chicken. Store each separately in sealable containers or plastic bags for up to 3 days in the refrigerator. When ready to finish the meal, cook as directed.

bank a batch Make a double batch of the stew and rice and store each separately for up to 3 months in the freezer. Thaw overnight in the refrigerator or in the microwave for 6 to 8 minutes on LOW. Reheat the stew in a large saucepan over medium heat or in the microwave for 3 to 4 minutes on HIGH. Reheat the rice in the microwave for a few minutes on HIGH.

. . . a hearty dish with loads of

vegetables, garlic, ginger, curry,

sweet coconut, and fresh cilantro.

Warm Chicken–Cherry Waldorf in Romaine

Waldorf salad is a signature combination of apples, walnuts, and chicken. My contribution to the dish is the addition of sweet dried cherries and anise-like fennel. Plus, I like to serve the salad warm. You can serve it warm or chilled—your choice.

Total Time: 18–23 minutes
Prep time: 10–15 minutes
Walk-away time: 8 minutes

Serves 4

1 1/4 pounds boneless, skinless chicken breasts

1 cup sweetened dried cherries or cranberries

2 Granny Smith apples, cored and chopped

1 bulb fennel, trimmed and chopped

1/2 cup walnut pieces

2 tablespoons chopped fresh chives

1/2 cup mayonnaise

1 tablespoon fresh lemon juice

1 teaspoon Dijon mustard

1/2 teaspoon finely grated lemon zest

Salt and freshly ground black pepper to taste

4 leaves romaine lettuce

1. Place the chicken in a large saucepan and pour over enough water to cover. Set over high heat and bring to a boil. Reduce the heat to medium and simmer until the chicken is cooked through, about 8 minutes.

2. Drain and, when cool enough to handle, cut the chicken into 1-inch pieces. Transfer the still warm chicken to a large bowl and add the cherries, apples, fennel, walnuts, and chives. Toss to combine.

3. In a small bowl, whisk together the mayonnaise, lemon juice, mustard, and lemon zest. Add to the chicken mixture and stir to coat. Season with salt and pepper.

4. Arrange the lettuce leaves on a serving platter or individual plates. Spoon the chicken mixture evenly into the lettuce leaves and serve. If serving chilled, you can make the chicken mixture up to 2 days in advance and store in a sealable container in the refrigerator.

make it a meal kit Poach the chicken and whisk together the mayonnaise, lemon juice, mustard, and lemon zest. Store each separately in sealable containers or plastic bags for up to 3 days in the refrigerator. When ready to finish the meal, cube the chicken and toss it with the mayonnaise mixture; add the remaining ingredients and serve.

morph it Poach a double batch of the chicken and store the extra for up to 3 months in the freezer. Thaw overnight in the refrigerator or in the microwave for a few minutes on LOW. Use the extra, cut into pieces, in Chicken with Pistachio–Parsley Pesto (page 104) or in place of the baked chicken in Baked Chicken with Green Spinach–Horseradish Sauce (page 112).

Cereal-Crusted Chicken with Curry Cream

Take that breakfast treat to a new level! You can use any unsweetened cereal, granola, or oats when you want to explore new flavors. (For the best results, place the cereal in a plastic bag and roll with a rolling pin until coarsely crushed or give it a quick spin in the food processor.) I like to serve this dish with Sautéed Carrots & Parsnips (page 252).

Total Time: 35 minutes
Prep time: 10 minutes
Walk-away time: 25 minutes

Serves 4

Cooking spray

2 cups crushed unsweetened cornflakes cereal

4 boneless, skinless chicken breast halves

Salt and freshly ground black pepper to taste

¼ cup orange marmalade

CURRY CREAM
½ cup sour cream

1 teaspoon curry powder

Pinch of paprika

1. Preheat the oven to 400°F. Coat a large baking sheet with cooking spray.

2. Place the crushed cereal in a shallow dish and set aside.

3. Season both sides of the chicken with salt and pepper. Brush the marmalade over both sides of the chicken. Add the chicken to the cereal and turn to coat both sides. Place the chicken on the prepared sheet and spray the tops with cooking spray. Bake until the crust is golden brown and chicken is cooked through, about 25 minutes.

4. In a small bowl, whisk together the sour cream, curry powder, and paprika.

5. Serve the chicken with the curry cream spooned over the top or on the side.

make it a meal kit Coat the chicken with the cereal as directed. Whisk together the curry cream. Store each separately (before cooking the chicken) in sealable containers or plastic bags for up to 3 days in the refrigerator. When ready to finish the meal, bake the chicken as directed and serve with the curry cream over the top.

bank a batch Make a double batch of the chicken and store it in a sealable container or plastic bag for up to 3 days in the refrigerator or 3 months in the freezer. Thaw overnight in the refrigerator or in the microwave for 4 to 6 minutes on LOW. Reheat in a 350°F oven for 10 to 15 minutes or in the microwave for a few minutes on HIGH.

morph it Make a double batch of the chicken and use the extra in place of the poached chicken in the Warm Chicken–Cherry Waldorf in Romaine (page 90) or in place of the deli-sliced turkey in Turkey–Spinach Salad with Strawberries, Kiwi & Cashews in Honey–Sesame Dressing (page 128), or simply top it with mango chutney, fresh tomato salsa, or diced mango and lime juice!

Make a double batch of the curry cream and use it as a dip for fresh vegetables, grilled shrimp, or chilled crab claws or as a topping for pork, turkey, or baked fish. Store the cream in a sealable container for up to 3 days in the refrigerator.

Thai Chicken & Noodles

Raid your pantry for this winner and you'll have dinner on the table in lightning speed. I love the fresh combination of Thai flavors—garlic, ginger, soy sauce, lime, and sesame. You can top the dish with salted peanuts for more flavor and crunch. Served over rice noodles, this is a complete, satisfying meal!

Total Time: 16–18 minutes

Prep time: 10 minutes

Active cooking time:
6–8 minutes

Serves 4

8 ounces rice noodles

1 tablespoon peanut oil

2 cloves garlic, minced

1 tablespoon peeled and minced fresh ginger

1¼ pounds boneless, skinless chicken breasts, cut into 1-inch pieces

¼ cup reduced-sodium soy sauce

2 teaspoons toasted sesame oil

2 tablespoons fresh lime juice

Dash of hot sauce

¼ cup chopped scallions (white and green parts)

Lime wedges for garnish (optional)

1. Cook the noodles according to the package directions. Drain, reserving ¼ cup of the cooking water.

2. Meanwhile, heat the peanut oil in a large skillet over medium-high heat. Add the garlic and ginger and cook for 1 minute. Add the chicken and cook until golden brown on all sides, 3 to 5 minutes. Add the reserved cooking water, the soy sauce, sesame oil, lime juice, and hot sauce and bring to a simmer. Add the noodles and cook for 2 minutes to heat through, stirring frequently.

3. Remove from the heat and stir in the scallions. Serve with lime wedges on the side if you like.

make it a meal kit Cook and drain the noodles and make the chicken mixture. Store each separately in sealable containers or plastic bags for up to 3 days in the refrigerator. When ready to finish the meal, reheat the chicken mixture in a large skillet over medium heat and finish as directed.

bank a batch Make a double batch of the entire meal and store the extra noodles and chicken mixture separately for up to 3 months in the freezer. Thaw overnight in the refrigerator or in the microwave for 5 to 7 minutes on LOW. Reheat the chicken mixture on the stovetop in a large saucepan or in the microwave for a few minutes on HIGH. Reheat the noodles in the microwave for a few minutes on HIGH.

. . . you'll have dinner on the

table in lightning speed.

Sicilian Chicken

I like to serve the dish with rigatoni tossed in a little olive oil and seasoned with salt and black pepper. For easy cleanup, pound the chicken between two pieces of plastic wrap or in a plastic bag (use the flat side of a meat mallet, the bottom of a heavy skillet, or a rolling pin to pound the chicken).

Total Time: 20–25 minutes

Prep time: 10–15 minutes

Active cooking time:
10 minutes

Serves 4

4 boneless, skinless chicken breast halves, pounded to a ½-inch thickness

Salt and freshly ground black pepper to taste

¼ cup all-purpose flour

1 tablespoon olive oil

½ cup dry white wine or dry vermouth

One 14-ounce can diced tomatoes, undrained

½ cup sliced pimiento-stuffed green olives

¼ cup golden raisins

1 tablespoon balsamic vinegar

1 teaspoon dried oregano

¼ cup chopped fresh basil

1. Season both sides of the chicken with salt and pepper. Place the flour in a shallow dish, add the chicken, and turn to coat evenly. Tap off any excess flour.

2. Heat the oil in a large skillet over medium-high heat. Add the chicken and cook until golden brown, about 2 minutes per side. Add the wine and cook for 1 minute. Add the tomatoes, olives, raisins, vinegar, and oregano and bring to a simmer. Partially cover the skillet and simmer until the chicken is cooked through and the sauce thickens, about 5 minutes. Remove from the heat, sprinkle with the basil, and serve.

morph it Brown a double batch of the chicken and remove half of it from the pan before adding the tomatoes and remaining ingredients. Let it cool, then store in a sealable container or plastic bag in the refrigerator for up to 3 days or in the freezer for up to 3 months. Cube the extra chicken and morph it into Mulligatawny Stew over Rice (page 88); eliminate the cooking time for the chicken and add the chicken when you add the vegetables.

Or, warm the extra chicken in the microwave for 1 minute on HIGH, slice into thin strips, and use it in Warm Chicken–Cherry Waldorf in Romaine (page 90) or in place of the turkey in Turkey–Spinach Salad with Strawberries, Kiwi & Cashews in Honey–Sesame Dressing (page 128).

Chicken with Chili con Queso Cream Sauce

This sauce is also an excellent dip with tortilla chips. For a complete meal, serve with instant brown rice on the side or underneath.

Total Time: 17–19 minutes

Prep time: 10 minutes

Active cooking time: 7–9 minutes

Serves 4

1 tablespoon olive oil

4 boneless, skinless chicken breast halves

Salt and freshly ground black pepper to taste

1 tablespoon chili powder

1 teaspoon ground cumin

CHILI CON QUESO CREAM SAUCE

1¼ cups milk (2% milk fat or higher works best)

1 cup shredded Monterey Jack cheese

One 10-ounce package frozen chopped spinach, thawed, drained well, and squeezed dry

One 6-ounce jar chopped pimientos, drained

One 4-ounce can diced green chiles, drained

1. Heat the oil in a large skillet over medium-high heat. Season the chicken all over with salt and pepper. In a small bowl, combine the chili powder and cumin; rub into both sides of the chicken. Add the chicken to the hot oil and cook until golden brown, about 2 minutes per side. Remove from the pan and set aside.

2. In the same pan over medium-low heat, combine the sauce ingredients. Bring to a simmer, stirring frequently and simmering until the cheese melts. Return the chicken to the pan and simmer until cooked through, 3 to 5 minutes.

make it a meal kit Season the chicken with salt and pepper and rub with the spices. Combine the sauce ingredients. Store each separately for up to 3 days in the refrigerator. When ready to finish the meal, brown the chicken as directed, add the cheese sauce to the pan, and finish cooking.

bank a batch Make a double batch of the entire meal and store the extra in a sealable container for up to 3 months in the freezer. Thaw overnight in the refrigerator or in the microwave for 5 to 7 minutes on LOW. Reheat in a large skillet or saucepan or in the microwave for a few minutes on HIGH.

Chicken Skewers with Spicy Raisin Ketchup

Meet your new barbecue sauce! You'll adore the combination of sweet raisins, earthy cumin, and tangy jalapeño pepper. Serve this with Toasted Coconut Rice (page 261). If using wooden skewers, soak them for at least 20 minutes before using to prevent scorching.

Total Time: 15–22 minutes

Prep time: 10–15 minutes

Active cooking time:
5–7 minutes

Serves 4

Cooking spray

1¼ pounds boneless, skinless chicken breasts, cut into 2-inch pieces

2 medium zucchini, cut into 2-inch pieces

Metal or wooden skewers

2 tablespoons olive oil

Salt and freshly ground black pepper

SPICY RAISIN KETCHUP

¾ cup ketchup

½ cup dark raisins

2 tablespoons balsamic vinegar

1 tablespoon minced fresh or pickled jalapeño chile pepper

1 teaspoon ground cumin

1. Coat a stovetop grill pan or griddle with cooking spray and set over medium-high heat.

2. Meanwhile, thread alternating pieces of chicken and zucchini onto the skewers. Brush them with the oil and season with salt and pepper. Place the skewers on the hot grill pan and cook until the chicken is cooked through, 5 to 7 minutes total, turning frequently.

3. Meanwhile, in a small saucepan, combine the spicy ketchup ingredients. Set the pan over medium heat, bring to a simmer, and continue to simmer until the raisins plump up, about 5 minutes.

4. Serve the spicy ketchup alongside the skewers for dunking.

make it a meal kit Assemble the skewers as directed. Make the spicy ketchup. Store each separately in sealable containers or plastic bags for up to 3 days in the refrigerator or up to 3 months in the freezer. Thaw overnight in the refrigerator or in the microwave for 5 minutes on LOW. When ready to finish the meal, cook the skewers as directed. Reheat the sauce on the stovetop in a small saucepan over medium heat or in the microwave for a few minutes on HIGH.

morph it Make a double batch of the ketchup and use it as a fantastic barbecue sauce for flank steak and turkey tenderloin (for a smooth sauce, puree it in a blender or food processor). Store the extra ketchup in a sealable container for up to 7 days in the refrigerator or up to 3 months in the freezer. Thaw overnight in the refrigerator or in the microwave for 3 minutes on LOW.

have it your way Instead of chicken, try medium shrimp (peeled and deveined), scallops, or cubed steak; instead of zucchini, use sliced red onion, cremini mushrooms, and/or sliced bell peppers.

Instead of the Spicy Raisin Ketchup, serve the skewers with the Orange–Ginger Sauce on page 102.

Meet your new barbecue sauce!

Chicken Breasts with Cranberry-Spiked Stuffing

Stuffing chicken breasts is easy and fun, and you can explore a variety of fillings when you're ready for a change. Excellent substitutions for the cranberries include dried cherries, currants, dried plums, and dried apples. I like to serve this with Garlic-Roasted Asparagus with Almonds (page 241).

Total Time: 45 minutes

Prep time: 15 minutes

Walk-away time: 30 minutes

Serves 4

Cooking spray

4 boneless, skinless chicken breast halves

1$\frac{1}{2}$ cups cubed dry stuffing or cubed day-old bread

$\frac{1}{2}$ cup sweetened dried cranberries

$\frac{1}{4}$ cup chopped scallions (white and green parts)

2 teaspoons dried sage

1 teaspoon dried oregano

$\frac{1}{2}$ teaspoon salt

$\frac{1}{4}$ teaspoon freshly ground black pepper

1 cup reduced-sodium chicken broth

1 tablespoon Dijon mustard

1. Preheat the oven to 400°F. Coat a large baking sheet with cooking spray.

2. Using a sharp knife, cut the chicken crosswise (as if cutting a bagel) almost through to the other side, but not all the way through. Open the chicken (as if opening a book) and transfer to the prepared sheet.

3. In a large bowl, combine the stuffing, cranberries, scallions, sage, oregano, salt, and pepper. Toss to combine. In a small bowl, whisk together the broth and mustard. Add this to the stuffing mixture and stir until blended and the mixture sticks together. Spoon the stuffing over the bottom half of each chicken breast. Fold the chicken over to cover the filling and season the top with salt and pepper. Secure the chicken closed with wooden toothpicks. Bake until the chicken is cooked through, about 30 minutes.

make it a meal kit Slice open the chicken breasts, make the stuffing, and store each separately in sealable containers or plastic bags for up to 3 days in the refrigerator (do not stuff the chicken until ready to bake).

bank a batch Make a double batch of the stuffed chicken and bake as directed. Store the extra cooked chicken for up to 3 days in the refrigerator or up to 3 months in the freezer. Thaw overnight in the refrigerator or in the microwave for 4 to 6 minutes on LOW. Reheat in a 350°F oven for about 15 minutes or in the microwave for a few minutes on HIGH.

. . . explore a variety of fillings . . .

Pan-Grilled Chicken with Orange–Ginger Sauce

What an amazing sauce for chicken. It's also a great sauce for pork and salmon. Serve this with rice or cellophane noodles for a complete meal.

Total Time: 16–21 minutes

Prep time: 10 minutes

Active cooking time:
6–11 minutes

Serves 4

Cooking spray

1 tablespoon toasted sesame oil

4 boneless, skinless chicken breast halves

Salt and freshly ground black pepper to taste

ORANGE–GINGER SAUCE

1 cup orange juice

2 tablespoons reduced-sodium soy sauce

1 tablespoon light brown sugar

1 tablespoon cornstarch

1 teaspoon peeled and finely grated fresh ginger

1. Coat a stovetop grill pan with cooking spray and set over medium heat.

2. Brush the sesame oil all over the chicken and season with salt and pepper. Place on the hot pan and cook until cooked through, 3 to 5 minutes per side.

3. Meanwhile, in a small saucepan, whisk together the sauce ingredients until blended. Set the pan over medium-high heat and bring to a simmer. Reduce the heat to medium and simmer until the sauce thickens, about 5 minutes. Spoon the sauce over the chicken and serve.

make it a meal kit Grill the chicken, make the sauce, and store each separately in sealable containers or plastic bags for up to 3 days in the refrigerator. Reheat the sauce in a medium saucepan or in the microwave for a few minutes on HIGH. Add the chicken to the warm sauce and simmer until heated through (or add the chicken to the sauce in the microwave and cook for 1 minute on HIGH, until hot).

morph it Grill a double batch of chicken and morph the extra into Chicken & Sausage Sandwiches with Fried Bell Peppers (page 116).

Seared Chicken with Merlot & Raspberry Sauce

If you don't have olive oil handy, substitute any oil you have. I like to serve this with regular couscous or Garlic–Herb Couscous (page 262).

Total Time: 13–15 minutes

Prep time: 5 minutes

Active cooking time: 8–10 minutes

Serves 4

1 tablespoon olive oil

4 boneless, skinless chicken breast halves

Salt and freshly ground black pepper to taste

1 cup merlot or other dry red wine

RASPBERRY SAUCE

½ cup raspberry preserves

½ cup reduced-sodium chicken broth or water

1 teaspoon finely grated orange zest (optional)

1. Heat the oil in a large skillet over medium heat. Season the chicken all over with salt and pepper and add to the hot pan. Sear until golden brown, about 2 minutes per side. Add the merlot and cook for 1 minute.

2. In a measuring cup, whisk together the sauce ingredients and add to the pan. Simmer until the sauce thickens and reduces and the chicken is cooked through, 3 to 5 minutes, then serve.

bank a batch Make a double batch of the entire meal and store the extra in a sealable container or plastic bag for up to 3 days in the refrigerator or up to 3 months in the freezer. Thaw overnight in the refrigerator or in the microwave for 5 to 7 minutes on LOW. Reheat in a large skillet or in the microwave for a few minutes on HIGH.

have it your way Feel free to substitute whatever fruit preserves you have handy. Strawberry, blackberry, and apricot preserves all work great, as does orange marmalade (and you can skip the addition of orange zest when you use orange marmalade).

Chicken with Pistachio–Parsley Pesto

Making pesto from scratch is a breeze when you use a blender or food processor. For variations on this pesto, instead of pistachios and parsley, try toasted slivered almonds (toast them in a small dry skillet over low heat for a few minutes, until golden brown) and basil, or walnuts and sage, or pine nuts and cilantro. I usually serve this over angel hair pasta, with Mixed Cherry Tomato Salad (page 281) on the side.

Total Time: 18–20 minutes

Prep time: 10–12 minutes

Active cooking time:
8 minutes

Serves 4

12 ounces angel hair pasta

2 teaspoons olive oil

$\frac{1}{2}$ cup chopped onion

$1\frac{1}{4}$ pounds boneless, skinless chicken breast halves, cut into 1-inch pieces

PISTACHIO–PARSLEY PESTO

1 packed cup fresh parsley leaves

$\frac{1}{3}$ cup sour cream

$\frac{1}{4}$ cup freshly grated Parmesan cheese

3 tablespoons olive oil, or more as needed

2 tablespoons salted dry-roasted pistachios

3 cloves garlic

$\frac{1}{2}$ teaspoon salt

1. Cook the pasta according to the package directions. Drain, transfer to a warm serving platter, and keep warm.

2. Heat the oil in a large skillet over medium heat. Add the onion and cook, stirring, for 2 minutes. Add the chicken and cook until golden brown on all sides, 5 minutes.

3. In a blender, combine the pesto ingredients and process until smooth, adding more oil if necessary to create a saucelike consistency.

4. Add the sauce to the chicken in the skillet and cook for 1 minute to heat through. Serve the chicken and sauce over the pasta.

make it a meal kit Cook and drain the pasta, cook the chicken mixture, and make the pesto. Store each separately in sealable containers or plastic bags, up to 3 days in the refrigerator for the pasta and chicken, up to 5 days in the refrigerator for the pesto. When ready to finish the meal, reheat the pasta in the microwave for a few minutes on HIGH. Toss the chicken and pesto together in a large skillet over medium heat until heated through, then pour over the pasta. You can also reheat the chicken and pesto together in the microwave for a few minutes on HIGH.

bank a batch Make a double batch of the pesto and use it over grilled fish, steamed or sautéed shrimp, pan-seared pork medallions, or in place of the Artichoke–Basil Pesto in Chicken with Artichoke–Basil Pesto (page 114). Store for up to 3 months in the freezer. Thaw overnight in the refrigerator or in the microwave for a few minutes on LOW.

. . . pesto from scratch is

a breeze in the blender

or food processor . . .

5-Ingredient Sweet-n-Sour Chicken

This is an excellent use of pantry staples. The sauce is also suitable for pork or shrimp. I like to serve this with steamed French-cut green beans and quinoa or jasmine rice.

Total Time: 15 minutes

Prep time: 5 minutes

Active cooking time: 10 minutes

Serves 4

2 teaspoons peanut or vegetable oil

1 ¼ pounds boneless, skinless chicken breasts, cut into 1-inch pieces

One 11-ounce can crushed pineapple in juice

¼ cup apricot preserves

¼ cup hoisin sauce

Heat the oil in a large skillet over medium-high heat. Add the chicken and cook until golden brown on all sides, about 5 minutes. Add the pineapple with the juice from the can, the apricot preserves, and the hoisin sauce and bring to a simmer. Let simmer until the chicken is cooked through and the sauce thickens and reduces, about 5 minutes.

bank a batch Make a double batch of the entire meal and store the extra in a sealable container for up to 3 days in the refrigerator or up to 3 months in the freezer. Thaw overnight in the refrigerator or in the microwave for 5 to 7 minutes on LOW. Reheat in a large skillet or saucepan or in the microwave for a few minutes on HIGH.

Sweet Potato Soup with Parmesan & Basil; see Have It Your Way variation, p. 17

Three-Onion Soup with Cheese-Smothered Toast, p. 20

White Bean Soup with Andouille & Collard Greens, p. 22

Red Pepper Hummus with Toasted Pita Triangles, p. 30

Quick Spanakopita, p. 32 and 5-Ingredient Wild Mushroom Turnovers with Romano Cheese, p. 34

Rotelle with Roasted Fennel, Baby Carrots &
Shaved Pecorino Romano, p. 49

Caramelized Onions with Red Peppers & Balsamic Vinegar over Spinach Fettucine, p. 70

Beet Ravioli in Gorgonzola Broth, p. 63

Artichoke Manicotti in Pesto Cream, p. 68

Bowties with Pancetta & Tuna, p. 75

Zucchini Risotto with Gorgonzola, p. 78

Spanish Chicken, p. 83

Seared Almond-Crusted Chicken with Baby Corn & Tomatoes, p. 84

Chicken Breasts with Cranberry-Spiked Stuffing, p. 100, and Garlic-Roasted Asparagus with Almonds, p. 241

Sesame Chicken with Bok Choy, p. 108

Roasted Turkey Tenderloin with New
Potatoes & Tarragon Broth, p. 126, and
Warm Spinach Salad with Pancetta,
Gorgonzola & Pine Nuts, p. 275

Turkey–Spinach Salad with Strawberries, Kiwi & Cashews in Honey–Sesame Dressing, p. 128

Parmesan–Sage Pork Loin, p. 134

Asian Pork Kebabs with Apricot Mayonnaise, p. 138, over Toasted Coconut Rice, p. 261

Chipotle Pork Soft Tacos, p. 144

Grilled Pork over Toasted Polenta, p. 140

Seared Ham with Jalapeño–Apple Chutney, p. 156, and German Potato Salad, p. 267

Anita's Slow Cooker Chili,
p. 166

Moroccan Beef Stew, p. 172

Steak & Shiitake Fried Rice, p. 184

Filet Mignon with Spicy Rémoulade,
p. 178, and Roasted Broccoli with
Red Onion & Walnuts, p. 246

5-Ingredient London Broil with Cumin-Roasted Tomatoes & Corn, p. 197

Bacon-Wrapped Scallops with Jalapeño–Papaya Salsa, p. 206

Halibut Nachos with Chipotle Aïoli, p. 226

Shrimp in Salsa Verde, p. 211, and Vegetable Sauté with Black Bean Sauce, p. 258

Herbed Fish Cakes with Cucumber–Mint Relish, p. 230

Braised Trout with Bacon & Mushrooms, p. 232, and Roasted Brussels Sprouts with Sun-Dried Tomatoes, p. 245

5-Ingredient Lemon Pepper Salmon, p. 236, and Sautéed Red Cabbage with Mandarins, p. 247

Twice-Baked Potatoes with Cheddar & Bacon, p. 253

Rosemary-Roasted Vegetable Medley, p. 259

Beet–Arugula Salad with Buttermilk–Blue Cheese Dressing, p. 270

Seared Goat Cheese over Greens, p. 276

Frozen Key Lime Pie, p. 288

Blueberry–Nectarine Galette, p. 291

Orange-Poached Pears with Fudge Sauce, p. 294

Roasted Chicken Breasts with Garlic, Rosemary & Lemon

To round out this meal, roast cubed red potatoes alongside the chicken. You'll get an instant side dish without dirtying another pan!

Total Time: 35 minutes

Prep time: 10 minutes

Walk-away time: 25 minutes

Serves 4

Cooking spray

4 boneless, skinless chicken breast halves

Salt and freshly ground black pepper to taste

1 tablespoon olive oil

2 tablespoons fresh lemon juice

1 tablespoon finely grated lemon zest

2 to 3 cloves garlic, to your taste, minced

2 tablespoons chopped fresh rosemary

1. Preheat the oven to 400°F. Coat a roasting pan with cooking spray.

2. Season the chicken all over with salt and pepper and place in the prepared pan. Brush the top of the chicken with the oil. Drizzle over the lemon juice, then sprinkle with the lemon zest, garlic, and rosemary. Roast until the chicken is golden brown and cooked through, 25 to 30 minutes.

morph it Make a double batch and morph the extra into Chicken & Sausage Sandwiches with Fried Bell Peppers (page 116) or Warm Chicken–Cherry Waldorf in Romaine (page 90).

Sesame Chicken with Bok Choy

The recipe calls for red curry paste, a wonderfully tangy ingredient sold with the Asian ingredients in the supermarket. If you can't find it, substitute curry powder for a different flavor. I like to serve this with rice noodles or cellophane noodles on the side.

Total Time: 18–22 minutes

Prep time: 10 minutes

Active cooking time:
8–12 minutes

Serves 4

1 tablespoon olive oil

4 cups chopped bok choy (stems and leaves)

1 medium red bell pepper, seeded and sliced into thin strips

4 boneless, skinless chicken breast halves

Salt and freshly ground black pepper to taste

1/2 cup reduced-sodium chicken broth

1/2 cup sake (rice wine)

1 tablespoon toasted sesame oil

1 tablespoon peeled and minced fresh ginger

1 teaspoon red curry paste

1/4 cup chopped fresh cilantro

1. Heat the oil in a large skillet over medium-high heat. Add the bok choy and bell pepper and cook, stirring, for 2 minutes. Remove the vegetables from the pan and set aside.

2. Season both sides of the chicken with salt and pepper and add to the hot pan. Cook until golden brown, about 2 minutes per side.

3. In a small bowl, whisk together the broth, sake, sesame oil, ginger, and curry paste, pour over the chicken, and bring to a simmer. Return the vegetables to the pan, partially cover, and simmer until the chicken is cooked through, 2 to 4 minutes. Remove from the heat, top with the cilantro, and serve.

make it a meal kit Chop the bok choy and slice the pepper. Whisk together the sauce ingredients (the broth through the curry paste). Store each separately in sealable containers or plastic bags for up to 3 days in the refrigerator. When ready to finish the meal, cook as directed.

slow cook it (And Bank a Batch by doubling the recipe in a large slow cooker—it's too easy not to!) Arrange the bok choy and red pepper in the bottom of a medium to large slow cooker. Season the chicken with salt and pepper and place on top of the bok choy. In a small bowl, whisk together the broth, sake, sesame oil, ginger, and curry paste and pour over the chicken. Cover and cook on LOW for 6 to 8 hours or HIGH for 3 to 4 hours. Top with the cilantro just before serving. When Banking a Batch, store the extra chicken and vegetables in a sealable container or plastic bags for up to 3 days in the refrigerator or up to 3 months in the freezer. Thaw overnight in the refrigerator or in the microwave for 5 minutes on LOW. Reheat in a large saucepan over medium heat or in the microwave for a few minutes on HIGH.

Bank a Batch by doubling

the recipe in a slow cooker . . .

Spicy Chicken Meatballs with Tomato–Lime Dip

My inspiration for this dish came from south of the border. The chicken meatballs are spiked with hot chiles, scallions, ginger, and garlic, then served with a tangy tomato sauce that's spruced up with fresh lime and cumin. I like to serve this with warm tortillas and Southwest Cabbage Slaw (page 268).

Total Time: 21–23 minutes

Prep time: 15 minutes

Active cooking time:
6–8 minutes

Makes 16 meatballs and
1¾ cups dip; serves 6 to 8

SPICY CHICKEN MEATBALLS

1¼ pounds ground chicken

¼ cup chopped fresh cilantro

1 fresh serrano or jalapeño chile pepper, seeded and minced

2 cloves garlic, minced

2 scallions (white and green parts), finely chopped

1 teaspoon peeled and finely grated fresh ginger

½ teaspoon salt

¼ teaspoon freshly ground black pepper

1 tablespoon olive oil

TOMATO–LIME DIP

One 15-ounce can tomato sauce

2 tablespoons fresh lime juice

1 teaspoon ground cumin

Salt and freshly ground black pepper to taste

1. In a large bowl, combine all the meatball ingredients except the oil. Mix well, then shape into golf ball–size meatballs.

2. Heat the oil in a large skillet over medium-high heat. Add the meatballs and cook until browned on all sides and cooked through, 5 to 7 minutes.

3. Meanwhile, in a small saucepan, combine the tomato sauce, lime juice, and cumin. Set the pan over medium heat and bring to a simmer. Partially cover and let simmer for 5 minutes. Season with salt and pepper.

4. Serve the meatballs with the tomato-lime dip on the side for dunking.

make it a meal kit Shape the meatballs and make the dip. Store each separately in sealable containers for up to 3 days in the refrigerator. When ready to finish the meal, brown the meatballs as directed and reheat the sauce in a small saucepan over medium heat or in the microwave for a few minutes on HIGH.

bank a batch Make a double batch of the entire meal and store the extra meatballs and sauce separately in sealable containers for up to 3 months in the freezer. Thaw overnight in the refrigerator or in the microwave for 5 to 7 minutes on LOW. Reheat the meatballs in a large saucepan (when reheating in a saucepan, add a little olive oil to the pan if necessary to keep the meatballs from sticking) or in the microwave for a few minutes on HIGH. Reheat the sauce in a small saucepan or in the microwave for a few minutes on HIGH.

morph it Make a double batch of the dip; it's great with grilled chicken or flank steak, steamed shrimp, or fresh vegetables (warm or chilled).

have it your way Feel free to swap ground turkey or lean ground beef for the chicken if desired.

Feel free to swap ground turkey

or lean ground beef for

the chicken . . .

Baked Chicken with Green Spinach–Horseradish Sauce

This is one meal that's sure to become one of your entertaining staples. Plus, thanks to the food processor, the room-temperature sauce comes together in seconds. I serve this with rice (regular or instant) or Black & Pink Beans with Rice (page 257).

Total Time: 30 minutes

Prep time: 5 minutes

Walk-away time: 25 minutes

Serves 4

Cooking spray

4 boneless, skinless chicken breast halves

Salt and freshly ground black pepper to taste

GREEN SPINACH–HORSERADISH SAUCE

One 10-ounce package frozen chopped spinach, thawed

1/2 cup mayonnaise

6 tablespoons prepared white horseradish

2 tablespoons chopped fresh parsley

Salt and freshly ground black pepper to taste

1. Preheat the oven to 400°F. Coat a large baking sheet with cooking spray.

2. Season the chicken all over with salt and pepper. Place the chicken on the prepared sheet and bake until golden brown and cooked through, about 25 minutes.

3. Meanwhile, in a food processor, combine the spinach, mayonnaise, horseradish, and parsley and process until smooth. Season with salt and pepper.

4. Spoon the sauce over the baked chicken and serve.

make it a meal kit Bake the chicken and make the sauce. Store each separately in sealable containers or plastic bags for up to 3 days in the refrigerator or up to 3 months in the freezer. Thaw overnight in the refrigerator (I don't recommend thawing the chicken in the microwave). Reheat the chicken in the microwave for a few minutes on HIGH. Spoon the sauce over the chicken just before serving (or, if desired, heat the sauce in the microwave for 2 minutes on HIGH). You can also serve the sauce over a rotisserie chicken, in which case you don't even have to turn on the oven!

morph it Bake a double batch of the chicken and use the extra to make Chicken with Artichoke–Basil Pesto (page 114) or Pan-Grilled Chicken with Orange–Ginger Sauce (page 102).

Make a double batch of the Green Spinach–Horseradish Sauce—it makes a great dip for fresh vegetables, crackers, or steamed shellfish. Store for up to 3 months in the freezer. Thaw overnight in the refrigerator or in the microwave for to 5 to 7 minutes on LOW.

. . . this sauce comes together

in seconds.

Chicken with Artichoke–Basil Pesto

Artichokes are amazing. I especially love the tender hearts when they're packaged in either olive oil (sold in jars) or brine (sold in cans). This pesto also makes a great dip alongside pita triangles. I like to serve this with 5-Ingredient Mashed Chipotle Sweet Potatoes with Lime (page 256).

Total Time: 16–18 minutes

Prep time: 10 minutes

Active cooking time:
6–8 minutes

Serves 4

2 teaspoons olive oil

4 boneless, skinless chicken breast halves

Salt and freshly ground black pepper to taste

1 tablespoon salt-free lemon-and-herb seasoning

ARTICHOKE–BASIL PESTO

One 14-ounce can or two 7-ounce jars artichoke hearts, drained

1 packed cup fresh basil leaves

2 cloves garlic

1/2 cup reduced-sodium chicken broth, or more as needed

2 tablespoons olive oil

2 tablespoons freshly grated pecorino romano or Parmesan cheese

1. Heat the oil in a large skillet over medium heat. Season the chicken all over with salt and pepper. Season both sides with the lemon-and-herb seasoning. Place the chicken in the hot pan and cook until golden brown and cooked through, 3 to 4 minutes per side.

2. Meanwhile, in a blender, combine the pesto ingredients and process until smooth, adding more broth if necessary to create a thick sauce.

3. Transfer the cooked chicken to a warm serving platter or individual plates and top with the pesto.

make it a meal kit Season the chicken with the salt, pepper, and seasoning. Prepare the pesto. Store each separately in sealable containers or plastic bags for up to 3 days in the refrigerator or up to 3 months in the freezer. Thaw overnight in the refrigerator (I don't recommend thawing either in the microwave). When ready to finish the meal, cook the chicken as directed and top with the pesto.

morph it Brown a double batch of the chicken and use it to make Seared Chicken with Sun-Dried Tomato Sauce (page 118).

Make a double batch of the pesto and use it as a sandwich topping (it's great with smoked turkey, ham, salami, provolone, and Parmesan cheese). It's also an excellent sauce for pasta (double the recipe to coat 1 pound of cooked pasta and top the pasta with extra grated cheese).

This pesto also makes a

great dip . . .

Chicken & Sausage Sandwiches with Fried Bell Peppers

This is a gourmet sandwich that makes a midweek mealtime feast! To save time, you can throw this together using rotisserie chicken meat, deli-sliced chicken, or leftover chicken and turkey from another meal. I often serve it with Fennel–Walnut Salad with Sweet Gorgonzola (page 277).

Total Time: 19–21 minutes

Prep time: 10 minutes

Active cooking time:
9–11 minutes

Serves 4

2 tablespoons olive oil, divided

2 medium red bell peppers, seeded and sliced into thin strips

1 cup onion sliced into half-moons

Salt and freshly ground black pepper to taste

1 pound boneless, skinless chicken breasts, cut into 1-inch pieces

1 cup diced chorizo, andouille, or other cooked spicy sausage

2 tablespoons balsamic vinegar

4 long rolls (submarine or hoagie rolls)

1. Heat 1 tablespoon of the oil in a large skillet over medium-high heat. Add the bell peppers and onion and cook, stirring, until softened, about 5 minutes. Season with salt and pepper. Remove the peppers and onion from the skillet and set aside.

2. Heat the remaining 1 tablespoon oil in the same skillet over medium-high heat. Add the chicken and cook until golden brown and cooked through, 3 to 5 minutes. Add the sausage and vinegar and cook for 1 minute to heat through.

3. Using tongs, arrange the chicken mixture on the open rolls, top with the fried peppers and onion, and serve.

morph it Make this with leftover cooked chicken from Pan-Grilled Chicken with Orange–Ginger Sauce (page 102) or Roasted Chicken with Buttery Chipotle, Cumin & Cilantro (at right), or swap in 3 cups shredded rotisserie chicken. When using already cooked chicken, after you sauté the peppers, sauté the sausage and vinegar, then add the chicken at the end just for a minute to reheat it.

Roasted Chicken with Buttery Chipotle, Cumin & Cilantro

Meet your Quick Fix butter sauce. This version is smoky and hot, but try other flavor combinations, like parsley and dill (great with fish or shellfish) or basil and mint (nice with pork or lamb). Since you're already using the oven, serve the dish with Saucy Roasted Eggplant with Toasted Polenta (page 248).

Total Time: 30 minutes
Prep time: 5 minutes
Walk-away time: 25 minutes

Serves 4

Cooking spray

4 boneless, skinless chicken breast halves

Salt and freshly ground black pepper to taste

2 tablespoons unsalted butter, softened

2 teaspoons minced canned chipotle chiles in adobo sauce

1 teaspoon ground cumin

¼ cup chopped fresh cilantro

1. Preheat the oven to 400°F. Coat a roasting pan with cooking spray.

2. Season the chicken all over with salt and pepper and place in the prepared pan.

3. In a small bowl, mix the butter, chipotles, and cumin until well blended. Spread the butter mixture evenly over the chicken in the pan. Roast until the chicken is cooked through, about 25 minutes.

4. Sprinkle the cilantro over the chicken just before serving.

morph it Make a double batch and use the extra chicken in Seared Chicken with Sun-Dried Tomato Sauce (page 118) or Chicken & Sausage Sandwiches with Fried Bell Peppers (at left).

Seared Chicken with Sun-Dried Tomato Sauce

Sun-dried tomatoes are the perfect pantry staple. Sweet and tangy, they whip up into a sauce in seconds. You can buy them dry or packed in oil, and both lend fantastic depth of flavor to a dish. Oil-packed tomatoes will keep in your refrigerator for a least a month.

I like to serve this dish with angel hair, or capellini, pasta tossed with olive oil and chopped fresh basil.

Total Time: 16–18 minutes
Prep time: 10 minutes
Active cooking time:
6–8 minutes

Serves 4

1 cup drained oil-packed sun-dried tomatoes, plus 1 tablespoon oil from the jar

4 boneless, skinless chicken breast halves

Salt and freshly ground black pepper to taste

1 cup reduced-sodium chicken broth

3 cloves garlic, peeled

¼ cup chopped fresh basil

1. Heat the sun-dried tomato oil in a large skillet over medium-high heat. Season both sides of the chicken with salt and pepper and add to the hot pan. Cook until golden brown, about 2 minutes per side.

2. Meanwhile, in a blender, combine the sun-dried tomatoes, broth, and garlic and process until smooth. Add the sauce to the chicken, bring to a simmer, and let simmer until the chicken is cooked through, about 2 minutes.

3. Remove from the heat, sprinkle with the basil, and serve.

make it a meal kit Season the chicken. Make the sun-dried tomato sauce. Store each separately in sealable containers or plastic bags for up to 3 days in the refrigerator or up to 3 months in the freezer. Thaw the chicken overnight in the refrigerator (I don't recommend thawing it in the microwave) and the sauce in the microwave for 4 to 6 minutes on LOW. When ready to finish the meal, cook the chicken as directed and add the sauce.

bank a batch Make a double batch of the entire meal and store for up to 5 days in the refrigerator or up to 3 months in the freezer. Thaw overnight in the refrigerator or in the microwave for 4 to 6 minutes on LOW. Reheat in the microwave for a few minutes on HIGH.

morph it Make a double batch of the sun-dried tomato sauce and use it as a topping for grilled or baked fish, turkey or beef burgers, or pasta. Reheat in a small saucepan or in the microwave for a few minutes on HIGH.

Sweet and tangy, sun-dried tomatoes

whip up into a sauce in seconds.

Mojito Chicken

This dish is inspired by the sweet and tangy drink of the same name. I often serve this with Roasted Butternut Squash with Cumin & Coriander (page 255) or Roasted Brussels Sprouts with Sun-Dried Tomatoes (page 245).

Total Time: 19–21 minutes

Prep time: 10 minutes

Active cooking time: 9–11 minutes

Serves 4

2 teaspoons olive oil

$\frac{1}{2}$ cup chopped onion

2 cloves garlic, minced

1 tablespoon sugar

$1\frac{1}{4}$ pounds boneless, skinless chicken breasts, cut into 1-inch pieces

$\frac{1}{2}$ cup spiced rum

$\frac{1}{4}$ cup fresh lime juice

1 teaspoon finely grated lime zest

$\frac{1}{4}$ cup chopped fresh mint

1. Heat the oil in a large skillet over medium heat. Add the onion, garlic, and sugar and cook, stirring, until softened, about 3 minutes. Add the chicken and cook, stirring a few times, until golden brown on all sides, 3 to 5 minutes. Add the rum, lime juice, and lime zest, bring to a simmer, and let simmer until the chicken is cooked through, 3 minutes.

2. Remove from the heat, stir in the mint, and serve.

bank a batch Make a double batch and store the extra in a sealable container or plastic bag for up to 3 days in the refrigerator or up to 3 months in the freezer. Thaw overnight in the refrigerator or in the microwave for 4 to 6 minutes on LOW. Reheat in a large skillet over medium heat for 5 minutes or in the microwave for a few minutes on HIGH.

morph it Make a double batch and morph the extra into Mulligatawny Stew over Rice (page 88). The flavors of lime and mint pair beautifully with the mulligatawny's ginger, curry, and coconut.

Turkey Tenderloin with Olives, Parsley & Lemon

Turkey tenderloin is a very lean cut of turkey that blends well with bold flavors. To finish the meal, the perfect side dish would be Twice-Baked Potatoes with Cheddar & Bacon (page 253) and steamed green beans or broccoli florets.

Total time: 55–60 minutes
Prep time: 10 minutes
Walk-away time: 35–40 minutes
Resting time: 10 minutes

Serves 4

Cooking spray

One 1½-pound turkey tenderloin

Salt and freshly ground black pepper to taste

2 tablespoons Dijon mustard

½ cup finely chopped kalamata olives

¼ cup chopped fresh parsley

2 tablespoons fresh lemon juice

2 teaspoons finely grated lemon zest

1. Preheat the oven to 400°F. Coat a roasting pan with cooking spray.

2. Season the turkey all over with salt and pepper and place in the prepared pan. Brush the mustard all over the top and sides of the turkey. Press the olives and parsley into the turkey, allowing the mustard to act as glue. Squeeze the lemon juice and sprinkle the lemon zest over the turkey. Roast until an instant-read thermometer inserted into the thickest part registers at least 160°F, 35 to 40 minutes. Let the turkey rest for 10 minutes before cutting it crosswise into ½-inch-thick slices.

morph it Make a double batch (roast two turkey tenderloins) and morph the extra into Turkey Tetrazzini with Green Peas (page 122), or use the turkey in place of the chicken in Warm Chicken–Cherry Waldorf in Romaine (page 90). Store the extra turkey in a sealable container or plastic bag for up to 5 days in the refrigerator or up to 3 months in the freezer. Thaw overnight in the refrigerator (I don't recommend thawing in the microwave). If you want to warm the turkey, reheat it in the microwave for a few minutes on LOW.

Turkey Tetrazzini with Green Peas

My mom made the best turkey tetrazzini when I was growing up—it was a childhood favorite. It's a great use of leftover roasted turkey and chicken, but you could also make the dish with leftover ham or cooked shrimp. I serve this with Red Lettuce with Honey–Maple Vinaigrette (page 282) or Mixed Cherry Tomato Salad (page 281).

Total Time: 30–33 minutes

Prep time: 10–11 minutes

Active cooking time:
10–12 minutes

Walk-away time: 10 minutes

Serves 4 to 6

12 ounces broad egg noodles

2 teaspoons olive oil

1/2 cup chopped onion

2 to 3 cloves garlic, to your taste, minced

1 cup sliced mushrooms (button, cremini, portabella, or any wild mushrooms)

One 1-pound turkey tenderloin, cut into 1-inch pieces (about 4 cups)

1 teaspoon dried thyme

1 teaspoon dried oregano

1/2 teaspoon salt

1/2 teaspoon freshly ground black pepper

2 cups reduced-sodium chicken broth

1/2 cup frozen green peas

1 1/2 cups sour cream

2 tablespoons chopped fresh parsley

1/4 cup freshly grated Parmesan cheese

1. Cook the egg noodles according to the package directions. Drain and set aside, covered with aluminum foil to keep warm.

2. Meanwhile, heat the oil in a large skillet over medium-high heat. Add the onion and garlic and cook, stirring, for 1 minute. Add the mushrooms and cook, stirring a few times, until they release their liquid. Add the turkey and cook, stirring a few times, until browned on all sides, about 5 minutes. Add the thyme, oregano, salt, and pepper and stir to coat. Cook, stirring, until the herbs are fragrant, about 1 minute. Add the broth, bring to a simmer, and continue to simmer until the turkey is cooked through, about 10 minutes.

3. Add the peas and simmer for 1 minute. Remove from the heat and stir in the sour cream and parsley. Add the cooked egg noodles, then season to taste with salt and pepper. Sprinkle with the Parmesan cheese just before serving.

make it a meal kit Cook and drain the egg noodles. Cook the onion, garlic, and mushrooms, then add the turkey and spices (thyme, oregano, salt, and pepper) and cook as directed (without adding the broth). Store each separately in sealable containers or plastic bags for up to 3 days in the refrigerator or up to 3 months in the freezer. Thaw the turkey mixture overnight in the refrigerator (I don't recommend thawing it in the microwave). When ready to finish the meal, return the turkey mixture to a large skillet over medium-high heat. When it's hot, add the broth. Reheat the noodles in the microwave for a few minutes on HIGH. Finish the meal as directed.

morph it Make the dish with extra turkey from Roasted Turkey Tenderloin with New Potatoes & Tarragon Broth (page 126) or Turkey Tenderloin with Olives, Parsley & Lemon (page 121). You can also make it with store-bought rotisserie chicken.

. . . tetrazzini is a great use of leftover

roasted turkey and chicken . . .

Pan-Seared Turkey Tenderloin with Herbs & Porcini Mushrooms

Since turkey tenderloin is lean and mild, I like to add the bold, woodsy flavor of dried wild mushrooms. I also liven up the dish with fresh and dried herbs. Serve this with egg noodles that have been tossed with butter, salt, and black pepper.

Total Time: 22–27 minutes
Prep time: 15–20 minutes
Active cooking time:
7 minutes

Serves 4

1 ounce dried porcini mushrooms

½ cup boiling water

One 1¼-pound turkey tenderloin, cut crosswise into 1-inch-thick slices

Salt and freshly ground black pepper to taste

¼ cup all-purpose flour

1 teaspoon dried thyme

1 teaspoon dried oregano

1 tablespoon olive oil

½ cup reduced-sodium chicken broth

¼ cup chopped fresh parsley

1. Place the dried mushrooms in a small bowl and pour the boiling water over them. Let stand until the mushrooms soften, about 10 minutes. Strain them through a sieve, reserving the soaking liquid. Chop the mushrooms into small pieces and set aside.

2. Meanwhile, season both sides of the turkey slices with salt and pepper. In a shallow dish, combine the flour, thyme, and oregano. Add the turkey slices and turn to coat both sides evenly.

3. Heat the oil in a large skillet over medium-high heat. Add the turkey and cook until golden brown, about 2 minutes per side. Add the mushrooms, the reserved soaking liquid, and the broth. Bring the liquid to a simmer, then continue to simmer until the turkey is cooked through and the sauce thickens, about 3 minutes.

4. Remove from the heat, sprinkle with the parsley, and serve.

make it a meal kit Soak the mushrooms in advance, strain, and transfer the mushrooms along with their soaking liquid to a sealable container. Coat the turkey with the flour mixture and store (uncooked) in a plastic bag. You can store both for up to 3 days in the refrigerator. When ready to finish the meal, cook the turkey as directed.

bank a batch Make a double batch of the entire meal and store the extra for up to 3 days in the refrigerator or up to 3 months in the freezer. Thaw overnight in the refrigerator or in the microwave for 5 to 7 minutes on LOW. Reheat in a large saucepan or skillet over medium heat or in the microwave for a few minutes on HIGH.

morph it Make a double batch of the turkey and use the extra instead of chicken in Chicken with Eggplant, Capers & Black Olives (page 86); cut the turkey into 1-inch pieces and add to the eggplant mixture when instructed to return the cooked chicken to the pan.

have it your way Feel free to substitute any dried wild mushrooms for the porcini. Shiitake, cremini, and oyster all work very well. You can also substitute sliced pork tenderloin or sliced boneless, skinless chicken breasts for the turkey.

Roasted Turkey Tenderloin with New Potatoes & Tarragon Broth

This dish sounds fancy, but the oven does most of the work. It braises the lean turkey meat while the tarragon (an anise-flavored herb) infuses itself into the broth. I serve this dish with a red lettuce salad with blue cheese dressing or Warm Spinach Salad with Pancetta, Gorgonzola & Pine Nuts (page 275).

Total Time: 55–60 minutes
Prep time: 10 minutes
Walk-away time: 35–40 minutes
Resting time: 10 minutes

Serves 4

Cooking spray

One 1¼-pound turkey tenderloin

Salt and freshly ground black pepper to taste

2 pounds small red potatoes, quartered (if bigger, cut into 2-inch pieces)

2 shallots, chopped

1 cup dry white wine

1 cup reduced-sodium chicken broth

2 tablespoons cider vinegar

2 tablespoons chopped fresh tarragon

1. Preheat the oven to 400°F. Coat a roasting pan with cooking spray.

2. Season the turkey all over with salt and pepper and place in the prepared pan. Arrange the potatoes all around the turkey, spray them with cooking spray, then season them with salt and pepper. Arrange the shallots over the potatoes.

3. In a small bowl, combine the wine, broth, vinegar, and tarragon. Pour this over the turkey.

4. Roast the turkey and potatoes until an instant-read meat thermometer inserted into the thickest part of the turkey registers at least 160°F, 35 to 40 minutes. Let the turkey rest for 10 minutes before cutting it crosswise into ½-inch-thick slices.

morph it Make a double batch (roast two turkey tenderloins, but don't make extra potatoes) and morph the extra turkey into Turkey–Spinach Salad with Strawberries, Kiwi & Cashews in Honey–Sesame Dressing (page 128) or Turkey Tetrazzini with Green Peas (page 122).

Turkey Tenderloin with Apricot Sauce

This is a wonderful sauce that's also fabulous with chicken and pork. I line the roasting pan with foil because the sauce is sticky, making for a difficult cleanup with an unlined pan. The oven's already hot, so serve this dish with Roasted Butternut Squash with Cumin & Coriander (page 255).

Total Time: 55–60 minutes
Prep time: 10 minutes
Walk-away time: 35–40 minutes
Resting time: 10 minutes

Serves 4

Cooking spray

One 1¼-pound turkey tenderloin

Salt and freshly ground black pepper to taste

APRICOT SAUCE

⅔ cup apricot preserves

2 cloves garlic, minced

2 tablespoons Dijon mustard

2 tablespoons reduced-sodium soy sauce

1. Preheat the oven to 400°F. Line a roasting pan with aluminum foil and spray the foil with cooking spray.

2. Season the turkey with salt and pepper and place it in the prepared pan.

3. In a small bowl, combine the sauce ingredients. Mix well and pour over the turkey. Roast until an instant-read thermometer inserted into the thickest part registers at least 160°F, 35 to 40 minutes, basting frequently with the apricot sauce.

4. Let the turkey rest for 10 minutes before cutting it crosswise into ½-inch-thick slices.

bank a batch Make a double batch of the entire meal and store the extra in a sealable container or plastic bag for up to 3 days in the refrigerator or up to 3 months in the freezer. Thaw overnight in the refrigerator or in the microwave for 5 to 7 minutes on LOW. Reheat in a large saucepan or skillet over medium heat or in the microwave for a few minutes on HIGH.

morph it Make a double batch and morph the extra turkey into Turkey–Spinach Salad with Strawberries, Kiwi & Cashews in Honey–Sesame Dressing (page 128).

Turkey–Spinach Salad with Strawberries, Kiwi & Cashews in Honey–Sesame Dressing

This will be your "go to" salad at least a few times each month. You can use leftover turkey or chicken or buy the turkey unsliced from the deli counter and cut it up yourself—or, morph extra cooked turkey tenderloin from any of the previous turkey recipes in this chapter. The salad is also great with pork or shrimp. Serve this with Parmesan-Crusted Rolls (page 263) or Onion Knots (page 264). Take note: This is an excellent recipe for morphing.

Total Time: 10 minutes

Prep time: 10 minutes

Serves 4

1 pound cooked turkey breast (from the deli), thickly sliced

6 cups baby spinach or lettuce leaves

1 cup hulled and sliced fresh strawberries

2 kiwis, peeled and cut crosswise into ¼-inch-thick slices

½ cup salted dry-roasted cashews

HONEY–SESAME DRESSING

½ cup reduced-sodium chicken broth

2 tablespoons honey

2 teaspoons toasted sesame oil

2 teaspoons honey mustard

Salt and freshly ground black pepper to taste

1. Cut the turkey into bite-size pieces and set aside. Arrange the spinach on salad plates or a large serving platter. Top with the turkey, strawberries, kiwi slices, and cashews.

2. In a small bowl, whisk together the dressing ingredients. Pour over the salad and serve.

morph it Make a double batch of the Honey–Sesame Dressing—it's excellent on all types of salads or as a marinade for chicken, pork, or fish. Store the extra in a sealable container for up to 5 days in the refrigerator.

have it your way You may also substitute an equal amount of store-bought rotisserie chicken or leftover turkey from a whole roasted turkey, roasted turkey breast, or any of the turkey tenderloin recipes in this chapter.

This will be your "go-to" salad . . .

4

Pork and Ham

PORK IS BACK.

I serve pork tenderloin and pork loin at least once a week, and almost always as a staple dinner-party food. Why? Because pork pairs well with a variety of ingredients, and grocery stores carry super-lean cuts of pork these days. The loin and tenderloin are especially lean, but even the chops are so well trimmed by the butcher that you rarely have to trim them at all. And you know me—any little bit of help I can get in the prep department is a welcome addition to meal-making.

I also like the pre-marinated pork tenderloins (sold next to the other pork products). I often add other ingredients for a deeper flavor, but since they're already marinated, you get a huge head start. Go for it if you see them!

When it comes to my Quick Fix strategies, pork is another leader of the pack. You can prep it ahead, it cooks quickly, you can prepare a double batch of an entire meal and refrigerate or freeze it, and you can morph leftover pork from one meal to the next, creating completely new dishes. Given that, the next time you're perusing the chicken chapter, switch over to the pork chapter and try something new. You can even substitute pork for chicken in most dishes.

One note of caution: Because pork is so lean, keep an eye on it while cooking. It's easy to turn a moist pork chop into a dry, chewy one. And if I want to chew on something for 20 minutes, I'll grab a piece of Bazooka®. Cook pork until an instant-read thermometer inserted into the thickest part registers 155°F to 160°F (the temperature will often rise 5°F once the pork is removed from the oven, getting you to the appropriate 160°F).

. . . grocery stores carry super-lean cuts

of pork these days.

Lemon–Rosemary Pork Loin

Combining the floral taste of rosemary with tangy lemon is like taking your palate for a refreshing walk in the garden! And mild-flavored pork loin is the perfect partner. I like to serve this with Roasted Butternut Squash with Cumin & Coriander (page 255).

Total Time: 55–60 minutes
Prep time: 10 minutes
Walk-away time: 35–40 minutes
Resting time: 10 minutes

Serves 4

Cooking spray

One 1¼-pound pork tenderloin

Salt and freshly ground black pepper to taste

¼ cup olive oil

2 tablespoons fresh lemon juice

2 tablespoons red wine vinegar

2 tablespoons chopped fresh rosemary

1 tablespoon Dijon mustard

1 teaspoon grated lemon zest

1. Preheat the oven to 400°F. Coat a shallow roasting pan with cooking spray. Season the pork all over with salt and pepper, then place it in the pan.

2. In a small bowl, whisk together the oil, lemon juice, vinegar, rosemary, mustard, and lemon zest. Pour the mixture over the pork. Place the pork in the oven and roast until an instant-read thermometer inserted into the thickest part registers 160°F, 35 to 40 minutes. Remove from the oven and let rest for 10 minutes before cutting crosswise into ½-inch-thick slices.

make it a meal kit Season the pork with salt and pepper. Whisk together the marinade (the oil through the lemon zest). Transfer the pork to a plastic bag and pour in the marinade. Store for up to 3 days in the refrigerator or up to 3 months in the freezer. Thaw overnight in the refrigerator (I don't recommend thawing in the microwave). Finish as directed.

morph it Make a double batch (roast 2 pork loins) and morph the extra into Pork Medallions with Cranberry–Horseradish Sauce (page 137) or Sweet & Tangy Pork Chops with Pineapple (page 147).

Parmesan–Sage Pork Loin

Load up your favorite roasting pan with vegetables, pork, and seasonings, and sit back and relax. The aromas emanating from the kitchen will knock your socks off. This meal gives you a slow-cooked taste without having to wait all day (unless you choose to slow cook it; see right). I like to serve Garlic-Roasted Asparagus with Almonds (page 241) or Roasted Green Beans with Grape Tomatoes & Olives (page 242) on the side.

Total Time: 70 minutes

Prep time: 15 minutes

Walk-away time: 45 minutes

Resting time: 10 minutes

Serves 4

2 cups diced red potatoes, unpeeled

1 cup chopped onion

1 cup chopped celery

1 cup chopped carrots

1½ cups reduced-sodium chicken broth

½ cup dry sherry

One 2-pound pork tenderloin, trimmed of silverskin

Salt and freshly ground black pepper to taste

2 tablespoons dried sage

1 tablespoon salt-free garlic-and-herb seasoning

¼ cup freshly grated Parmesan cheese

1. Preheat the oven to 400°F.

2. Arrange the potatoes, onion, celery, and carrots in a large roasting pan. Pour the broth and sherry over them. Season the pork all over with salt and pepper and sprinkle with the sage and garlic-and-herb seasoning. Place the pork on top of the vegetables and sprinkle with the Parmesan (press the cheese into the meat). Roast until an instant-read thermometer inserted into the thickest part registers 160°F, about 45 minutes.

3. Let the pork rest for 10 minutes, then cut crosswise into ½-inch-thick slices and serve with the vegetables and brothy sauce.

morph it Leftover pork? Morph the extra into Grilled Pork over Toasted Polenta (page 140); skip the grilling of the pork step and toast the polenta as directed; top the polenta with the leftover pork and other ingredients as directed.

have it your way If you don't want to add sherry, substitute an equal amount of orange or pineapple juice, or add ½ teaspoon vanilla extract when you add the broth; any of these ingredients will add the sweetness you'd get from the sherry.

slow cook it Follow the directions above, except arranging the ingredients in a large slow cooker instead of a roasting pan. Cover and cook on LOW for 6 to 8 hours or HIGH for 3 to 4 hours.

. . . slow-cooked taste without

having to wait all day . . .

Pork with Rhubarb Chutney

You can buy rhubarb fresh or frozen. I like to serve this with quinoa or Sautéed Carrots & Parsnips (page 252).

Total Time: 50–65 minutes
Prep time: 10–15 minutes
Walk-away time: 30–40 minutes
Resting time: 10 minutes

Serves 4

Cooking spray

One 1¼-pound pork tenderloin, trimmed of silverskin

Salt and freshly ground black pepper to taste

RHUBARB CHUTNEY

2 cups cored and chopped Granny Smith or McIntosh apples

1 cup chopped fresh or thawed frozen rhubarb stalks

⅔ cup apple juice

¼ cup chopped shallots

¼ cup golden or dark raisins

2 tablespoons brown sugar

2 tablespoons cider vinegar

2 teaspoons ground cumin

1. Preheat the oven to 400°F. Coat a shallow roasting pan with cooking spray.

2. Season the pork all over with salt and pepper. Place in the pan and roast until an instant-read thermometer inserted into the thickest part registers 160°F, 30 to 40 minutes. Remove from the oven and let rest for 10 minutes before cutting crosswise into ½-inch-thick slices.

3. Meanwhile, in a medium saucepan over medium heat, combine the chutney ingredients. Bring to a simmer, reduce the heat to medium-low, and let simmer until the apples break down and the chutney thickens, about 15 minutes. Serve the chutney over the sliced pork.

make it a meal kit Make the chutney and store it in a sealable container for up to 5 days in the refrigerator or up to 3 months in the freezer. Thaw overnight in the refrigerator or in the microwave for a few minutes on LOW. Reheat in a small saucepan over medium heat or in the microwave for 2 minutes on HIGH.

morph it Make a double batch of the entire recipe. Use the extra chutney to spoon over grilled or roasted chicken, turkey, fish, and shellfish. Morph the extra pork into Chipotle Pork Soft Tacos (page 144) or Hot Chile Grilled Pork Medallions with Avocado–Mango Salsa (page 143).

Pork Medallions with Cranberry–Horseradish Sauce

I like to use a stovetop grill pan or griddle for this because it gets superhot and sears the pork to perfection in lightning speed. You can also use leftover pork loin or tenderloin; just sear the outside of each slice until golden brown (no need to cook it through since it's already cooked). In the sauce, cranberries lend a sweet contrast to the pungent horseradish, but you could also use dried blueberries, dried cherries, or diced dried mango. A nice side dish for this is German Potato Salad (page 267).

Total Time: 16 minutes
Prep time: 10 minutes
Active cooking time: 6 minutes

Serves 4

1 tablespoon olive oil

One 1¼-pound pork tenderloin, trimmed of silverskin and cut crosswise into 1-inch-thick rounds

Salt and freshly ground black pepper to taste

CRANBERRY–HORSERADISH SAUCE

One 16-ounce can whole-berry cranberry sauce

2 to 3 tablespoons prepared horseradish

1 teaspoon Dijon mustard

1. Heat the oil in a large skillet or a stovetop grill pan or griddle over medium-high heat for 3 to 5 minutes. Season the pork on both sides with salt and pepper. Add to the hot pan and cook until just cooked through, about 3 minutes per side.

2. Meanwhile, in a small saucepan, combine the sauce ingredients. Set the pan over medium heat, bring to a simmer, and let simmer for 5 minutes.

3. Serve the medallions with the sauce spooned over the top.

make it a meal kit Cut the pork into medallions and season it, combine the sauce ingredients, and store each separately in sealable containers or plastic bags for up to 5 days in the refrigerator or up to 3 months in the freezer. Thaw both overnight in the refrigerator or in the microwave for a few minutes on LOW. Cook the pork as directed above. Heat the sauce in a small saucepan over medium heat or in the microwave for 2 minutes on LOW.

morph it Make a double batch of the sauce. It makes a great topping (warm or chilled) for chicken, fish, pork, and ham, or served alongside cheese and crackers.

Asian Pork Kebabs with Apricot Mayonnaise

The combination of mayo, sweet apricot preserves, salty soy sauce, and sharp Dijon mustard is fabulous, and it makes a wonderful dipping sauce for kebabs of any kind. I serve this with Toasted Coconut Rice (page 261). If you're using wooden skewers, soak them in water for at least 20 minutes before using, to keep them from scorching.

Total Time: 20–22 minutes

Prep time: 15 minutes

Active cooking time:
5–7 minutes

Serves 4

Cooking spray

APRICOT MAYONNAISE

1 cup mayonnaise

¼ cup apricot preserves

1 tablespoon reduced-sodium soy sauce

1 tablespoon Dijon mustard

1 teaspoon garlic powder

½ teaspoon ground ginger

One 1¼-pound pork tenderloin, trimmed of silverskin and cut into 2-inch cubes

1 medium red bell pepper, seeded and cut into 2-inch pieces

Metal or wooden skewers

Salt and freshly ground black pepper to taste

1. Coat a stovetop grill pan or griddle with cooking spray and preheat over medium-high heat until hot, 3 to 5 minutes.

2. In a medium bowl, combine the Apricot Mayonnaise ingredients. Mix well, then remove and reserve ⅓ cup of the mayonnaise.

3. Alternate pieces of pork and bell pepper on the skewers. Season the skewers with salt and pepper. Brush the remaining mayonnaise mixture all over the pork and pepper pieces. Place the skewers in the hot grill pan and cook until the pork is just cooked through (still slightly pink in the center), 5 to 7 minutes, turning frequently.

4. Serve the kebabs with the reserved Apricot Mayonnaise on the side for dipping.

make it a meal kit Prepare the mayonnaise and store in a sealable container. Skewer the pork and peppers and wrap in plastic wrap. The mayonnaise will keep for up to 3 days in the refrigerator, the skewers up to 2 days. When ready to finish the meal, cook as directed above.

morph it Make a double batch of the Apricot Mayonnaise; it's an amazing sandwich spread when paired with smoked turkey, roast beef, and Swiss cheese!

Make a double batch of the pork kebabs and serve the extra pork and peppers over the polenta in Grilled Pork over Toasted Polenta (page 140), or dunk the skewers in the Cranberry–Horseradish Sauce from Pork Medallions with Cranberry–Horseradish Sauce (page 137), or use the pork and peppers to make Chipotle Pork Soft Tacos (page 144).

Grilled Pork over Toasted Polenta

Packaged polenta is a Quick Fix cook's best pal because it's precooked and ready to eat in just minutes. You can find it in the refrigerated section of the produce aisle or in the rice aisle. I serve this with 5-Ingredient Watercress Salad with Pears, Goat Cheese & Pine Nuts (page 283).

Total Time: 20–25 minutes

Prep time: 10–15 minutes

Active cooking time: 10 minutes

Serves 4

Cooking spray

One 24-ounce log prepared corn polenta, plain or flavored, cut crosswise into ½-inch-thick slices

Salt and freshly ground black pepper to taste

⅓ cup freshly grated Parmesan cheese, or more as needed

One 1¼-pound pork tenderloin, trimmed of silverskin and cut crosswise into ½-inch-thick rounds

1 cup chopped roasted red peppers (from a water-packed jar)

¼ cup drained capers

¼ cup chopped fresh basil

1. Preheat the oven to 425°F. Coat a large baking sheet with cooking spray.

2. Arrange the polenta rounds on the sheet; season with salt and pepper. Sprinkle with the Parmesan. Bake until the cheese is golden brown, about 10 minutes.

3. Meanwhile, coat a stovetop grill pan or griddle with cooking spray and preheat over medium-high heat until hot, 3 to 5 minutes. Season the pork on both sides with salt and pepper. Add the pork to the hot pan and cook until golden brown and just cooked through (still slightly pink in the center), 2 to 3 minutes per side.

4. Arrange the warm polenta rounds on a platter and top with the pork. Top with the roasted red peppers, capers, and basil just before serving.

make it a meal kit Prepare the polenta. Slice and season the pork. Store each separately in sealable containers in the refrigerator for up to 3 days (I don't recommend freezing). When ready to finish the meal, reheat the polenta slices on a baking sheet (in a single layer) in a 300°F oven for 10 minutes or in the microwave for 2 minutes on HIGH. Finish the pork as directed.

have it your way If you don't have polenta handy, serve the pork over toasted cornbread or thin slices of any toasted bread or baguette.

Pork Tenderloin with Raisin–Cognac Sauce

Since most of the prep time for this dish is "walk-away" time, this is a great meal to serve guests—as the pork cooks, you can entertain. I like to serve this with mashed potatoes or Roasted Broccoli with Red Onion & Walnuts (page 246).

Total Time: 50–60 minutes
Prep time: 10 minutes
Walk-away time:
30–40 minutes
Resting time: 10 minutes

Serves 4

Cooking spray

One 1¼-pound pork tenderloin

Salt and freshly ground black pepper to taste

RAISIN–COGNAC SAUCE

One 14-ounce can reduced-sodium chicken broth

¼ cup Cognac or brandy

½ cup golden or dark raisins

2 tablespoons minced shallot

1 teaspoon dried thyme

Salt and freshly ground black pepper to taste

1. Preheat the oven to 400°F. Coat a shallow roasting pan with cooking spray.

2. Season the pork all over with salt and pepper. Place the pork in the pan and roast until an instant-read thermometer inserted into the thickest part registers 160°F. Remove from the oven and let rest for 10 minutes before cutting crosswise into ½-inch-thick slices.

3. Meanwhile, in a small saucepan, combine the broth, Cognac, raisins, shallot, and thyme. Set the pan over medium-high heat and bring to a simmer. Let simmer until the raisins are plump and the sauce reduces to about 1 cup, about 10 minutes. Season with salt and pepper. Keep warm until ready to use. Spoon the sauce over the pork just before serving.

make it a meal kit Make the sauce and store in a sealable container for up to 5 days in the refrigerator or up to 3 months in the freezer. Thaw overnight in the refrigerator or in the microwave for a few minutes on LOW. Reheat in a small saucepan over medium heat or in the microwave for 2 minutes on HIGH.

morph it Make a double batch of the sauce; spoon it over roast chicken or turkey or steak.

Roasted Pork Tenderloin with Strawberry Glaze

I recommend lining the roasting pan with foil because otherwise the sugar in the strawberry preserves will stick to the bottom of your pan, making for lengthy cleanup. When you're ready for a change, seedless raspberry or blackberry preserves work great too. I like to serve this with quinoa or oven-roasted potatoes (roasted alongside the pork to soak up the strawberry glaze).

Total Time: 50–60 minutes
Prep time: 10 minutes
Walk-away time: 30–40 minutes
Resting time: 10 minutes

Serves 4

Cooking spray

One 1¼-pound pork tenderloin, trimmed of silverskin

Salt and freshly ground black pepper to taste

2 tablespoons chopped fresh thyme or 2 teaspoons dried

STRAWBERRY GLAZE

⅔ cup seedless strawberry preserves or jam

½ cup dry sherry, red wine, or reduced-sodium chicken broth

1 tablespoon Dijon mustard

1. Preheat the oven to 400°F. Line a shallow roasting pan with aluminum foil, then coat the foil with cooking spray. Season the pork all over with salt and pepper and the thyme and place in the pan.

2. In a small bowl, combine the glaze ingredients. Mix well, then brush all over the pork. Roast until an instant-read thermometer inserted into the thickest part registers 160°F, 30 to 40 minutes. Remove from the oven and let rest for 10 minutes before cutting crosswise into ½-inch-thick slices.

bank a batch Season the pork and transfer to a plastic bag. Prepare the glaze and add to the bag. Refrigerate for up to 3 days or freeze for up to 3 months. Thaw overnight in the refrigerator. Roast as directed.

morph it Make a double batch (roast 2 pork tenderloins) and morph the extra into Chipotle Pork Soft Tacos (page 144). Once baked and sliced, store the extra pork in a sealable container or plastic bag for up to 3 days in the refrigerator or up to 3 months in the freezer. Thaw overnight in the refrigerator or in the microwave for a few minutes on LOW. Reheat the pork in the microwave for a few minutes on LOW.

Hot Chile Grilled Pork Medallions with Avocado–Mango Salsa

Hot chile oil is a one-stop shop for flavor. I serve this with instant rice or warm tortillas, or both.

Total Time: 21 minutes
Prep time: 15 minutes
Active cooking time: 6 minutes

Serves 4

One 1¼-pound pork tenderloin, trimmed of silverskin and cut crosswise into 1-inch-thick rounds

1 tablespoon hot chile oil

Salt and freshly ground black pepper to taste

AVOCADO–MANGO SALSA

1 cup peeled, pitted, and diced ripe mango

1 cup peeled, pitted, and diced ripe avocado

2 tablespoons minced red onion

2 tablespoons fresh lime juice

2 tablespoons chopped fresh cilantro

1 fresh serrano or jalapeño chile pepper, seeded and minced

¼ teaspoon ground cumin

Salt and freshly ground black pepper to taste

1. Preheat a stovetop grill pan over medium-high heat until hot, 3 to 5 minutes. Brush both sides of the pork with the chile oil and season with salt and pepper. Put the rounds in the hot pan and cook until golden brown and just cooked through (still slightly pink in the center), about 3 minutes per side.

2. Meanwhile, in a medium bowl, combine the salsa ingredients. Serve the salsa spooned over the pork slices.

make it a meal kit Slice the pork and season it, make the salsa, and store each separately in sealable containers or plastic bags for up to 2 days in the refrigerator.

morph it Make this using leftover pork from Pork with Rhubarb Chutney (page 136) or Beer-Braised Pork over Coriander Potato–Carrot Puree (page 152). Brush the slices with chile oil, season, and cook as directed above. Or, microwave the pork for 2 minutes on HIGH before topping with the salsa.

Make a double batch of the chutney and serve it with grilled or roasted chicken, fish, or shellfish, or alongside cheese and crackers.

Chipotle Pork Soft Tacos

The chipotle chiles add smoky heat to the sauce for the pork, so plan to serve "cooling" ingredients alongside; sour cream, tomatoes, and avocado are perfect! I also serve Black Bean & Corn Salad (page 271) or Black & Pink Beans with Rice (page 257) on the side.

Total Time: 21–26 minutes

Prep time: 10–15 minutes

Active cooking time: 11 minutes

Serves 4

1 tablespoon olive oil

2 cloves garlic, minced

One 1¼-pound pork tenderloin, trimmed of silverskin and cut into 1-inch cubes

One 8-ounce can tomato sauce

1 tablespoon minced canned chipotle chiles in adobo sauce

1 teaspoon dried oregano

Eight 6-inch flour tortillas

½ cup crumbled queso fresco or shredded Monterey Jack cheese

ADDITIONAL TOPPINGS (OPTIONAL)

Sour cream

Shredded lettuce

Diced tomatoes

Sliced avocado

1. Heat the oil in a large skillet over medium-high heat. Add the garlic and cook for 1 minute. Add the pork and cook until golden brown on all sides, about 5 minutes. Add the tomato sauce, chipotles, and oregano, bring to a simmer, and let simmer until the pork is just cooked through (still slightly pink in the center) and the sauce has reduced and thickened, about 5 minutes.

2. If desired, for warm tortillas, wrap them in a clean kitchen towel and warm them in the microwave for 30 seconds on HIGH.

3. Arrange the pork on the tortillas, top with the cheese and other toppings as desired, and serve.

make it a meal kit Brown the pork with the garlic. Combine the tomato sauce, chiles, and oregano. Store each separately in sealable containers for up to 3 days in the refrigerator or up to 3 months in the freezer. Thaw overnight in the refrigerator or in the microwave for a few minutes on LOW. When ready to finish the meal, combine the pork and sauce in a large skillet over medium heat and simmer until hot, or reheat both together in the microwave for a few minutes on HIGH. Serve as directed.

morph it Make the dish with leftover pork from Beer-Braised Pork over Coriander Potato–Carrot Puree (page 152). Add it to the pan when you add the garlic.

have it your way This dish is an ideal way to use up leftover cooked chicken, shrimp, fish, or beef. Add the cooked poultry, seafood, or beef when you add the garlic.

Apricot-Glazed Pork

This is sure to become one of your weekly go-to recipes. The contrast of sweet apricot preserves and salty tamari sauce is amazing. Since you shouldn't spend more time on the side dish than the main course, quick-cooking couscous is perfect.

Total Time: 14 minutes

Prep time: 5 minutes

Active cooking time: 9 minutes

Serves 4

2 teaspoons toasted sesame oil

One 1¼-pound pork tenderloin, trimmed of silverskin and cut crosswise into ½-inch-thick rounds

Salt and freshly ground black pepper to taste

1¼ cups apricot preserves

¼ cup reduced-sodium soy sauce or tamari

1 tablespoon chopped pickled ginger

Heat the oil in a large skillet over medium-high heat. Season both sides of the pork with salt and pepper. Add the pork to the hot pan and sear for 2 minutes per side. Add the apricot preserves, soy sauce, and ginger, bring to a simmer, and let simmer until the pork is just cooked through (still slightly pink in the center) and the sauce has reduced, about 5 minutes.

bank a batch Make a double batch of the entire recipe and store the extra in a sealable container or plastic bag for up to 3 days in the refrigerator or up to 3 months in the freezer. Thaw overnight in the refrigerator or in the microwave for 4 to 6 minutes on LOW. Reheat in a large skillet over medium heat or in the microwave for 2 to 3 minutes on HIGH.

have it your way No apricot preserves in the house? Orange marmalade makes a great substitute.

Sweet & Tangy Pork Chops with Pineapple

Since pork is mild, it shines when served with fruity sauces, which you can whip up in a flash with canned fruit. Canned fruits like pineapple and mandarin oranges are packaged when ripe, so their quality and sweetness don't suffer. I like to serve this with Toasted Coconut Rice (page 261).

Total Time: 19–24 minutes

Prep time: 10–15 minutes

Active cooking time:
9 minutes

Serves 4

1 tablespoon peanut or olive oil

4 boneless pork loin chops (about 5 ounces each)

Salt and freshly ground black pepper to taste

One 8-ounce can crushed pineapple, undrained

2/3 cup orange juice

2 tablespoons light or dark brown sugar

2 tablespoons reduced-sodium soy sauce

1 tablespoon cornstarch

1/4 cup chopped scallions (white and green parts)

1. Heat the oil in a large skillet over medium-high heat. Season the pork chops on both sides with salt and pepper. Add the chops to the hot pan and cook until golden brown, about 2 minutes per side.

2. Meanwhile, in a medium bowl, combine the pineapple, orange juice, brown sugar, soy sauce, and cornstarch and stir until the cornstarch dissolves. Add this to the pork in the pan, bring to a simmer, and let simmer until the pork is just cooked through (still slightly pink in the center) and the sauce has thickened, about 5 minutes.

3. Serve the chops with a spoonful of sauce, sprinkled with the scallions.

make it a meal kit Combine the sauce ingredients (the pineapple through the cornstarch) and store in a sealable container for up to 3 days in the refrigerator.

morph it Make a double batch of the recipe and use the extra sauce to spoon over grilled or rotisserie chicken or turkey meatballs. Use the extra pork, sliced up, instead of the ham in Open-Faced Ham Sandwiches with Jack Cheese & Ancho Slaw (page 155).

Hazelnut-Crusted Pork Chops with Cherry–Port Sauce

A simple chop taken over the top! I love sweet hazelnuts for their crunchy contribution to this dish. If you like, you can substitute almonds or pecans. And, if you don't want to use alcohol, substitute apple or grape juice. I often serve this with Rosemary-Roasted Vegetable Medley (page 259).

Total Time: 22 minutes

Prep time: 10 minutes

Active cooking time:
12 minutes

Serves 4

4 boneless pork loin chops (about 5 ounces each)

Salt and freshly ground black pepper to taste

1 large egg white, lightly beaten

1 cup finely chopped hazelnuts

1 tablespoon olive oil

¼ cup chopped shallots

2 cloves garlic, minced

⅓ cup port wine or sweet sherry

1 cup reduced-sodium chicken broth

½ cup sweetened dried cherries

1 teaspoon dried thyme

1. Season the pork all over with salt and pepper. Place the egg white in a shallow dish, add the pork chops, and turn to coat evenly. Place the hazelnuts in a shallow dish, add the chops, and turn to coat both sides with the nuts.

2. Heat the oil in a large skillet over medium-high heat. Add the pork chops and cook until golden brown, about 2 minutes per side. Remove them from the pan and set aside.

3. To the same pan over medium-high heat, add the shallots and garlic and cook, stirring, until softened, about 2 minutes. Add the port and cook for 1 minute. Add the broth, cherries, and thyme and bring to a simmer. Return the chops to the pan and simmer until just cooked through (still slightly pink in the center), about 5 minutes. Serve immediately.

make it a meal kit Coat the pork with the egg white and hazelnuts and wrap them individually in plastic wrap. Store for up to 3 days in the refrigerator before finishing the meal.

have it your way This dish also works with boneless, skinless chicken breasts. Pound the breasts to a $\frac{1}{2}$-inch thickness before dunking them in the egg white and hazelnuts, then proceed with the recipe as directed.

This dish also works with boneless, skinless chicken breasts.

Pork Chops with Mustard–Sage Sauce

The blend of flowery sage and tangy mustard provides a hint of the holidays, but you should make this dish year-round. Serve this up with Sautéed Carrots & Parsnips (page 252) or Garlic-Roasted Asparagus with Almonds (page 241).

Total Time: 19 minutes

Prep time: 10 minutes

Active cooking time: 9 minutes

Serves 4

1 tablespoon vegetable oil

4 boneless pork loin chops (about 5 ounces each)

Salt and freshly ground black pepper to taste

MUSTARD–SAGE SAUCE

1 cup reduced-sodium chicken broth

1 tablespoon Dijon mustard

2 teaspoons cornstarch

1 tablespoon chopped fresh sage or 1 teaspoon dried

1/2 teaspoon garlic powder

1. Heat the oil in a large skillet over medium-high heat. Season both sides of the pork chops with salt and pepper. Add the chops to the hot pan and cook until golden brown, about 2 minutes per side.

2. In a medium bowl, whisk the sauce ingredients until the cornstarch dissolves. Add to the skillet, and simmer until the pork is just cooked through (still slightly pink in the center) and the sauce has thickened, about 5 minutes.

make it a meal kit Season the chops. Whisk together the sauce ingredients. Store each separately in sealable containers for up to 3 days in the refrigerator. When ready to finish the meal, cook the pork as directed, adding the sauce once the chops are browned.

bank a batch Make a double batch and freeze the extra pork in its sauce for up to 3 months. Thaw overnight in the refrigerator or in the microwave for a few minutes on LOW. Reheat in a large skillet over medium heat or in the microwave for a few minutes on HIGH.

morph it Make a double batch of the sauce—it's fantastic over grilled or rotisserie chicken or sliced deli ham (for added flavor, sear thick ham slices in a hot skillet over medium-high heat until browned on both sides; top with the sauce before serving). Store in a sealable container for up to 3 days in the refrigerator (I don't recommend freezing the sauce on its own).

Pork Chops with Orange–Hoisin Glaze

Prepared hoisin sauce is a thick and rich blend of fermented beans, soy sauce, garlic, and seasonings. The sweet-salty blend is excellent whisked into orange juice, creating a hearty sauce in just minutes. I like to pair this with rice and Roasted Brussels Sprouts with Sun-Dried Tomatoes (page 245).

Total Time: 17 minutes
Prep time: 10 minutes
Active cooking time: 7 minutes

Serves 4

1 tablespoon peanut or olive oil

4 boneless pork loin chops (about 5 ounces each)

Salt and freshly ground black pepper to taste

ORANGE–HOISIN GLAZE

$\frac{2}{3}$ cup orange juice

2 tablespoons brown sugar

2 tablespoons hoisin sauce

2 teaspoons balsamic vinegar

1. Heat the oil in large skillet over medium-high heat. Season the pork on both sides with salt and pepper and add it to the hot pan. Cook until golden brown, about 2 minutes per side.

2. In a small bowl, whisk together the glaze ingredients. Add the glaze to the pork and bring to a simmer. Let simmer until the pork is just cooked through (still slightly pink in the center) and the glaze has thickened, about 3 minutes.

make it a meal kit Season the pork. Whisk together the glaze ingredients. Store each separately in sealable containers for up to 3 days in the refrigerator. When ready to finish the meal, cook the pork and add the glaze as directed.

bank a batch Make a double batch of the entire meal and freeze the pork in the glaze for up to 3 months. Thaw overnight in the refrigerator or in the microwave for a few minutes on LOW. Reheat in a large skillet over medium heat or in the microwave for a few minutes on HIGH.

have it your way The glaze is also great with chicken, shrimp, or a hearty white fish, such as monkfish, cod, or halibut. Substitute an equal amount of any of these items (5-ounce boneless chicken breasts, 1¼ pounds large shrimp, or 5-ounce fish fillets) and proceed as directed.

Beer-Braised Pork Chops over Coriander Potato–Carrot Puree

Braising keeps the lean pork chops moist during cooking. Partner this up with Red Lettuce with Honey–Maple Vinaigrette (page 282) or Seared Goat Cheese over Greens (page 276).

Total Time: 20–25 minutes

Prep time: 10–15 minutes

Active cooking time:
10 minutes

Serves 4

CORIANDER POTATO–CARROT PUREE

2 medium Idaho potatoes, peeled and cut into 2-inch chunks

2 medium carrots, peeled and cut into 2-inch chunks

¼ cup sour cream

2 teaspoons sugar

1 teaspoon ground coriander

Salt and freshly ground black pepper to taste

4 boneless pork loin chops (about 5 ounces each)

Salt and freshly ground black pepper to taste

1 tablespoon olive oil

One 12-ounce can or bottle beer (preferably ale or lager)

1. In a medium saucepan, combine the potatoes and carrots. Pour over enough water to cover and set the pan over high heat. Bring to a boil and let boil until the potatoes and carrots are fork-tender, about 8 minutes. Drain and mash with the sour cream, sugar, and coriander until smooth. Season with salt and pepper; keep warm.

2. Meanwhile, season the pork on both sides with salt and pepper. Heat the oil in a large skillet over medium-high heat. Add the pork to the hot pan and cook until golden brown, about 2 minutes per side. Add the beer and simmer until the pork is just cooked through (still slightly pink in the center), about 5 minutes.

3. Spoon a dollop of puree onto each serving plate, top with a chop, and serve.

make it a meal kit Make the puree and store in a sealable container for up to 3 days in the refrigerator. Reheat in the microwave for a few minutes on HIGH before serving.

have it your way No beer? Substitute reduced-sodium chicken broth or ginger ale.

Pork Chops with Maple–Mustard Sauce

I adore maple syrup. When you buy 100% real maple syrup, you can enjoy a rich flavor and sweet partner for fresh dill and tangy mustard. This sauce is also great with chicken. I often serve this with Mushrooms with Garlic, Parmesan & Bread Crumbs (page 250).

Total Time: 19 minutes

Prep time: 10 minutes

Active cooking time:
9 minutes

Serves 4

1 tablespoon olive oil

4 boneless pork loin chops (about 5 ounces each)

Salt and freshly ground black pepper to taste

MAPLE–MUSTARD SAUCE

1 cup reduced-sodium chicken broth

3 tablespoons maple syrup

1 tablespoon Dijon mustard

2 teaspoons cornstarch

2 tablespoons chopped fresh dill

1. Heat the oil in a large skillet over medium-high heat. Season the pork on both sides with salt and pepper. Add the chops to the hot pan and cook until golden brown, about 2 minutes per side.

2. In a small bowl, whisk together the sauce ingredients until the cornstarch dissolves. Add to the pork, bring to a simmer, and let simmer until the pork is just cooked through (still slightly pink in the center) and the sauce has thickened, about 5 minutes. Remove from the heat and serve, sprinkled with the dill.

make it a meal kit Season the pork. Whisk together the sauce ingredients. Store each separately in sealable containers for up to 3 days in the refrigerator. When ready to finish the meal, cook the pork and add the sauce as directed.

bank a batch Make a double batch of the entire meal and freeze the extra pork in the sauce for up to 3 months. Thaw overnight in the refrigerator or in the microwave for a few minutes on LOW. Reheat in a large skillet over medium heat or in the microwave for a few minutes on HIGH.

Baked Ham-Stuffed Endive

Endive leaves lend a mild pepper flavor to the creamy ham filling here. Think of this for your next lunch or brunch party. I like to serve it with 5-Ingredient Mashed Chipotle Sweet Potatoes with Lime (page 256).

Total Time: 25–30 minutes
Prep time: 10–15 minutes
Walk-away time: 15 minutes

Serves 4

Cooking spray

4 cups diced ham (from deli or ham steaks or any leftover ham)

1/2 cup sour cream

1/4 cup diced red onion

2 teaspoons Dijon mustard

1 teaspoon dried oregano

12 endive leaves

2 tablespoons Italian-seasoned dry bread crumbs

2 tablespoons freshly grated Parmesan cheese

1. Preheat the oven to 400°F. Coat a shallow roasting pan with cooking spray.

2. In a large bowl, combine the ham, sour cream, onion, mustard, and oregano. Spoon the mixture equally into the endive leaves, then arrange the stuffed leaves in the prepared pan.

3. In a small bowl, combine the bread crumbs and Parmesan and sprinkle over the ham filling. Bake until the tops are golden brown and the leaves wilt, about 15 minutes.

make it a meal kit Prepare the ham filling, separate, wash, and dry the endive leaves, combine the bread crumbs and Parmesan, and store each component separately in sealable containers or plastic bags for up to 3 days in the refrigerator. Stuff the leaves and sprinkle with the topping just before baking as directed above.

have it your way Instead of ham, substitute diced smoked turkey (from the deli or meat section), diced rotisserie chicken, or diced steamed or grilled shrimp.

Open-Faced Ham Sandwiches with Jack Cheese & Ancho Slaw

Open-faced sandwiches turn midweek meals into something special, especially when they boast hearty bread, salty ham, sweet cheese, and a slaw with cilantro and smoky ancho chiles. I often serve these sandwiches with Garlicky Cream of Broccoli Soup (page 19) or Cream of Asparagus Soup (page 14).

Total Time: 12–18 minutes

Prep time: 10–15 minutes

Active cooking time: 2–3 minutes

Serves 4

ANCHO SLAW

1 cup store-bought cole slaw mix (shredded cabbage and carrots)

¼ cup mayonnaise

1 tablespoon chopped fresh cilantro

1 tablespoon red wine vinegar

1 teaspoon ground ancho chiles, Tabasco® chipotle sauce, or minced canned chipotle chiles in adobo sauce

½ teaspoon ground cumin

Salt and freshly ground black pepper to taste

4 thick slices country bread or rye bread

12 ounces thinly sliced deli ham

8 slices Monterey Jack cheese

1. In a medium bowl, combine the slaw mix, mayonnaise, cilantro, vinegar, ground ancho, and cumin and mix well to coat the slaw. Season with salt and pepper.

2. Preheat the broiler. Line a baking sheet with aluminum foil.

3. Place the bread slices on the sheet. Top the bread with equal portions of the slaw mixture, then with the ham and cheese slices. Place the sandwiches under the broiler until the cheese melts, 2 to 3 minutes.

make it a meal kit The slaw gets better with age (the cabbage softens), so make it in advance and store in a sealable container for up to 3 days in the refrigerator.

morph it Instead of ham, make the sandwiches with leftover pork from Parmesan–Sage Pork Loin (page 134).

Seared Ham with Jalapeño–Apple Chutney

What an excellent use for leftover baked ham! You can also use ¼- to ½-inch-thick ham slices (purchased either from the meat section or the deli department) instead of a sliced baked ham. I serve this with German Potato Salad (page 267) on the side.

Total Time: 20–30 minutes
Prep time: 10–15 minutes
Active cooking time:
10–15 minutes

Serves 4

JALAPEÑO–APPLE CHUTNEY

2 cups peeled, cored, and diced McIntosh or Granny Smith apples

½ cup chopped yellow onion

⅔ cup water

2 tablespoons brown sugar

2 tablespoons cider vinegar

1 fresh jalapeño chile pepper, seeded and minced

1½ teaspoons ground cumin

Salt and freshly ground black pepper to taste

Cooking spray

1 pound boneless leftover ham, cut into ¼-inch-thick slices

1. To make the chutney, combine the apples, onion, water, brown sugar, vinegar, jalapeño, and cumin in a medium saucepan. Set the pan over medium heat and bring to a simmer. Reduce the heat to medium-low and let simmer until the apples break down and the mixture thickens, 10 to 15 minutes. Season with salt and pepper.

2. Meanwhile, coat a stovetop grill pan or griddle with cooking spray and preheat over medium-high heat until hot, 3 to 5 minutes. Add the ham slices to the hot pan and cook until golden brown, 2 to 3 minutes per side.

3. Serve the ham slices with the chutney spooned over the top.

make it a meal kit Slice the ham, make the chutney, and store in separate sealable containers or plastic bags for up to 5 days in the refrigerator.

bank a batch Make a double batch of the entire meal and store the extra ham and chutney together for up to 3 months in the freezer. Thaw overnight in the refrigerator or in the microwave for a few minutes on LOW. Reheat in a large skillet over medium heat or in the microwave for 2 minutes on HIGH.

morph it Make a double batch of the chutney—it's amazing over grilled chicken or fish. It will keep for up to 3 months in the freezer. Thaw overnight in the refrigerator or in the microwave for a few minutes on LOW. Reheat in a small saucepan over medium heat or in the microwave for 2 minutes on HIGH.

. . . an excellent use for leftover

baked ham!

5

Beef

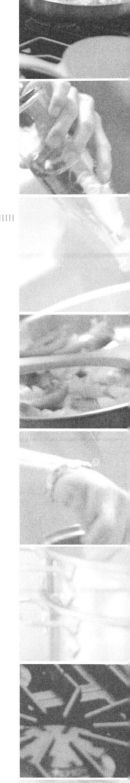

NO MATTER THE CUT, BEEF ADDS richness to any dish.

That's why I try to serve some sort of beef or steak dish at least once a week. (I think many of us fall into a chicken rut.) And since you can find super-lean cuts of beef at the grocery store these days, dealing with fattier cuts of meat doesn't seem to be an issue. Despite the lack of marbling (the fat striations in meat), the leaner cuts aren't tough, meaning they don't require the long cooking or marinating times our mothers used to deal with. Thank goodness!

Beef is a terrific Quick Fix ingredient because you can prep ahead (including marinating, since it won't break down like seafood) and it cooks fast, whether you're pan-searing, grilling, roasting, or broiling. Beef is great for morphing too—steak rounds out a warm pasta salad or fried rice, and extra meatballs can be nestled into turnovers or combined with mushrooms in a tart. (Just don't tell anyone those are yesterday's meatballs and you'll wow the crowd!) Beef also freezes very well, so when you're cooking one meal, think ahead and bank a batch or two for future Quick Fix Meals.

. . . beef cooks fast, whether you're

pan-searing, grilling, roasting, or broiling.

Beef & Mushroom Tart

Not just a special meal for the family, this is also the perfect party food because it serves a lot of people when you cut the tart into smaller squares. An excellent partner is 5-Ingredient Watercress Salad with Pears, Goat Cheese & Pine Nuts (page 283).

Total Time: 42 minutes

Prep time: 15 minutes

Active cooking time:
12 minutes

Walk-away time:
15 minutes

Serves 4 to 6

1 sheet frozen puff pastry, thawed according to package directions

2 teaspoons olive oil

½ cup chopped shallots

1 pound lean ground beef

2 cups sliced mushrooms (any variety)

1 teaspoon dried thyme

½ teaspoon salt

½ teaspoon freshly ground black pepper

1 cup crumbled goat cheese

1. Preheat the oven to 400°F. Unroll the puff pastry onto a large baking sheet and roll it out into a 10x16 inch rectangle. Set aside.

2. Heat the oil in a large skillet over medium-high heat. Add the shallots and cook, stirring, until softened, about 3 minutes. Add the beef and cook until no longer pink, about 5 minutes, breaking up the meat as it cooks. Add the mushrooms and cook until softened, about 3 minutes. Add the thyme, salt, and pepper and cook for 1 minute, until the thyme is fragrant.

3. Arrange the beef mixture over the puff pastry, to within ¼ inch of the edges. Top with the goat cheese. Bake until the pastry is golden brown, about 15 minutes. Let rest for 3 to 5 minutes before cutting and serving.

make it a meal kit Assemble the tart in advance, cover with plastic wrap, and store for up to 3 days in the refrigerator before baking. I don't recommend freezing the tart once it's filled.

have it your way For a vegetarian tart, eliminate the ground beef and double the amount of mushrooms; use a variety of wild mushrooms for a taste explosion!

Alphabets with Mini Meatballs

I spent many childhood dinners eating canned Spaghetti-Os® with meatballs. I ate Spaghetti-Os not because my mom took the night off from cooking, but because the soft pasta and tender little meatballs were the only foods I could handle after a trip to the orthodontist! Serve my take on that meal with a mixed green salad on the side.

Total Time: 20–22 minutes

Prep time: 10 minutes

Active cooking time:
10–12 minutes

Serves 4

1 pound alphabet-shaped pasta

1¼ pounds lean ground beef

1½ teaspoons dried Italian seasoning

1 tablespoon olive oil

One 28-ounce can crushed tomatoes

One 6-ounce can tomato paste

1 teaspoon dried oregano

1 teaspoon dried thyme

1 teaspoon garlic powder

1 teaspoon onion flakes

Salt and freshly ground black pepper to taste

¼ cup freshly grated Parmesan cheese

1. Cook the pasta according to the package directions. Drain and set aside.

2. Meanwhile, in a large bowl, combine the beef and Italian seasoning. Mix well and shape into small meatballs, each about the size of a marble.

3. Heat the oil in a large skillet over medium-high heat. Add the meatballs and cook until golden brown on all sides, about 3 minutes. Add the tomatoes, tomato paste, oregano, thyme, garlic powder, and onion flakes and bring to a simmer. Reduce the heat to medium-low and continue to simmer until the meatballs are cooked through, about 5 minutes. Add the cooked pasta and cook for 1 minute to heat through. Season with salt and pepper and top with the Parmesan just before serving.

make it a meal kit Shape the meatballs in advance, combine (don't cook) the sauce ingredients (the crushed tomatoes through the onion flakes), and cook and drain the pasta in advance. Store each separately in sealable containers or plastic bags for up to 3 days in the refrigerator. When ready to finish the meal, brown the meatballs as directed and add the premixed sauce to the pan. Add the pasta as directed before seasoning and topping with the cheese.

bank a batch Make a double batch of the meatballs and sauce and store them separately for up to 3 months in the freezer. Thaw overnight in the refrigerator or in the microwave for 6 minutes on LOW. Reheat in a large saucepan or in the microwave for a few minutes on LOW, then add the cooked pasta.

morph it Cook a double batch of the meatballs (they'll keep for 5 days in the refrigerator or up to 3 months in the freezer), toss the extras into a pasta sauce, and morph them into super-easy spaghetti and meatballs.

. . . morph this into super-easy

spaghetti and meatballs . . .

Meatballs with Root Beer BBQ Sauce

I grew up drinking root beer, and I still adore throwing one back with my dad! So, I thought, why not make a sauce with my favorite beverage? The meatballs and sauce are excellent over mashed potatoes with Green Beans with Pineapple Vinaigrette (page 243) on the side.

Total Time: 20–25 minutes

Prep time: 10–15 minutes

Active cooking time:
10 minutes

Serves 4

1¼ pounds lean ground beef

2 teaspoons salt-free garlic-and-herb seasoning

½ teaspoon salt

¼ teaspoon freshly ground black pepper

1 tablespoon olive oil

ROOT BEER BBQ SAUCE

One 15-ounce can tomato sauce

One 12-ounce can or bottle root beer

2 tablespoons cider vinegar

2 tablespoons reduced-sodium soy sauce

1 tablespoon Worcestershire sauce

2 teaspoons chili powder

1½ teaspoons ground cumin

1 teaspoon dry mustard

Dash of hot sauce

1. In a large bowl, combine the beef, garlic-and-herb seasoning, salt, and pepper. Mix well and shape into 16 to 20 meatballs, each 2 to 3 inches in diameter.

2. Heat the oil in a large skillet over medium-high heat. Add the meatballs and cook until browned on all sides, about 5 minutes.

3. In a medium bowl, whisk together the sauce ingredients, then add to the meatballs and bring to a simmer. Reduce the heat to medium-low and continue to simmer until the meatballs are cooked through, about 5 minutes.

make it a meal kit Shape the meatballs, combine (don't cook) the sauce ingredients, and store them separately in sealable containers or plastic bags for up to 3 days in the refrigerator. When ready to finish the meal, brown the meatballs, then add the premixed sauce and cook as directed.

bank a batch Make a double batch of the entire meal and store the extra for up to 3 months in the freezer. Thaw overnight in the refrigerator or in the microwave for 4 to 6 minutes on LOW. Reheat in a large saucepan or in the microwave for 3 to 5 minutes on HIGH.

. . . why not make a sauce with

my favorite beverage?

Anita's Slow Cooker Chili

My friend Anita is a busy mom and she often uses her slow cooker to make mealtime come together fast. You can brown the meat first (in a large skillet over medium-high heat), or combine the raw meat with the other ingredients and let the slow cooker do all the work. You can save even more time by combining all the ingredients in the slow cooker insert up to 2 days ahead and storing it in the refrigerator.

Total Time: 4 hours on HIGH;
6 hours on LOW

Prep time: 10–15 minutes

Serves 8

1¼ pounds ground beef

¼ cup dry red wine

1 tablespoon chili powder

1 teaspoon sugar

1 teaspoon ground cumin

¼ teaspoon salt

¼ teaspoon ground cinnamon

1 clove garlic, minced

One 15-ounce can red kidney beans, rinsed and drained

One 15-ounce can black beans, rinsed and drained

One 14-ounce can Mexican-style stewed tomatoes with jalapeño chile peppers and spices, undrained

6 tablespoons shredded Cheddar cheese

MUST-HAVE SIDES AND TOPPINGS

Sour cream

Diced onion

Diced tomato

Diced avocado

Shredded cheddar Cheese

Warmed tortillas with honey and butter (Anita's favorite)

Combine all of the ingredients except for the sides and toppings in a medium to large slow cooker and mix well. Cover and cook on HIGH for 4 hours or on LOW for 6 hours. Serve with the sides and toppings in bowls on the side.

bank a batch **Make a double batch and store the extra in a sealable container (or portion out individual servings and store in several smaller containers) for up to 3 days in the refrigerator or up to 3 months in the freezer. Thaw overnight in the refrigerator or in the microwave for 4 to 6 minutes on LOW. Reheat in a large saucepan or in the microwave for 3 to 5 minutes on HIGH.**

make it on the stovetop **Heat 2 teaspoons vegetable oil in a large pot over medium-high heat. Add the beef and cook until no longer pink, about 5 minutes, breaking up the meat as it cooks. Add the remaining ingredients except for the sides and toppings and bring to a simmer. Reduce the heat to medium-low, partially cover, and simmer for 20 minutes.**

. . . let the slow cooker do all the work.

Tex-Mex Stuffed Peppers

You can also make these peppers with ground turkey or ground chicken. When I make these, I like to use red peppers for their sweetness, but you can substitute green peppers (or any other color). And you can swap shredded Cheddar cheese for the Jack if desired.

Total Time: 52 minutes

Prep time: 15 minutes

Active cooking time:
7 minutes

Walk-away time: 30 minutes

Serves 4

Cooking spray

1 cup instant rice (white or brown)

2 teaspoons olive oil

½ pound lean ground beef

1 tablespoon chili powder

1 teaspoon ground cumin

1 teaspoon dried oregano

½ teaspoon garlic powder

½ teaspoon salt

¼ teaspoon freshly ground black pepper

One 15-ounce can Santa Fe corn, Fiesta Corn (Del Monte®), or regular canned corn, drained

One 15-ounce can pink beans, rinsed and drained

½ cup sour cream

¼ cup chopped fresh cilantro

4 large red or green bell peppers, stems ends neatly cut out

½ cup shredded Monterey Jack cheese

1. Preheat the oven to 375°F. Coat a shallow roasting pan with cooking spray.

2. Cook the rice according to the package directions.

3. Meanwhile, heat the oil in a large skillet over medium heat. Add the beef and cook until no longer pink, about 5 minutes, breaking up the meat as it cooks. Add the chili powder, cumin, oregano, garlic powder, salt, and pepper and cook for 1 minute. Add the cooked rice, corn, beans, and sour cream and cook for 1 minute to heat through. Remove from the heat and stir in the cilantro.

4. Stuff the beef mixture into the bell peppers and arrange them side by side in the prepared pan. Top with the shredded cheese. Bake until the peppers are soft and the cheese is golden and bubbly, about 30 minutes.

make it a meal kit Make the rice, cook the beef with the spices (up to and before adding the cooked rice), and store them separately in sealable containers or plastic bags for up to 3 days in the refrigerator. When you're ready to finish the meal, combine the rice and beef with the corn and beans and follow the recipe as directed.

You can also make these peppers with

ground turkey or ground chicken.

Italian Braised Beef over Egg Noodles

You can serve this over any pasta, such as penne or capellini, instead of egg noodles. To round out the meal (and add color), serve Mixed Cherry Tomato Salad (page 281) on the side.

Total Time: 32–34 minutes

Prep time: 15 minutes

Active cooking time:
7–9 minutes

Walk-away time: 10 minutes

Serves 4

1 tablespoon olive oil

1¼ pounds cubed stew beef (1-inch cubes)

Salt and freshly ground black pepper to taste

¼ cup all-purpose flour

1 cup chopped onion

1 cup chopped carrots

1 cup sliced button mushrooms

1 stalk celery, chopped

2 cloves garlic, minced

1 teaspoon dried thyme

1 teaspoon dried oregano

1 cup dry red wine, such as Sangiovese or Zinfandel

One 14-ounce can reduced-sodium beef broth

One 6-ounce can tomato paste

2 bay leaves

1 pound wide egg noodles

¼ cup chopped fresh parsley

1. Heat the oil in a large saucepan over medium-high heat. Season the beef all over with salt and pepper. Place the flour in a shallow dish, add the beef, and turn to coat evenly, tapping off any excess. Add the beef to the hot pan and cook until browned on all sides, 3 to 5 minutes total. Using a slotted spoon, remove the beef from the pan and set aside. To the same pan, add the onion, carrots, mushrooms, celery, and garlic and cook, stirring, until the vegetables soften, 3 minutes. Return the beef to the pan, add the thyme and oregano, and stir to coat. Add the wine and cook for 1 minute. Add the broth, tomato paste, and bay

leaves and bring to a simmer. Reduce the heat to medium-low, partially cover, and simmer until the beef is cooked through, about 10 minutes.

2. Meanwhile, cook the egg noodles according to the package directions. Drain and set aside.

3. Remove the beef mixture from the heat, remove the bay leaves, and stir in the parsley.

4. Arrange the egg noodles on a warm serving platter, top with the beef mixture, and serve.

make it a meal kit Make the egg noodles, cook the beef with the vegetables and spices (up to and before adding the parsley), and store them separately in sealable containers or plastic bags for up to 3 days in the refrigerator. When you're ready to finish the meal, reheat the egg noodles in the microwave for 2 minutes on HIGH. Remove the bay leaves from the beef mixture and reheat in a large saucepan or in the microwave for 3 to 5 minutes on HIGH. Serve the beef over the egg noodles and top with the parsley.

bank a batch Make a double batch of the beef and egg noodles and store the extras separately in sealable containers or plastic bags for up to 3 days in the refrigerator or up to 3 months in the freezer. Thaw overnight in the refrigerator or in the microwave for 4 to 6 minutes on LOW. Reheat the beef portion in a large saucepan or in the microwave for 3 to 5 minutes on HIGH. Reheat the egg noodles in the microwave for 2 minutes on HIGH. Serve the beef over the egg noodles and top with the parsley.

have it your way Feel free to serve the braised beef over rice, quinoa, or couscous instead of egg noodles.

slow cook it Brown the beef as directed above. Remove the beef from the pan and transfer to a medium to large slow cooker. Add all the remaining ingredients except the egg noodles and parsley. Cover and cook on HIGH for 4 hours or on LOW for 6 to 8 hours. Cook the egg noodles just before serving. Remove the bay leaves, serve the beef over the egg noodles, and top with the parsley.

Moroccan Beef Stew

Head to Morocco with chickpeas, olives, raisins, and cilantro simmered in a rich broth, the flavors deepened with the warmth of cinnamon. This dish is fantastic over couscous. Another great side dish would be Cucumber Salad with Oranges & Mint (page 272).

Total Time: 25–30 minutes

Prep time: 10–15 minutes

Active cooking time:
15 minutes

Serves 4

1 tablespoon olive oil

1¼ pounds lean beef steak (such as sirloin, rib-eye, or round), cut into 1-inch cubes

1 cup chopped yellow onion

2 medium carrots, chopped

4 cloves garlic, minced

2 teaspoons paprika

2 teaspoons ground cumin

1 teaspoon ground cinnamon

½ teaspoon salt

½ teaspoon freshly ground black pepper

2 cups reduced-sodium beef broth

One 15-ounce can chickpeas, rinsed and drained

1 cup pitted kalamata olives, drained and halved

½ cup golden or dark raisins

¼ cup chopped fresh cilantro

1. Heat the oil in a large stockpot or Dutch oven over medium-high heat. Add the beef and cook until browned on all sides, about 5 minutes total. Remove the beef from the pan and set aside.

2. To the same pan, add the onion, carrots, and garlic and cook, stirring, until softened, about 3 minutes. Add the paprika, cumin, cinnamon, salt, and pepper and cook for 1 minute, until the spices are fragrant. Return the beef to the pan and add the broth, chickpeas, olives, and raisins. Bring to a simmer, reduce the heat to medium-low, and continue to simmer until the beef is cooked through, about 5 minutes. Remove from the heat, stir in the cilantro, and serve.

bank a batch **Make a double batch of the entire meal and store the extra in a seal-able container or plastic bag for up to 3 days in the refrigerator or up to 3 months in the freezer. Thaw overnight in the refrigerator or in the microwave for 4 to 6 minutes on LOW. Reheat in a large saucepan or in the microwave for 3 to 5 minutes on HIGH.**

have it your way **Feel free to substitute an equal amount of boneless, skinless chicken breasts, cut into cubes, for the beef.**

This dish is fantastic

over couscous.

Quick Fix Beef Bourguignon

Classic Beef Bourguignon is beef stewed in red wine with bacon, mushrooms, and onions. In my version, I swap carrots and peas for mushrooms and use pearl onions for their sweetness and fun size and shape. This is wonderful served over egg noodles. I also like to serve it with crusty bread or Parmesan-Crusted Rolls (page 263).

Total Time: 45–47 minutes

Prep time: 15 minutes

Active cooking time: 10–12 minutes

Walk-away time: 20 minutes

Serves 6

4 slices bacon, diced

1¼ pounds beef tenderloin, sirloin, rib-eye, or round, cut into 1-inch cubes

Salt and freshly ground black pepper to taste

¼ cup all-purpose flour

2 cloves garlic, minced

1 teaspoon dried thyme

1 cup dry red wine

2 cups reduced-sodium beef broth

2 tablespoons tomato paste

3 medium carrots, chopped

2 cups frozen pearl onions

1 cup frozen green peas

1. In a large stockpot or Dutch oven over medium-high heat, cook the bacon until browned and crisp. Remove the bacon from the pan with a slotted spoon and set aside to drain on paper towels.

2. Season the beef all over with salt and pepper. Place the flour in a shallow dish, add the beef, and turn to coat evenly, tapping off any excess. Add the beef to the hot pan and cook until golden brown on all sides, about 5 minutes total. Add the garlic and cook for 1 minute. Add the thyme and cook for 1 minute, until fragrant. Add the wine and bring to a simmer. Add the broth, tomato paste, carrots, pearl onions, and reserved bacon and bring to a simmer. Reduce the heat to medium-low and continue to simmer until the beef is cooked through and the sauce thickens, about 20 minutes.

3. Add the peas and simmer for 1 minute, until hot. Ladle the beef mixture into bowls or over egg noodles and serve.

bank a batch Make a double batch of the entire meal and store the extra in a sealable container for up to 3 days in the refrigerator or up to 3 months in the freezer. Thaw overnight in the refrigerator or in the microwave for 5 to 7 minutes on LOW. Reheat in a large saucepan or in the microwave for a few minutes on HIGH.

slow cook it Fry the bacon and brown the beef as directed. Remove the beef from the pan and transfer to a medium to large slow cooker. Add the remaining ingredients, except the peas. Cover and cook on HIGH for 4 hours or on LOW for 6 to 8 hours. Add the peas and cook for 5 minutes to heat through.

This is wonderful served

over egg noodles.

Mesquite Burgers with Grilled Onions & Provolone

Mesquite seasoning is a great flavor booster, and sweet provolone is the perfect balance for mesquite's sharpness. Feel free to make this dish with ground turkey breast if you prefer turkey burgers. I like to serve sliced tomatoes or Black Bean & Corn Salad (page 271) on the side.

Total Time: 19–28 minutes

Prep time: 10–15 minutes

Active cooking time: 9–13 minutes

Serves 4

Cooking spray

1¼ pounds lean ground beef

1½ teaspoons mesquite seasoning

1 large yellow onion, sliced crosswise into ½-inch-thick rounds

Salt and freshly ground black pepper to taste

4 to 6 ounces sliced provolone cheese

4 Kaiser rolls or large hamburger buns

1. Coat an outdoor grill or stovetop grill pan with cooking spray and preheat over medium-high heat.

2. Meanwhile, in a large bowl, combine the beef and mesquite seasoning, then shape into 4 burgers, each about 1 inch thick. Add the burgers to the hot pan and cook for 4 to 6 minutes per side for medium doneness.

3. Meanwhile, season both sides of the onion rounds with salt and pepper. Place the rounds in the pan next to the burgers and cook until golden brown and slightly soft, 3 to 5 minutes per side. Place the onions on top of the burgers, top with the cheese, and cook for 1 minute, until the cheese melts. Serve immediately on the rolls.

make it a meal kit Make the burgers and onions and store them separately (cooked or uncooked) in sealable containers or plastic bags for up to 3 days in the refrigerator or up to 3 months in the freezer. Thaw overnight in the refrigerator or in the microwave for 4 to 6 minutes on LOW. Finish cooking as directed above, or, if cooked, reheat in a 350°F oven for 15 minutes or in the microwave for 1 to 2 minutes on HIGH.

morph it Make a double batch of the burgers and morph the extras into Beef & Mushroom Tart (page 161); add the crumbled-up burgers to the pan when you add the mushrooms.

Beef Medallions with Chorizo Baked Beans

These baked beans are also amazing with burgers (beef and turkey) and grilled chicken breasts. Since this is such a comfort meal, I like to serve it with Traditional Potato Salad (page 266) and 5-Ingredient Broccoli Ranch Slaw (page 269).

Total Time: 16–25 minutes

Prep time: 10–15 minutes

Active cooking time: 6–10 minutes

Serves 4

CHORIZO BAKED BEANS

Two 15-ounce cans red beans, rinsed and drained

$\frac{1}{2}$ cup diced chorizo or other cooked spicy sausage, such as andouille

$\frac{1}{3}$ cup minced onion

One 8-ounce can tomato sauce

$\frac{1}{3}$ cup ketchup

2 tablespoons brown sugar

1 teaspoon chili powder

$\frac{1}{2}$ teaspoon ground cumin

$\frac{1}{2}$ teaspoon paprika

4 filets mignons

Salt and cracked black peppercorns to taste

1 tablespoon Worcestershire sauce

2 teaspoons olive oil

1. To make the beans, in a medium saucepan, combine the beans, sausage, onion, tomato sauce, ketchup, brown sugar, chili powder, cumin, and paprika. Set over medium heat and bring to a simmer.

2. Meanwhile, season both sides of the beef with salt and cracked pepper. Brush the Worcestershire over both sides of the beef. Heat the oil in a large skillet over medium-high heat. Add the steaks and cook for 3 to 5 minutes per side for medium doneness. Serve the beef with the beans on the side.

bank a batch **Make a double batch of the beans and store the extra for up to 3 days in the refrigerator or 3 months in the freezer. Thaw overnight in the refrigerator or in the microwave for 4 to 6 minutes on LOW. Reheat in a saucepan or in the microwave for 3 to 5 minutes on HIGH.**

Filet Mignon with Spicy Rémoulade

Think of rémoulade, a mayo-based condiment, as France's version of tartar sauce. I kick mine up with hot chipotle chiles, making it the perfect partner for steak. I like to serve this with Roasted Broccoli with Red Onion & Walnuts (page 246) or Mushrooms with Garlic, Parmesan & Bread Crumbs (page 250).

Total Time: 16–20 minutes

Prep time: 5 minutes

Active cooking time:
6–10 minutes

Resting time: 5 minutes

Serves 4

1 tablespoon olive oil

4 filets mignons or boneless sirloin steaks

Salt and cracked black peppercorns to taste

SPICY RÉMOULADE

1 cup mayonnaise

1 tablespoon minced cornichons or gherkin pickles

2 teaspoons drained capers

1½ teaspoons minced canned chipotle chiles in adobo sauce

2 teaspoons chopped fresh parsley

1 clove garlic, minced

1. Heat the oil in a large skillet over medium-high heat until hot, 1 to 2 minutes. Season both sides of the steaks with salt and cracked pepper. Add the steaks to the hot pan and cook for 3 to 5 minutes per side for medium doneness. Remove from the pan and let stand for 5 minutes.

2. Meanwhile, in a small bowl, combine the rémoulade ingredients until well mixed.

3. Serve the steak with the rémoulade spooned over the top of each one.

make it a meal kit Prepare the rémoulade up to 3 days in advance and refrigerate in a sealable container until ready to serve.

morph it Make a double batch of the steaks and morph the extra into Warm Steak & Penne Salad with Tomato Soup French Dressing (page 194).

5-Ingredient Rib-Eye with Garlic–Rosemary Marinade

Rib-eye steaks are fairly lean cuts of beef with just enough marbling (fat) to create a tender, mouthwatering meal, but feel free to make this with your favorite steak. I often serve this with orzo or Black & Pink Beans with Rice (page 257).

Total Time: 37–46 minutes

Prep time: 5–10 minutes

Marinating time: 15 minutes

Active cooking time: 12–16 minutes

Resting time: 5 minutes

Serves 4

4 boneless rib-eye steaks

Salt and cracked black peppercorns or coarsely ground black pepper to taste

GARLIC–ROSEMARY MARINADE

¼ cup olive oil

2 cloves garlic, minced

2 tablespoons chopped fresh rosemary

Cooking spray

1. Season the steaks all over with salt and cracked pepper. In a shallow dish, combine the oil, garlic, and rosemary. Add the steaks and turn to coat. Let marinate for 15 minutes (or up to 24 hours; refrigerate if marinating more than an hour).

2. Coat a stovetop grill pan or griddle with cooking spray and preheat over medium-high heat until hot, 3 to 5 minutes. Add the steaks to the hot pan and cook for 3 to 5 minutes per side for medium doneness. Remove from the heat and let the steaks rest for 5 minutes before serving.

morph it Make a double batch of the steak and morph the extra into Multicolored Ponzu Beef Kebabs (page 186); just assemble the kebabs as instructed, sear them in a hot pan, and serve.

Chili-Rubbed Steak

This is a Quick Fix spice rub for any busy weeknight. For variety, try coarse salt and cracked black pepper and vary the spices—thyme, rosemary, oregano, cumin, tarragon, basil, curry, and fennel all work great. On the side, try Saucy Roasted Eggplant with Toasted Polenta (page 248) or 5-Ingredient Mashed Chipotle Sweet Potatoes with Lime (page 256).

Total Time: 16–20 minutes

Prep time: 5–10 minutes

Active cooking time:
6–10 minutes

Resting time: 5 minutes

Serves 4

2 tablespoons chili powder

1 teaspoon ground coriander

½ teaspoon salt

½ teaspoon freshly ground black pepper

4 boneless rib-eye steaks

1 tablespoon olive oil

1. In a shallow dish, combine the chili powder, coriander, salt, and pepper. Add the steaks and turn to coat both sides evenly, pressing the mixture into the meat.

2. Heat the oil in a large skillet over medium-high heat. Add the steaks and cook for 3 to 5 minutes per side for medium doneness. Remove from the heat and let rest for 5 minutes before serving.

morph it Make a double batch of the steak and morph the extra into Beef & Mushroom Tart (page 161), using the steak, cut into dice, instead of the ground beef; add it to the pan when you add the mushrooms.

Sesame-Crusted Steaks with Buttermilk–Horseradish Sauce

A word regarding the steak: don't select a double-cut thick steak for this recipe because the sesame seeds will burn before the steak gets cooked through. The perfect side dish is Rosemary-Roasted Vegetable Medley (page 259).

Total Time: 16–20 minutes

Prep time: 5 minutes

Active cooking time:
6–10 minutes

Resting time: 5 minutes

Serves 4

4 boneless sirloin steaks

Salt and freshly ground black pepper to taste

⅓ cup sesame seeds

1 tablespoon olive oil

BUTTERMILK–HORSERADISH SAUCE

½ cup buttermilk

½ cup sour cream

2 tablespoons prepared horseradish

1 teaspoon Dijon mustard

1 teaspoon minced fresh chives

Salt and freshly ground black pepper to taste

1. Season the steaks all over with salt and pepper. Press the sesame seeds into both sides of the steaks.

2. Heat the oil in a large skillet over medium-high heat until hot, 1 to 2 minutes. Add the steaks and cook for 3 to 5 minutes per side for medium doneness. Remove from the heat and let stand for 5 minutes before serving.

3. Meanwhile, in a medium bowl, whisk together the buttermilk, sour cream, horseradish, mustard, and chives. Season with salt and pepper.

4. Serve the steaks with the sauce spooned over the top.

make it a meal kit Prepare the sauce and store it in a sealable container for up to 3 days in the refrigerator.

morph it Make a double batch of the steaks and morph the extra into Warm Steak & Penne Salad with Tomato Soup French Dressing (page 194), or swap this steak for the flank steak in Flank Steak with Sautéed Edamame & Wasabi–Mustard Dressing (page 188).

Coconut Beef Satay with Thai Peanut Sauce

As if the marinade, a unique coconut cream sauce, isn't enough to send your palate soaring, the sweet, salty, peanutty dipping sauce puts everything over the top. I like to serve this with instant rice or soba or somen noodles on the side.

Total Time: 13–20 minutes

Prep time: 10–15 minutes

Active cooking time:
3–5 minutes

Serves 4

Cooking spray

½ cup canned unsweetened coconut milk

1½ teaspoons curry powder

1 teaspoon ground coriander

½ teaspoon chile oil

1¼ pounds lean beef steak (such as sirloin, rib-eye, or round), cut into 2-inch cubes

Salt and freshly ground black pepper to taste

Metal or wooden skewers

THAI PEANUT SAUCE

½ cup reduced-sodium chicken broth

¼ cup creamy peanut butter

¼ cup reduced-sodium soy sauce

2 teaspoons toasted sesame oil

2 tablespoons chopped fresh cilantro

1. Coat a large stovetop grill pan or griddle with cooking spray and preheat over medium-high heat.

2. In a shallow dish, whisk together the coconut milk, curry powder, coriander, and chile oil.

3. Season the beef all over with salt and pepper. Add the beef to the coconut milk mixture and turn to coat. Thread the beef on skewers and place in the hot pan. Cook until browned and cooked through, 3 to 5 minutes, turning frequently.

4. Meanwhile, in a small saucepan, whisk together the broth, peanut butter, soy sauce, and sesame oil. Set over medium heat and bring to a simmer. Remove from the heat and stir in the cilantro.

5. Serve the beef skewers with the peanut sauce on the side in small bowls for dipping.

make it a meal kit Prepare the coconut mixture and add it to the beef as instructed. Make the peanut sauce. Store each separately in sealable containers or plastic bags for up to 3 days in the refrigerator. When ready to finish the meal, skewer the beef and cook as instructed. Reheat the peanut sauce in a small saucepan over low heat or in the microwave for 1 minute on HIGH.

morph it Make a double batch of the steak and morph the extra into Steak & Shiitake Fried Rice (page 184).

Steak & Shiitake Fried Rice

Fried rice is an ideal vehicle for leftovers. You can morph leftover steak, chicken, shrimp, or pork into fried rice and everyone at the table will think it's a completely new meal, made from scratch. I like to use regular rice in this recipe because it's bit "chewier" than instant, so factor that into your prep time, or prep ahead and make the rice up to 5 days in advance (store it in a sealable container in the fridge). I like to serve this with steamed snap peas on the side.

Total Time: 17–25 minutes

Prep time: 10–15 minutes

Active cooking time: 7–10 minutes

Serves 4

1 cup rice (white, basmati, or jasmine)

1 tablespoon olive oil

2 large eggs, lightly beaten

2 cloves garlic, minced

1 tablespoon peeled and minced fresh ginger

8 ounces steak of your choice, cut into 1-inch cubes

2 medium carrots, chopped, or 1/2 cup shredded carrots

1 cup snow peas, strings removed

1 cup sliced shiitake mushrooms or any mushroom variety

1/4 cup reduced-sodium soy sauce

2 teaspoons toasted sesame oil

1/4 cup chopped scallions (white and green parts)

1. Cook the rice according to the package directions.

2. Meanwhile, heat the olive oil in a large skillet over medium-high heat. Add the eggs and swirl to coat the bottom of the pan. Cook until the eggs are firm and set, 1 to 2 minutes. Transfer the eggs to a cutting board and set aside.

3. To the same skillet, add the garlic and ginger and cook for 1 minute. Add the steak and cook until cooked through, 3 to 5 minutes. Add the carrots, snow peas, and mushrooms and cook until the mushrooms are softened, about 3 minutes. Add the soy sauce and sesame oil and bring to a simmer. Stir in the rice and heat through. Remove from the heat and stir in the scallions.

4. Slice the eggs into thin strips. Spoon the fried rice onto a serving platter, top with the eggs, and serve.

make it a meal kit Make the rice, chop all the vegetables, and cut up the beef. Store each separately in sealable containers or plastic bags for up to 3 days in the refrigerator. When you're ready to finish the meal, make the dish as directed (with all the prep work completed!).

morph it Use cooked steak from any other steak recipe and add it when you add the carrots.

Make a double batch of the rice and morph the extra into Asparagus–Wild Mushroom Risotto with Parmesan (page 76). Cut the cooking time down to 8 to 10 minutes and add all the broth (2½ cups) at once, instead of adding it in ½-cup measurements.

Fried rice is an ideal

vehicle for leftovers.

Multicolored Ponzu Beef Kebabs

Ponzu sauce is a citrusy bottled sauce you can find in the Asian food section of the grocery store. It lends tremendous flavor to these kebabs. In fact, make an extra batch of the marinade and enjoy it with pork or chicken later in the week! Serve the kebabs with Toasted Coconut Rice (page 261).

Total Time: 23–25 minutes

Prep time: 15 minutes

Active cooking time: 8–10 minutes

Cooking spray

1¼ pounds lean beef steak, cut into 2-inch cubes

1 pint cherry or grape tomatoes

1 medium yellow or orange bell pepper, seeded and cut into 2-inch pieces

1 cup small button or cremini mushrooms, trimmed

4 to 6 scallions, cut into 2-inch lengths

Wooden or metal skewers

⅓ cup ponzu sauce

1 tablespoon Chinese black bean sauce

¼ teaspoon red pepper flakes

1. Coat a large stovetop grill pan or griddle with cooking spray and preheat over medium-high heat.

2. Alternate pieces of steak, tomatoes, bell pepper, mushrooms, and scallions on the skewers. Place the skewers in a large plastic bag.

3. In a small bowl, whisk together the ponzu sauce, black bean sauce, and red pepper flakes. Pour into the bag with the skewers, seal, and shake to coat the beef. Remove the kebabs from the bag, place them in the hot pan, and cook until the beef is browned and cooked through, 8 to 10 minutes, turning frequently.

make it a meal kit Assemble the kebabs and add the ponzu mixture as instructed. Store in the sealed bag for up to 3 days in the refrigerator before cooking as directed.

morph it Grill a double batch of the skewers, dice the extra beef and vegetables, and use the mixture instead of ground beef in Anita's Slow Cooker Chili (page 166).

have it your way Try serving the skewers with the Spicy Rémoulade on page 178. Swap the veggies if desired; excellent variations include zucchini, yellow squash, eggplant, and a variety of wild mushrooms.

Broiled Flank Steak with Ancho–Honey Mayo

Ancho chiles are dried poblano chile peppers and they have a subtle, paprika-like flavor and mild to moderate heat. They make a great base for sauces and toppings. For a color and flavor blast, serve the steak with Balsamic Roasted Beets (page 244) and steamed broccoli on the side.

Total Time: 30 minutes

Prep time: 10 minutes

Active cooking time: 10 minutes

Resting time: 10 minutes

Serves 4

One 1¼-pound flank steak

Salt and freshly ground black pepper to taste

1 teaspoon garlic powder

ANCHO–HONEY MAYO

½ cup mayonnaise

2 tablespoons honey

1 teaspoon ground ancho chiles

2 tablespoons chopped fresh cilantro

1. Preheat the broiler. Line a baking sheet with aluminum foil.

2. Season the steak all over with salt and pepper and the garlic powder. Transfer the steak to the baking sheet and place under the broiler for 5 minutes per side for medium doneness. Remove from the oven and let rest for 10 minutes before cutting crosswise into ¼-inch-thick slices.

3. Meanwhile, in a medium bowl, whisk together the mayonnaise, honey, and ground ancho.

4. Top the steak slices with the ancho-honey mayo and the cilantro just before serving.

morph it **Make a double batch of the Ancho–Honey Mayo—it makes an amazing (and uplifting!) sandwich spread. It will keep in a sealable container for up to 7 days in the refrigerator.**

Flank Steak with Edamame & Wasabi–Mustard Dressing

This is elegant enough for guests, and you'll love the combination of spicy and warming wasabi and sweet, nutty edamame. I like to round out the dish with instant brown rice or Toasted Coconut Rice (page 261).

Total Time: 26–30 minutes

Prep time: 10 minutes

Active cooking time:
6–10 minutes

Resting time: 10 minutes

Serves 4

Cooking spray

One 1¼-pound flank steak

Salt and freshly ground black pepper to taste

Mesquite seasoning to taste

2 teaspoons toasted sesame oil

2 cloves garlic, minced

1 tablespoon peeled and minced fresh ginger

One 10-ounce package fresh or thawed frozen shelled edamame

2 tablespoons reduced-sodium soy sauce

WASABI–MUSTARD DRESSING

¼ cup rice vinegar

3 tablespoons olive oil

2 teaspoons country-style Dijon mustard

1 teaspoon wasabi paste

1. Coat a large stovetop grill pan or griddle with cooking spray and preheat over medium-high heat until hot, 3 to 5 minutes. Season both sides of the flank steak with salt, pepper, and mesquite seasoning. Place the steak in the hot pan and cook for 3 to 5 minutes per side for medium doneness. Remove from the heat and let rest for 10 minutes before slicing crosswise into ½-inch-thick slices.

2. Meanwhile, heat the sesame oil in a large skillet over medium heat. Add the garlic and ginger and cook for 1 minute. Add the edamame and soy sauce and cook until the edamame are golden brown, 2 to 3 minutes, stirring frequently. Remove from the heat.

3. In a small bowl, whisk together the dressing ingredients.

4. Arrange the flank steak slices on a serving platter. Top with the sautéed edamame, then spoon the dressing over the top and serve.

morph it Make a double batch of the steak and morph the extra into Warm Steak & Penne Salad with Tomato Soup French Dressing (page 194) or Beef & Mushroom Tart (page 161).

Make a double batch of the edamame and morph the extra into Orzo with Spicy Edamame (page 47) or Warm Edamame–Rice Salad with Teriyaki Tuna (page 234).

Make a double batch of the dressing; it makes a fabulous dip for chilled shrimp, crab claws, or grilled chicken skewers. It will keep in a sealable container in the refrigerator for up to 5 days.

. . . the dressing makes a fabulous

dip for shrimp, crab claws, or

chicken skewers . . .

Grilled Flank Steak with Mint–Cilantro Mojo

You'll love this combination of a ginger-soy steak topped with the cilantro-mint sauce. And there's no need to clean the blender in between making the marinade and the mojo. I like to serve this with Vegetable Fricassée with Saffron Cream (page 260), but it's also great with the Chorizo Baked Beans from Beef Medallions with Chorizo Baked Beans (page 177).

Total Time: 46–50 minutes

Prep time: 15 minutes

Marinating time: 15 minutes

Active cooking time:
6–10 minutes

Resting time: 10 minutes

Serves 4

¼ cup reduced-sodium soy sauce

1 tablespoon peeled and chopped fresh ginger

1 tablespoon honey

2 teaspoons toasted sesame oil

1 clove garlic

¼ teaspoon freshly ground black pepper

One 1¼-pound flank steak

MINT–CILANTRO MOJO

⅓ cup fresh cilantro leaves

⅓ cup fresh mint leaves

¼ cup chopped scallions (white and green parts)

3 tablespoons water

1 tablespoon fresh lemon juice

2 teaspoons olive oil

1 clove garlic

Cooking spray

1. In a blender or food processor, combine the soy sauce, ginger, honey, sesame oil, garlic, and pepper and process until smooth. Pour the mixture into a plastic bag, add the flank steak, seal, and shake to coat. Let marinate for at least 15 minutes (and up to 24 hours; if marinating for more than an hour, put it in the refrigerator).

2. Combine the mojo ingredients in the blender or food processor and process until smooth.

3. Coat an outdoor grill or stovetop grill pan with cooking spray and preheat over medium-high heat until hot, 3 to 5 minutes. Remove the steak from the marinade (discard the marinade) and grill for 3 to 5 minutes per side for medium doneness. Remove from the heat and let the steak stand for 10 minutes before cutting crosswise into ¼-inch-thick slices.

4. Serve the steak with the mojo spooned over the top.

make it a meal kit Combine the marinade in a plastic bag, add the flank steak, seal, and refrigerate up to a day in advance. Make the mojo and store in a sealable container in the refrigerator for up to 3 days.

morph it Grill a double batch of the steak and morph the extra into Moroccan Beef Stew (page 172); skip the cooking the steak step and add the steak to the pan when you add the onion and other vegetables. Make a double batch of the mojo and use the extra with grilled chicken or fish.

Flank Steak with Parsley–Basil Chimichurri

Chimichurri is a topping that's typically made with parsley, oregano, garlic, salt, and pepper. In my version, I include basil for its fresh taste. You'll love the jolt of flavor it adds, so don't stop at steak—use the chimichurri to top chicken and fish as well. I like to serve this with Beet–Arugula Salad with Buttermilk–Blue Cheese Dressing (page 270).

Total Time: 21–25 minutes

Prep time: 5 minutes

Active cooking time:
6–10 minutes

Resting time: 10 minutes

Serves 4

Cooking spray

One 1¼-pound flank steak

Salt and freshly ground black pepper to taste

PARSLEY–BASIL CHIMICHURRI

½ cup fresh parsley leaves

½ cup fresh basil leaves

¼ cup olive oil

3 cloves garlic, coarsely chopped

Salt and freshly ground black pepper to taste

1. Coat a stovetop grill pan or griddle with cooking spray and preheat over medium-high heat until hot, 3 to 5 minutes. Season both sides of the steak with salt and pepper, then add to the hot pan and cook for 3 to 5 minutes per side for medium doneness. Let the steak rest for 10 minutes before slicing crosswise into ¼-inch-thick slices.

2. Meanwhile, to make the chimichurri, in a food processor or blender, combine the parsley, basil, oil, and garlic and process until smooth. Season with salt and pepper. Spoon the chimichurri over the steak just before serving.

make it a meal kit Make the chimichurri and store in a sealable container for up to 3 days in the refrigerator.

morph it Make a double batch of the steak and morph the extra into Tex-Mex Stuffed Peppers (page 168). Skip cooking the ground beef from scratch; instead, dice the cooked steak and add it to the pan when you add the rice and other ingredients.

Chile–Lime Marinated Skirt Steak

Chile peppers and lime have a natural affinity and the combo is fantastic with red meat. For the best flavor, let the steak marinate for at least 15 minutes and up to 24 hours (in the refrigerator). The marinade is also perfect for chicken and shrimp. I like to serve this with Toasted Coconut Rice (page 261). Other great partners are Sautéed Red Cabbage with Mandarins (page 247) or Vegetable Sauté with Black Bean Sauce (page 258).

Total Time: 41–43 minutes
Prep time: 10 minutes
Marinating time: 15 minutes
Active cooking time:
6–8 minutes
Resting time: 10 minutes

Serves 4

CHILE–LIME MARINADE

3 tablespoons fresh lime juice

1 tablespoon reduced-sodium soy sauce

2 cloves garlic, minced

1 fresh serrano chile pepper, seeded and minced

1 teaspoon ground coriander

One 1¼-pound skirt or flank steak

Salt and freshly ground black pepper to taste

Cooking spray

1. In a blender or small food processor, combine the marinade ingredients and process until smooth. Transfer to a shallow dish or plastic bag. Season the steak all over with salt and pepper and add to the marinade. Turn to coat both sides. Let marinate for at least 15 minutes (and up to 24 hours; if marinating more than an hour, put it in the refrigerator).

2. Coat a stovetop grill pan or griddle with cooking spray and preheat over medium-high heat until hot, 3 to 5 minutes. Add the steak to the hot pan and cook for 3 to 4 minutes per side for medium doneness. Remove from the heat and let rest for 10 minutes before cutting crosswise into ¼-inch-thick slices.

morph it Make a double batch of the steak and morph the extra into Steak & Shiitake Fried Rice (page 184).

Warm Steak & Penne Salad with Tomato Soup French Dressing

My version of that thick orange dressing I adored as a child is sweet and tangy and amazing on salads and pasta dishes like this one. I like to serve this with Garlic-Roasted Asparagus with Almonds (page 241).

Total Time: 16–25 minutes

Prep time: 5–10 minutes

Active cooking time:
6–10 minutes

Resting time: 5 minutes

Serves 4

1 pound penne pasta

Cooking spray

One 1¼-pound flank steak

Salt and freshly ground black pepper to taste

1 teaspoon dried oregano

TOMATO SOUP FRENCH DRESSING

One 10-ounce can condensed cream of tomato soup

½ cup reduced-sodium chicken broth or water

¼ cup sherry vinegar

1 tablespoon sugar

1 teaspoon sweet paprika

1 teaspoon dry mustard

¼ cup chopped scallions (white and green parts)

1. Cook the pasta according to the package directions. Drain and transfer to a large bowl.

2. Meanwhile, coat a large stovetop grill pan or griddle with cooking spray and preheat over medium-high heat until hot, 3 to 5 minutes. Season the flank steak all over with salt and pepper and the oregano. Add the steak to the hot pan and cook for 3 to 5 minutes per side for medium doneness. Remove from the heat and let stand for 5 minutes before slicing.

3. Meanwhile, in a medium bowl, whisk together the dressing ingredients. Add the dressing to the pasta and stir to coat. Cut the steak crosswise into ¼-inch-thick slices and then each slice into 1-inch pieces. Add the steak to the pasta and stir to combine. Fold in the scallions and serve.

make it a meal kit Cook and drain the pasta, cook the steak, combine the dressing ingredients, and store each separately in sealable containers or plastic bags in the refrigerator, the pasta and steak for up to 3 days, the dressing for up to 7 days. When ready to finish the meal, combine all the ingredients in a large saucepan over medium heat and reheat for a few minutes, until hot. Or, combine in a microwave-safe bowl and microwave for 3 to 5 minutes on HIGH, until hot.

bank a batch Make a double batch of the dressing—it's fantastic (warm or chilled) over chicken, lettuce, steamed vegetables, or baked fish. Store any extra dressing in a sealable container for up 3 months in the freezer. Thaw overnight in the refrigerator or in the microwave for 3 minutes on LOW.

. . . the dressing is fantastic over

chicken, lettuce, steamed vegetables,

or baked fish . . .

London Broil with Balsamic Onion Rings

These onions are also fabulous over seared chicken breasts or pork chops. An excellent accompaniment is Twice-Baked Potatoes with Cheddar & Bacon (page 253).

Total Time: 21–25 minutes

Prep time: 10 minutes

Active cooking time:
6–10 minutes

Resting time: 5 minutes

Serves 4

Cooking spray

One 1¼-pound London broil or flank steak

Salt, cracked black peppercorns, and freshly ground black pepper to taste

BALSAMIC ONION RINGS

1 tablespoon olive oil

1 large yellow onion, cut into ¼-inch-thick slices and separated into rings

2 tablespoons sugar

¼ cup balsamic vinegar

1. Coat a large stovetop grill pan or griddle with cooking spray and preheat over medium-high heat until hot, 3 to 5 minutes. Season both sides of the steak with salt and cracked pepper and add to the hot pan. Cook for 3 to 5 minutes per side for medium doneness. Remove from the heat and let stand for 5 minutes.

2. Meanwhile, heat the oil in a large skillet over medium-high heat. Add the onion rings and sugar and cook until golden brown and tender, about 5 minutes, stirring. Add the vinegar and cook until the liquid is absorbed, about 2 minutes. Season with salt and ground pepper.

3. Cut the steak crosswise into ½-inch-thick slices and serve with the onion rings over the top.

morph it Make a double batch of steak and morph the extra into Pan-Seared BBQ Beef on Garlic Crostini (page 198).

Make a double batch of the onion rings and morph the extra into Three-Onion Soup with Cheese-Smothered Toast (page 20); use the balsamic onions instead of cooking the onions from scratch.

5-Ingredient London Broil with Cumin-Roasted Tomatoes & Corn

London broil is a lean, wonderful piece of meat. You can also buy flank, skirt, or hanger steak for this recipe and enjoy the same result. The perfect side dishes are couscous along with Seared Goat Cheese over Greens (page 276) or Mushrooms with Garlic, Parmesan & Bread Crumbs (page 250).

Total Time: 30–32 minutes

Prep time: 10 minutes

Active cooking time: 10–12 minutes

Resting time: 10 minutes

Serves 4

Cooking spray

4 cups halved cherry or grape tomatoes

1 cup frozen white corn, thawed

Salt and freshly ground black pepper to taste

2 teaspoons ground cumin

One 1¼-pound London broil

1. Preheat the oven to 400°F. Coat a large baking sheet with cooking spray. Coat a stovetop grill pan or griddle with cooking spray and preheat over medium-high heat.

2. Arrange the tomatoes and corn on the prepared sheet and season with salt and pepper. Sprinkle over the cumin, then roast the tomatoes and corn until golden brown, about 15 minutes.

3. Meanwhile, season both sides of the London broil with salt and pepper. Add the steak to the hot pan and cook for 5 to 6 minutes per side for medium doneness. Remove from the heat and let rest for 10 minutes before cutting crosswise into ¼-inch-thick slices.

4. Arrange the steak slices on a warm serving platter, top with the tomato-corn mixture, and serve.

morph it Make a double batch of the steak and morph the extra into Steak & Shiitake Fried Rice (page 184), Warm Steak & Penne Salad with Tomato Soup French Dressing (page 194), or Beef & Mushroom Tart (page 161). In the tart use the steak, cut into dice, instead of the ground beef; add it to the pan when you add the mushrooms.

Pan-Seared BBQ Beef on Garlic Crostini

My smoky ketchup-based sauce is so good that you'll want to make a double batch so you can simmer meatballs in it. In this recipe, I suggest buying deli-sliced beef for a super time-saver. Try Roasted Green Beans with Grape Tomatoes & Olives (page 242) on the side.

Total Time: 15–20 minutes
Prep time: 10–15 minutes
Active cooking time: 5 minutes

Serves 4

1 French baguette, cut on the diagonal into ½-inch-thick slices

2 tablespoons olive oil, divided

2 cloves garlic, minced

1 pound thickly sliced deli roast beef

½ cup ketchup

2 tablespoons water

2 tablespoons reduced-sodium soy sauce

1 teaspoon Dijon mustard

1 teaspoon liquid smoke seasoning

1 teaspoon chili powder

Salt and freshly ground black pepper to taste

1. Preheat the oven to 400°F.

2. Arrange the bread slices on a large baking sheet and brush the tops with 1 tablespoon of the oil. Top with the garlic. Bake until golden brown, 6 to 8 minutes.

3. Meanwhile, heat the remaining 1 tablespoon oil in a large skillet over medium-high heat. Add the roast beef and cook until lightly browned, about 3 minutes, stirring a few times.

4. In a small bowl, whisk together the ketchup, water, soy sauce, mustard, liquid smoke, and chili powder, then add to the roast beef, bring to a simmer, and continue to simmer to heat through, about 2 minutes. Season with salt and pepper.

5. Serve the roast beef and sauce from the pan over the toasted garlic crostini.

make it a meal kit Make the garlic crostini up to 2 days in advance and store at room temperature in a sealable container or plastic bag. Combine the sauce ingredients (the ketchup through the chili powder) and store for up to 3 days in the refrigerator. When ready to finish the meal, heat the roast beef as directed, add the sauce and simmer as directed, and serve over the crostini (there's no need to reheat them).

. . . buy deli-sliced beef for a

super time-saver.

6

Fish and Shellfish

THERE ARE FEW THINGS IN THE Quick Fix kitchen that cook faster than seafood.

Since most fish is ready in much less than 20 minutes, it's a great choice for a protein-rich Quick Fix meal. With that in mind, plan on preparing the fish the day you will eat it (or within a day of prepping). You can certainly prep all the other ingredients (marinades, sauces, vegetables, etc.) in advance, and I've given you lots of tips throughout this chapter on how to do that. But when it comes to the fish portion, hold off until you're ready to cook. Why? The protein in fish is different than the protein in beef, pork, or chicken and it breaks down more quickly when combined with other ingredients, especially acidic ingredients like marinades with citrus juice and/or vinegar. That's why ceviche, an uncooked seafood dish, seems cooked, because the acidic ingredients (typically lemon and lime juice) actually interact with the protein and essentially cook the fish before it's served.

Aside from speeding from the stove to the table, seafood is super-adaptable to Quick Fix cooking in other ways. When I buy or cook with seafood, I always think "Bank a Batch." Fish and shellfish freeze very well, so either I make a double batch of an entire meal for the freezer or I make extra fish or shellfish to morph into another meal down the road. If you ever get stumped with morphing ideas (beyond what I suggest in this chapter), think "What would I do with chicken?" Cooked fish and shellfish can quickly transform a recipe meant to use chicken into a completely new, flavorful creation in a fraction of the time.

Cooked fish and shellfish can quickly

transform a recipe meant to use chicken . . .

Clams Rockefeller

I like to serve these tender baked clams (nestled under garlicky spinach, bread crumbs, and Parmesan cheese) with angel hair or capellini pasta tossed with olive oil and fresh basil.

Total Time: 28 minutes
Prep time: 10 minutes
Active cooking time: 10 minutes
Walk-away time: 8 minutes

Serves 4

2 dozen littleneck clams

2 teaspoons olive oil

3 cloves garlic, minced

One 10-ounce package frozen chopped spinach, thawed, drained well, and squeezed dry

2 tablespoons Italian-seasoned dry bread crumbs

2 slices bacon, cooked in the microwave or on the stovetop until crisp and crumbled

Salt and freshly ground black pepper to taste

2 tablespoons freshly grated Parmesan cheese

Hot sauce (optional)

1. Preheat the oven to 500°F.

2. Place the clams in a large stockpot and pour over enough water to cover. Set the pot over high heat and bring to a boil. Remove from the heat, drain, and discard any clams that haven't opened. When cool enough to handle, remove and discard the top shell from the clams. Arrange the clams (in their shells) on a large baking sheet and set aside.

3. Meanwhile, heat the oil in a large skillet over medium-high heat. Add the garlic and cook for 1 minute. Add the spinach and cook until hot, about 1 minute. Add the bread crumbs and bacon and cook 1 to 2 more minutes, until any liquid evaporates. Season with salt and pepper.

4. Top the clams with the spinach mixture, then sprinkle with the Parmesan. Bake until the cheese is golden brown, about 8 minutes. Drizzle with hot sauce before serving if desired.

make it a meal kit Assemble the clams as instructed and, before baking, cover the baking sheet with plastic wrap and store for up to 2 days in the refrigerator. When ready, bake as directed, adding a few minutes to the cooking time if necessary, until the filling is hot.

Vongole Pizza with Andouille, Clams & Scallops

Shellfish pizza: sounds crazy but it's wildly delicious. I like to serve Mixed Cherry Tomato Salad (page 281) or Baby Spinach Salad with Strawberry–Sherry Vinaigrette (page 279) on the side.

Total Time: 23–30 minutes

Prep time: 10–15 minutes

Active cooking time: 3 minutes

Walk-away time: 10–12 minutes

Serves 4

1 cup diced andouille or chorizo sausage

$\frac{1}{2}$ pound bay scallops

$\frac{1}{4}$ pound shelled clams or one 6-ounce can baby clams, drained

1 teaspoon dried oregano

1 pound refrigerated or frozen bread or pizza dough, thawed according to package directions

$\frac{1}{2}$ cup thawed frozen chopped spinach, drained well and squeezed dry

1 cup diced oil-packed sun-dried tomatoes

2 cups shredded mozzarella cheese

2 tablespoons freshly grated Parmesan cheese

1. Preheat the oven to 450°F.

2. Cook the sausage in a large skillet over medium-high heat until browned and crisp. Add the scallops and clams and cook for 2 minutes. Add the oregano and stir to coat. Cook for 1 minute, until the oregano is fragrant. Remove from the heat.

3. On a lightly floured work surface, roll the dough out into a 15-inch circle and transfer to a large baking sheet. Top the dough with the spinach, then the sun-dried tomatoes, leaving a $\frac{1}{2}$-inch border around the edges. Top with the sausage-seafood mixture, then both the cheeses. Bake until the crust is golden brown underneath and the cheeses melt, 10 to 12 minutes.

make it a meal kit Cook the andouille, scallops, clams, and oregano. Dice the tomatoes and prep the cheeses. Thaw the spinach. Store each separately in sealable containers or plastic bags in the refrigerator for up to 3 days.

bank a batch Assemble the pizza and, before baking, cover with plastic wrap, then aluminum foil, and store for up to 3 months in the freezer. Thaw overnight in the refrigerator and bake just before serving. You could also make two to four smaller pizzas that you can freeze and then stack to save space or have available as a quick snack.

morph it Use extra scallops from Bacon-Wrapped Scallops with Jalapeño–Papaya Salsa (page 206) to make this; you can eliminate the andouille since there's bacon wrapped around the scallops!

Use extra scallops from Bacon-Wrapped

Scallops with Jalapeño–Papaya Salsa

to make this . . .

Bacon-Wrapped Scallops with Jalapeño–Papaya Salsa

Scallops are sweet and buttery and shine on the plate when wrapped with smoky, salty bacon. You can use turkey bacon if you want to dodge some calories and fat. I love to serve this with Roasted Butternut Squash with Cumin & Coriander (page 255).

Total Time: 26–30 minutes

Prep time: 15 minutes

Active cooking time: 11–15 minutes

Serves 4

8 slices bacon

1¼ pounds sea scallops

Wooden toothpicks if necessary

1 tablespoon olive oil

JALAPEÑO–PAPAYA SALSA

1 medium ripe papaya, peeled, seeded, and diced

2 tablespoons chopped fresh cilantro

1 tablespoon fresh lime juice

1 tablespoon minced and seeded fresh jalapeño chile pepper

½ teaspoon ground cumin

Salt and freshly ground black pepper to taste

1. Preheat the oven to 400°F.

2. Halve the bacon slices crosswise and wrap one around each sea scallop. Secure with a toothpick if necessary.

3. Heat the oil in a large, ovenproof skillet over medium heat. Add the scallops and cook until the scallops are golden brown and the bacon is cooked, 3 to 5 minutes per side. Place the skillet in the oven and bake until the scallops are opaque and cooked through, about 5 minutes.

4. Meanwhile, in a small bowl, combine the papaya, cilantro, lime juice, jalapeño, and cumin. Mix well and season with salt and pepper.

5. Arrange the scallops on a serving platter and top with the salsa.

make it a meal kit Wrap the scallops with the bacon and make the papaya salsa. Store each separately in sealable containers or plastic bags; the scallops will keep for up to 2 days in the refrigerator, the salsa up to 5 days. When ready to finish the meal, cook the scallops as directed and serve with the salsa.

morph it Make a double batch of the scallops and use the extra in Vongole Pizza with Andouille, Clams & Scallops (page 204). Since there's bacon wrapped around the scallops, you can eliminate the andouille from the recipe, saving you another step!

Make a double batch of the Jalapeño–Papaya Salsa; it's a great topping for pan-seared chicken or pork chops or baked fish, such as flounder, tilapia, and halibut.

You can use turkey bacon if you

want to dodge some calories and fat.

Oyster Cracker & Dijon Herb-Crusted Scallops

When we were dating, my husband and I used to meet at a restaurant in Philadelphia that served oyster crackers and horseradish at the bar. I could eat the entire container of horseradish in just one sitting! I love oyster crackers, and tried to find a way to work them into a coating for fish. Well, here they are, in a crunchy crust for tender scallops. I like to serve this dish with Saucy Roasted Eggplant with Toasted Polenta (page 248) and Pear–Cucumber Salad with Balsamic & Shaved Romano Cheese (page 274).

Total Time: 16–21 minutes

Prep time: 10–15 minutes

Active cooking time: 6 minutes

Serves 4

4 cups oyster crackers (enough to yield 1 cup crushed)

1 teaspoon dried oregano

1 teaspoon dried basil

1 teaspoon garlic powder

½ teaspoon onion powder

¼ teaspoon sweet paprika

1¼ pounds bay scallops

2 tablespoons Dijon mustard

1 to 2 tablespoons olive oil

1. Place the oyster crackers in a plastic bag or food processor and mash with a rolling pin or the flat side of a meat mallet or process until you have fine crumbs. Add the oregano, basil, garlic powder, onion powder, and paprika and combine. Transfer to a plastic bag if it isn't already in one.

2. In a separate plastic bag, combine the scallops and mustard. Seal the bag and shake to coat the scallops evenly with the mustard. Add the scallops to the cracker mixture, seal the bag, and shake to coat the scallops.

3. Heat the oil in a large skillet over medium heat. Add the scallops, in batches if necessary to prevent overcrowding the pan—the scallops should cook in a single layer—and cook until golden brown and just cooked through, about 3 minutes per side.

make it a meal kit Prepare the cracker coating and store in a sealable container or plastic bag at room temperature for up to 1 week. When ready to finish the meal, coat the scallops with the mustard, add to the cracker mixture, and proceed as directed.

have it your way This dish also works well with fish fillets. Coat fillets with the mustard and cracker coating as directed for the scallops, then cook the fillets in the hot oil for about 3 minutes per side, until fork-tender.

This dish also works

well with fish fillets.

Parmesan-Seared Scallops with Tangy Tomato Dipping Sauce

Sweet scallops sparkle under a golden brown, salty crusting of Parmesan cheese. I love to serve this with orzo pasta that's been tossed with olive oil and fresh basil and Onion Knots (page 264).

Total Time: 16–21 minutes

Prep time: 10–15 minutes

Active cooking time: 6 minutes

Serves 4

1 tablespoon Dijon mustard

1¼ pounds sea scallops

½ cup freshly grated Parmesan cheese

TANGY TOMATO DIPPING SAUCE

One 8-ounce can tomato sauce

1 tablespoon fresh lemon juice

½ teaspoon chili powder

½ teaspoon hot sauce

¼ teaspoon freshly ground black pepper

2 teaspoons olive oil

1. Place the mustard in a shallow dish, add the scallops, and turn to coat evenly. Place the Parmesan in a separate shallow dish, add the scallops, and turn to coat. Set aside.

2. In a small saucepan, combine the sauce ingredients. Set the pan over medium heat, bring to a simmer, and let simmer for 5 minutes to allow the flavors to blend.

3. Meanwhile, heat the oil in a large skillet over medium heat. Add the scallops and cook until opaque and just cooked through, about 3 minutes per side.

4. Serve the scallops with the sauce on the side for dipping.

make it a meal kit Coat the scallops with the mustard and Parmesan and prepare the dipping sauce. Store each separately in sealable containers or plastic bags; the scallops will keep for up to 2 days in the refrigerator, the sauce up to 5 days. When ready to finish the meal, cook the scallops as directed and reheat the sauce in a small saucepan over medium heat or in the microwave for a few minutes on HIGH. Serve as directed.

Shrimp in Salsa Verde

Salsa verde is a green salsa made from serrano chiles, green tomatoes, cilantro, and lime juice and wonderful with seafood. If you can't find green tomatoes, you may use husked tomatillos or regular, ripe red tomatoes. I like to serve this dish with instant rice and Vegetable Sauté with Black Bean Sauce (page 258).

Total Time: 13 minutes
Prep time: 10 minutes
Active cooking time: 3 minutes

Serves 4

SALSA VERDE

2 large green tomatoes

1 fresh serrano or jalapeño chile pepper, seeded and minced

2 tablespoons chopped fresh cilantro

2 tablespoons fresh lime juice

Salt and freshly ground black pepper to taste

2 teaspoons olive oil

1½ pounds large shrimp, peeled and deveined

¼ cup chopped scallions (white and green parts)

1. In a large bowl, combine the salsa ingredients. Set aside.

2. Heat the oil in a large skillet over medium heat. Add the shrimp and cook until opaque and just cooked through, about 3 minutes.

3. Spoon the salsa verde onto a serving platter and top with the shrimp. Sprinkle the scallions over the top and serve.

make it a meal kit Make the **Salsa Verde** and store in a sealable container or plastic bag for up to 3 days in the refrigerator.

morph it Make a double batch of the Salsa Verde and serve it with corn chips, toasted pita wedges, and/or a fresh cheese platter. It's also terrific spooned over chicken or fish.

Or, double the entire recipe and morph the extra into Shrimp Tacos by serving the shrimp in flour tortillas and spooning the salsa over the top; serve with sour cream and guacamole on the side.

Curried Shrimp with Cilantro, Lime & Garlic

In just 16 minutes, you can enjoy a creamy shrimp dish that boasts the flavors of garlic, curry, lime, and cilantro. The combination is light and fresh. Try it with Toasted Coconut Rice (page 261)—the sweet rice is a nice balance for the tart lime.

Total Time: 16 minutes

Prep time: 10 minutes

Active cooking time: 6 minutes

Serves 4

2 teaspoons olive oil

3 shallots, minced

2 cloves garlic, minced

1 teaspoon curry powder

1 cup reduced-sodium vegetable or chicken broth

1½ pounds medium or large shrimp, peeled and deveined

1 tablespoon fresh lime juice

½ cup sour cream

¼ cup chopped fresh cilantro

Salt and freshly ground black pepper to taste

1. Heat the oil in a large skillet over medium heat. Add the shallots and garlic and cook, stirring, for 2 minutes. Stir in the curry powder and cook for 1 minute, until it is fragrant. Add the broth and bring to a simmer. Add the shrimp and lime juice and simmer until the shrimp are opaque and just cooked through, about 3 minutes, stirring or turning them over as necessary.

2. Remove the pan from the heat and stir in the sour cream and cilantro. Season with salt and pepper and serve.

have it your way Got extra cooked chicken? Perfect—use shredded or cubed chicken instead of the shrimp and add the chicken when you add the lime juice. Since the chicken is already cooked, you just need to heat it through with the other ingredients before stirring in the sour cream and cilantro.

Orange–Garlic Shrimp

I like to serve these shrimp with cellophane noodles tossed with a little sesame oil and soy sauce. Try substituting fresh cilantro for the basil.

Total Time: 16 minutes
Prep time: 10 minutes
Active cooking time: 6 minutes

Serves 4

¼ cup orange juice

4 cloves garlic, minced

½ teaspoon salt

¼ teaspoon freshly ground black pepper

2 teaspoons olive oil

1¼ pounds large or jumbo shrimp, peeled and deveined

2 tablespoons chopped fresh basil

1. In a shallow dish, whisk together the orange juice, garlic, salt, and pepper. Set aside.

2. Heat the oil in a large skillet over medium-high heat. Add the shrimp and cook for 2 minutes per side. Add the orange juice mixture and simmer until the shrimp are opaque and just cooked through, 1 to 2 minutes. Remove from the heat, stir in the basil, and serve.

make it a meal kit Make the sauce and peel and devein the shrimp. Store each separately in sealable containers or plastic bags; the sauce will keep for up to 3 days in the refrigerator, and the shrimp should be prepped no longer than a day ahead.

bank a batch Make a double batch of the entire meal and store the extra in a sealable container or plastic bag for up to 3 days in the refrigerator or up to 3 months in the freezer. Thaw overnight in the refrigerator or in the microwave for a few minutes on LOW. Reheat in a large skillet over medium-high heat or in the microwave for a few minutes on HIGH.

have it your way For a thicker sauce, add ¼ cup orange marmalade to the sauce and proceed as directed.

Also, try this sauce over grilled or pan-seared chicken or pork.

Coconut Shrimp with Curried Tomato, Lime & Roasted Garlic Coulis

Don't be afraid, *coulis* is just a fancy word for a thick sauce made with puréed vegetables or fruits. Mine boasts tomatoes, lime, curry powder, and sweet roasted garlic. For this meal, I like to serve Garlic–Herb Couscous (page 262) on the side.

Total Time: 19–24 minutes
Prep time: 15–20 minutes
Active cooking time:
4 minutes

Serves 4

CURRIED TOMATO, LIME & ROASTED GARLIC COULIS

½ cup garlic cloves, peeled

2 medium ripe beefsteak tomatoes, chopped

1 tablespoon fresh lime juice

1 teaspoon curry powder

Salt and freshly ground black pepper to taste

1 large egg

¾ cup all-purpose flour, divided

⅔ cup beer (any variety)

1½ teaspoons baking powder

2 cups unsweetened flaked coconut

24 large shrimp, peeled and deveined, tails left on

¼ cup olive oil

1. Preheat the oven to 400°F.

2. Wrap the garlic cloves in aluminum foil and roast until tender, 15 minutes.

3. In a food processor, combine the roasted garlic, tomatoes, lime juice, and curry powder and process until almost smooth. Season with salt and pepper. Set aside.

4. In a medium bowl, whisk together the egg, $\frac{1}{2}$ cup of the flour, the beer, and the baking powder. Place the remaining $\frac{1}{4}$ cup flour in a shallow dish. Place the coconut in a separate shallow dish. Dredge the shrimp in the flour, shaking off any excess. Then dunk the shrimp in the beer mixture and turn to coat. Finally, roll them in the coconut until all sides are coated.

5. Heat the oil in a large skillet over medium-high heat. Add the shrimp and cook until opaque and just cooked through, about 2 minutes per side.

6. Serve the shrimp with the coulis on the side for dunking.

make it a meal kit Make the coulis. Flour, dunk, and roll the shrimp in the coconut. Store each separately in sealable containers or plastic bags in the refrigerator; the shrimp will keep for up to 2 days, the coulis up to 3 days. When ready to finish the meal, cook the shrimp as directed and serve with the coulis on the side.

morph it Make a double batch of the coulis and use the extra as a topping for roasted turkey tenderloin, grilled flank steak, or broiled or baked fish. It will keep for up to 3 days in the refrigerator or up to 3 months in the freezer. Thaw overnight in the refrigerator before using.

Make a double batch of the roasted garlic and use the extra in Herb-Crusted Flounder Fillets in Roasted Garlic Sauce (page 222), Rotelle with Braised Zucchini, Roasted Garlic, Oregano & Feta (page 52), or Roasted Garlic–Artichoke Dip (page 28). It will last for up to 5 days in the refrigerator. You can also freeze the roasted garlic for up to 3 months; thaw overnight in the refrigerator before using.

Greek Shrimp & Rice

I like to serve this with Bruschetta with Chipotle–Cilantro Butter (page 265) or Fennel–Walnut Salad with Sweet Gorgonzola (page 277).

Total Time: 15–20 minutes
Prep time: 10 minutes
Active cooking time:
5–10 minutes

Serves 4

One 7-ounce package rice pilaf mix

2 teaspoons olive oil

1¼ pounds medium shrimp, peeled and deveined

One 14-ounce can diced tomatoes with green pepper and onion

½ cup sliced kalamata olives, drained

1 tablespoon onion flakes

1 teaspoon dried oregano

2 tablespoons chopped fresh mint

Salt and freshly ground black pepper to taste

1. In a medium saucepan, cook the rice pilaf according to the package directions.

2. Meanwhile, heat the oil in a large skillet over medium-high heat. Add the shrimp and cook for 2 minutes. Add the tomatoes, olives, onion flakes, and oregano, bring to a simmer, and let simmer until the shrimp are opaque and just cooked through, about 2 minutes. Fold in the rice and mint and cook for 1 minute to heat through. Season with salt and pepper. Serve the shrimp mixture over the rice pilaf.

make it a meal kit Cook the rice pilaf and let cool. Combine the tomatoes, olives, onion flakes, and oregano. Peel and devein the shrimp. Store each separately in sealable containers or plastic bags. The rice will keep for up to 4 days in the refrigerator and the tomato mixture for up to 3 days; the shrimp should be prepped no more than a day ahead. Reheat the rice in the microwave and cook the shrimp in the sauce as directed. Serve the shrimp mixture over the rice pilaf.

bank a batch Make a double batch of the entire meal and store the extra for up to 3 days in the refrigerator or up to 3 months in the freezer. Thaw overnight in the refrigerator or in the microwave for 3 to 4 minutes on LOW. Reheat in the microwave for 2 to 3 minutes on HIGH.

Grilled Shrimp with Ginger–Hoisin Glaze

Enjoy the flavor of hoisin sauce kicked up with the addition of sweet rice vinegar and pungent ginger. I would serve this with either Toasted Coconut Rice (page 261) or Garlic–Herb Couscous (page 262).

Also, this makes an excellent party food! Serve it as an impressive hors d'oeuvres, leaving the tails on the shrimp for a striking presentation.

Total Time: 14 minutes
Prep time: 10 minutes
Active cooking time: 4 minutes

Serves 4

GINGER–HOISIN GLAZE

2 tablespoons hoisin sauce

1 tablespoon rice vinegar

2 teaspoons peeled and finely grated fresh ginger

1 teaspoon reduced-sodium soy sauce

2 teaspoons peanut or olive oil

1¼ pounds large or jumbo shrimp, peeled and deveined

¼ cup chopped scallions (white and green parts)

1. In a small bowl, whisk together the glaze ingredients and set aside.

2. Heat the oil in a large skillet over medium-high heat. Add the shrimp to the hot pan and cook for 2 minutes. Turn the shrimp over, add the glaze, and simmer until the shrimp are opaque and just cooked through, about 2 minutes. Remove from the heat, top with the scallions, and serve.

make it a meal kit Make the glaze, peel and devein the shrimp, and chop the scallions. Store each separately in sealable containers or plastic bags; the glaze will keep for up to 3 days in the refrigerator, the scallions up to 2 days, and the shrimp should be prepped no longer than a day ahead.

bank a batch Make a double batch of the entire meal and store the extra in a sealable container or plastic bag for up to 3 days in the refrigerator or up to 3 months in the freezer. Thaw overnight in the refrigerator or in the microwave for a few minutes on LOW. Reheat in a large skillet over medium-high heat or in the microwave for a few minutes on HIGH.

have it your way Make this dish with chunks of chicken, pork, or tofu.

Fish Soft Tacos with Pico de Gallo–Black Bean Aïoli & Mixed Vegetables

In my fish tacos, I blend golden brown fish with pico de gallo sauce (a salsa-like sauce sold with the salsas and picante sauces), a black bean-spiked mayonnaise, and fresh, colorful vegetables. I love to serve them with Black & Pink Beans with Rice (page 257) or Mesclun Greens with Avocado & Corn in Citrus Vinaigrette (page 280).

Total Time: 13–15 minutes

Prep time: 10 minutes

Active cooking time: 3–5 minutes

Serves 4

2 teaspoons olive oil

1 pound fish fillets, such as flounder, cod, halibut, or trout, cut into 2-inch pieces

Salt and freshly ground black pepper to taste

PICO DE GALLO–BLACK BEAN AÏOLI

½ cup prepared pico de gallo sauce

½ cup canned black beans, rinsed and drained

½ teaspoon ground cumin

½ cup mayonnaise

Eight 6-inch flour tortillas, warmed if desired wrapped in paper towels in the microwave for 15 to 30 seconds

1 cup red onion thinly sliced into half-moons

½ cup grated carrot

1 medium green bell pepper, seeded and cut into thin strips

1 medium red bell pepper, seeded and cut into thin strips

1. Heat the oil in large skillet over medium-high heat. Add the fish pieces and cook until golden brown and fork-tender, 3 to 5 minutes, stirring frequently. Season with salt and pepper and remove from the heat.

2. Meanwhile, in a small saucepan, combine the pico de gallo, black beans, and cumin. Set the pan over medium heat and bring to a simmer. Remove from the heat and stir in the mayonnaise.

3. Arrange the fish on the tortillas, top with the vegetables and pico de gallo–black bean aïoli, and serve.

make it a meal kit Cook the fish as directed, make the aïoli, and slice and grate the vegetables; store them separately in sealable containers or plastic bags for up to 3 days in the refrigerator. When ready to finish the meal, reheat the fish in the microwave for 2 minutes on HIGH. Reheat the aïoli in the microwave for 1 to 2 minutes on HIGH. Assemble the tacos as directed and serve.

morph it Instead of cooking raw fish from scratch, use extra fish from Pan-Seared Flounder with Shallot–Lemon Butter (page 224) or Chipotle–Lime Glazed Halibut (page 225).

Baked Fish 'n' Chips with Honey Vinegar

Since I don't often deep-fry foods (too messy), I bake my fish and potatoes in a hot oven. The result is crunchy-crusted fish and golden brown "chips." I like to serve this with Romaine Salad with Roasted Cherry Tomatoes & Blue Cheese (page 273).

Total Time: 30–35 minutes

Prep time: 15–20 minutes

Walk-away time: 25 minutes

Serves 4

Cooking spray

2 large russet potatoes, peeled and cut into ½-inch-thick slices

Salt and freshly ground black pepper to taste

1 cup all-purpose flour

1 teaspoon baking powder

1 cup milk

1 large egg, lightly beaten

1¼ pounds cod or halibut fillets, cut into thin strips

¼ cup cider vinegar

2 tablespoons honey

1. Preheat the oven to 425°F. Coat a large baking sheet with cooking spray.

2. Arrange the potato slices on the sheet and spray their tops with cooking spray. Season with salt and pepper. Bake for 10 minutes and pull out of the oven. Leave the oven on.

3. Meanwhile, in a shallow dish, whisk together the flour, baking powder, and ½ teaspoon salt. Whisk in the milk and egg. Add the cod fillets and turn to coat with the batter. Arrange the cod in a single layer on the baking sheet with the partially cooked potatoes and bake until the fish and potatoes are golden brown and the fish is fork-tender, about 15 minutes.

4. Meanwhile, in a small bowl, whisk together the vinegar and honey. Serve the fish and chips with the honey vinegar on the side for dunking.

make it a meal kit Fully bake the potato slices (25 minutes) and let cool. Make the honey vinegar. Dunk the fish strips in the batter. Store each of the components separately in sealable containers or plastic bags. The potatoes and fish will keep for up to 2 days in the refrigerator, the honey vinegar up to 3 days. When ready to finish the meal, bake the fish as directed, adding the cooked potatoes to the baking sheet for the last few minutes so that they can reheat. Serve as directed.

morph it Cook a double batch of fish and use the extra in Fish Soft Tacos with Pico de Gallo–Black Bean Aïoli & Mixed Vegetables (page 218).

Herb-Crusted Flounder Fillets in Roasted Garlic Sauce

Coating a mild-tasting fish like flounder with a variety of herbs and spices is a quick and easy way to turn a simple meal into a stellar one. The sweet, caramelized garlic sauce is the icing on the cake. I like to serve this with Parmesan-Crusted Rolls (page 263), Garlic–Herb Couscous (page 262), or a prepackaged rice pilaf mix.

Total Time: 30–35 minutes

Prep time: 15–20 minutes

Active cooking time:
5 minutes

Walk-away time: 10 minutes

Serves 4

Cooking spray

$1/2$ cup garlic cloves, peeled

4 flounder or halibut fillets (about 5 ounces each)

Salt and freshly ground black pepper to taste

1 tablespoon spicy brown mustard

$1/4$ cup all-purpose flour

1 tablespoon chopped fresh parsley

1 teaspoon garlic powder

$1/2$ teaspoon onion powder

$1/2$ teaspoon dried oregano

$1/2$ teaspoon dried thyme

1 cup reduced-sodium chicken broth, divided

2 teaspoons cornstarch

1. Preheat the oven to 400ºF. Coat a large baking sheet with cooking spray.

2. Wrap the garlic cloves in aluminum foil and roast until golden brown and tender, about 15 minutes. Remove from the oven and keep the oven at 400ºF.

3. Meanwhile, season both sides of the fish fillets with salt and pepper. Brush both sides with the mustard. Set aside.

4. In a shallow dish, combine the flour, parsley, garlic powder, onion powder, oregano, thyme, and ¼ teaspoon each salt and pepper. Mix well. Add the mustard-coated fish to the flour mixture and turn to coat evenly. Place the fillets on the prepared baking sheet and spray their surfaces with cooking spray. Bake until fork-tender, 10 to 12 minutes.

5. Meanwhile, transfer the roasted garlic to a small saucepan and add ¾ cup of the broth. Set the pan over medium-high heat and bring to a simmer, stirring with a whisk to break up the garlic. Dissolve the cornstarch in the remaining ¼ cup broth and add to the simmering liquid. Cook for 1 to 2 minutes, whisking, until the mixture thickens to the consistency of gravy.

6. Serve the fish with the roasted garlic sauce spooned over the top.

make it a meal kit Coat the fish with the mustard and herb crust and wrap each fillet individually in plastic wrap to protect the crust. Prepare the sauce and store in a sealable plastic container. Both will keep in the refrigerator for up to 2 days. When ready to finish the meal, bake the fish as directed and reheat the sauce in the microwave for 2 to 3 minutes on LOW. Serve as directed.

morph it Make a double batch of the roasted garlic and use the extra in Rotelle with Braised Zucchini, Roasted Garlic, Oregano & Feta (page 52), Roasted Garlic–Artichoke Dip (page 28), or Coconut Shrimp with Curried Tomato, Lime & Roasted Garlic Coulis (page 214).

Pan-Seared Flounder with Shallot–Lemon Butter

Spiked butters turn this mild-flavored fish from bland to brilliant in just seconds with the addition of sweet shallots, fresh parsley, and lively lemon juice. I love to *serve* this with Braised Spinach with Pink Beans & Ham (page 254).

Total Time: 16 minutes
Prep time: 10 minutes
Active cooking time: 6 minutes

Serves 4

SHALLOT–LEMON BUTTER
2 tablespoons unsalted butter, softened
2 tablespoons minced shallot
2 tablespoons chopped fresh parsley
1 tablespoon fresh lemon juice

2 teaspoons olive oil
4 flounder fillets (about 5 ounces each)
Salt and freshly ground black pepper to taste

1. In a small bowl, combine the butter, shallot, parsley, and lemon juice.

2. Heat the oil in a large skillet over medium-high heat. Season both sides of the flounder fillets with salt and pepper. Add the flounder to the hot pan and cook until browned, about 2 minutes per side. Add the butter mixture and cook until it makes a sauce and the fish is fork-tender, about 2 minutes.

make it a meal kit Make the Shallot–Lemon Butter and store in a sealable container in the refrigerator for up to 5 days or the freezer for up to 3 months.

morph it Make a double batch of the entire meal and morph the extra into Fish Soft Tacos with Pico de Gallo–Black Bean Aïoli & Mixed Vegetables (page 218). The fish will last for up to 3 days in the refrigerator.

have it your way Make the dish with tilapia, halibut, salmon, trout, or even boneless, skinless chicken breasts (pound the chicken to a 1-inch thickness so it will cook faster).

Chipotle–Lime Glazed Halibut

Chipotle chiles are smoked jalapeño peppers and are sold canned in adobo, a vinegar-spiked tomato sauce. Adding fresh lime and cilantro to this sauce sends flavors soaring to a new level of freshness! I like to serve this with instant rice or Black & Pink Beans with Rice (page 257).

Total Time: 16 minutes

Prep time: 10 minutes

Active cooking time: 6 minutes

Serves 4

½ cup fresh lime juice (about 2 limes)

1 tablespoon light or dark brown sugar

2 teaspoons minced canned chipotle chiles in adobo sauce

½ teaspoon finely grated lime zest

4 halibut steaks (about 5 ounces each)

Salt and freshly ground black pepper to taste

2 teaspoons olive oil

1 lime, cut into wedges

¼ cup chopped fresh cilantro

1. In a shallow dish, whisk together the lime juice, brown sugar, chipotles, and lime zest.

2. Season the halibut on both sides with salt and pepper. Add the halibut to the lime juice mixture and turn to coat both sides.

3. Heat the oil in a large skillet over medium-high heat until hot, 1 to 2 minutes. Remove the halibut from the glaze (reserve the glaze) and add the steaks to the hot pan. Cook until golden brown, about 2 minutes per side. Add the glaze to the skillet, bring to a simmer, and let simmer until the sauce reduces and the fish is just cooked through and fork-tender, about 2 minutes.

4. Serve the halibut with the lime wedges on the side. Sprinkle the cilantro over the top just before serving.

morph it Make a double batch of the entire meal and morph the extra into Fish Soft Tacos with Pico de Gallo–Black Bean Aïoli & Mixed Vegetables (page 218).

have it your way Make the dish with flounder, tilapia, trout, or salmon instead.

Halibut Nachos with Chipotle Aïoli

I love turning nachos into a main course, and you can easily do that when you flavor the fish with smoky mesquite seasoning and serve it over the chips with a variety of toppings and a cilantro-and-chipotle-spiked mayo. If you like, serve the mixture over whole-wheat tortillas or baked corn chips instead of the tortilla chips. I like to partner this with Black Bean & Corn Salad (page 271) or Black & Pink Beans with Rice (page 257).

Total Time: 16–25 minutes

Prep time: 10–15 minutes

Active cooking time:
6–10 minutes

Serves 4

Cooking spray

1¼ pounds halibut fillets or steaks

1 tablespoon mesquite seasoning

2 tablespoons fresh lime juice

CHIPOTLE AÏOLI

¼ cup mayonnaise

¼ cup sour cream

1 tablespoon chopped fresh cilantro

2 teaspoons minced canned chipotle chiles in adobo sauce

Tortilla chips

TOPPINGS (OPTIONAL)

Shredded lettuce

Diced tomatoes

Prepared salsa

Shredded Cheddar cheese

Sliced black olives

Sliced pickled jalapeño chile peppers

1. Coat a stovetop grill pan or griddle with cooking spray and preheat over medium-high heat until hot, 3 to 5 minutes.

2. Sprinkle both sides of the halibut with the mesquite seasoning. Drizzle both sides with the lime juice. Place the fish in the hot pan and cook until just cooked through and fork-tender, 3 to 5 minutes per side. Using two forks, pull the halibut apart into small, bite-size pieces.

3. Meanwhile, in a medium bowl, whisk together the aïoli ingredients and set aside.

4. Arrange the chips on a serving platter or individual plates and top with the grilled fish. Arrange the desired toppings over the fish and drizzle the aïoli over everything.

make it a meal kit Cook the halibut, then break it into pieces as directed. Prepare the aïoli and prep the toppings as needed. Store the components separately in sealable containers or plastic bags. The fish and toppings will keep for up to 2 days in the refrigerator, the aïoli up to 3 days. When ready to finish the meal, reheat the fish in the microwave for 2 to 3 minutes on HIGH and serve over the chips with the toppings and aïoli.

have it your way If you want the traditional melted cheese on top of your nachos, place the nachos in a baking dish and top with the desired toppings, ending with the shredded cheese, and place under the broiler for 2 to 3 minutes, until the cheese melts.

Pan-Seared Tilapia with Mango–Ginger Sauce

Tilapia is such a mild-flavored fish, which is why I blast it with super-flavorful sauces. This one is a unique blend of succulent mango, salty soy sauce, pungent ginger and garlic, and fresh chives. I like to serve Garlic–Herb Couscous (page 262) or Toasted Coconut Rice (page 261) on the side. Or you can simply toss cooked somen or soba noodles with sesame or walnut oil.

Total Time: 15–23 minutes

Prep time: 10–15 minutes

Active cooking time: 5–8 minutes

Serves 4

MANGO–GINGER SAUCE

1 large ripe mango, peeled, seeded, and chopped

1 tablespoon reduced-sodium soy sauce

1 tablespoon water, or more as needed

1 tablespoon peeled and minced fresh ginger

1 clove garlic

4 tilapia or halibut fillets (about 5 ounces each)

Salt and freshly ground black pepper to taste

2 teaspoons olive oil

2 tablespoons chopped fresh chives

1. In a blender or food processor, combine the sauce ingredients and process until smooth, adding more water as necessary to create a thick sauce.

2. Season both sides of the tilapia with salt and pepper. Heat the oil in a large skillet over medium-high heat. Add the tilapia to the hot pan and cook until golden brown, 2 to 3 minutes per side. Add the sauce to the tilapia, bring to a simmer, and let simmer until the fish is fork-tender, 1 to 2 minutes.

3. Transfer the tilapia and sauce to a warm serving platter, top with the chives, and serve.

make it a meal kit Prepare the sauce and store in a sealable container for up to 5 days in the refrigerator or up to 3 months in the freezer. Thaw overnight in the refrigerator or in the microwave for a few minutes on LOW. Reheat in a small saucepan or in the microwave for 1 to 2 minutes on HIGH.

morph it Make a double batch of the sauce and use the extra as a simmer sauce for shrimp, scallops, pork medallions, or chunks of chicken, or as a warm dipping sauce for grilled chicken, pork, fish, or vegetable kebabs.

. . . make extra sauce to simmer

with shrimp, scallops, pork medallions,

or chunks of chicken . . .

Herbed Fish Cakes with Cucumber–Mint Relish

Thanks to the food processor, you can make these fish cakes in just minutes, in one bowl! Even if you don't have a food processor, you can whip them up with ease. I like to serve Traditional Potato Salad (page 266) on the side to round out the meal.

Total Time: 29 minutes
Prep time: 15 minutes
Active cooking time:
4 minutes
Walk-away time: 10 minutes

Serves 4

Cooking spray

4 trout fillets (about 5 ounces each), skin removed if necessary and coarsely chopped

2 tablespoons chopped fresh basil

2 tablespoons minced red onion

2 tablespoons mayonnaise

Pinch of salt

Pinch of freshly ground black pepper

2 teaspoons olive oil

CUCUMBER–MINT RELISH

1 cup peeled, seeded, and finely diced cucumber

2 tablespoons chopped fresh mint

2 teaspoons olive oil

2 teaspoons red wine vinegar

1 teaspoon Dijon mustard

Salt and freshly ground black pepper to taste

1. Preheat the oven to 400°F. Coat a large baking sheet with cooking spray.

2. In a food processor, combine the trout, basil, onion, and mayonnaise. Add the salt and pepper. Pulse on and off until the mixture comes together, then shape into 4 cakes, each about 1 inch thick.

3. Heat the oil in a large skillet over medium-high heat. Add the cakes and cook until golden brown, about 2 minutes per side. Transfer the fish cakes to the prepared baking sheet and bake until cooked through, about 10 minutes.

4. Meanwhile, combine the relish ingredients in a small bowl.

5. Serve the fish cakes with the relish spooned over the top.

make it a meal kit Make and shape the fish cakes and, before cooking, wrap them in plastic wrap. Make the relish and store in a sealable container. Both will keep for up to 3 days in the refrigerator. When ready to finish the meal, cook the fish cakes as directed and serve with the relish.

morph it Make a double batch of the relish; it's amazing over grilled chicken, seared pork chops, and turkey burgers, or served alongside cheese and crackers or as the dipping sauce for chilled shrimp cocktail.

have it your way I call for trout, but you can use flounder, halibut, tuna, or salmon instead.

Braised Trout with Bacon & Mushrooms

Trout is my husband's favorite fish. The sauce for this is so good that I like to serve mashed potatoes on the side to soak up any extra drips. Round out the meal with Roasted Brussels Sprouts with Sun-Dried Tomatoes (page 245).

Total Time: 28 minutes
Prep time: 10 minutes
Active cooking time: 18 minutes

Serves 4

½ cup diced bacon or pancetta

1 cup sliced mushrooms (button, cremini, or shiitake, or any combination you prefer)

⅓ cup thinly sliced shallots

1 teaspoon dried thyme

2 teaspoons olive oil

4 trout or striped bass fillets (about 5 ounces each)

Salt and freshly ground black pepper to taste

1 cup dry vermouth or dry white wine

2 tablespoons chopped fresh parsley

1. Cook the bacon in a large skillet over medium heat. When browned and crisp, add the mushrooms and shallots and cook, stirring a few times, until the mushrooms release their juice, about 5 minutes. Add the thyme and cook for 1 minute. Remove the mixture from the pan and set aside.

2. Heat the oil in the same skillet over medium-high heat. Season both sides of the trout fillets with salt and pepper. Add the fillets to the hot pan and cook until golden brown, about 2 minutes per side. Return the mushroom mixture to the skillet, add the vermouth, and simmer until the liquid reduces and the trout is just cooked through and fork-tender, about 3 minutes. Sprinkle with the parsley.

make it a meal kit Cook the mushroom-shallot mixture and store for up to 3 days in the refrigerator. When you're ready, cook the fish as directed and add the mushroom mixture.

morph it Make a double batch of the mushroom-shallot mixture; it's excellent over pan-seared pork chops, grilled chicken breasts, or roasted turkey. It will keep for up to 3 months in the freezer. Thaw overnight in the refrigerator or in the microwave for a few minutes on LOW. Reheat in a large skillet over medium heat or in the microwave for 1 to 2 minutes on HIGH.

Grilled Tuna Steaks with Chipotle–Citrus Sauce

As if grilled tuna steaks weren't yummy enough, the mildly hot, slightly sweet, tangy sauce sends flavors soaring. I like to serve this dish with soba noodles tossed with sesame oil and fresh cilantro.

Total Time: 20–25 minutes
Prep time: 10–15 minutes
Active cooking time: 10 minutes

Serves 4

Cooking spray

4 tuna steaks (about 5 ounces each)

Salt and freshly ground black pepper to taste

CHIPOTLE–CITRUS SAUCE

½ cup orange juice

¼ cup fresh lime juice

¼ cup reduced-sodium soy sauce

1 tablespoon minced shallot

2 teaspoons peeled and finely grated fresh ginger

2 teaspoons minced canned chipotle chiles in adobo sauce

1 clove garlic, chopped

1. Coat the grates of an outdoor grill or a stovetop grill pan with cooking spray and preheat to medium high.

2. Season both sides of the tuna with salt and pepper. Grill the tuna steaks for 5 minutes per side for medium-rare doneness.

3. Meanwhile, in a blender or food processor, combine the sauce ingredients and process until smooth.

4. Serve the tuna steaks with the ponzu sauce drizzled over the top.

make it a meal kit Make the sauce and store in a sealable container for up to 1 week in the refrigerator.

morph it Make a double batch of the tuna and morph into Warm Edamame–Rice Salad with Teriyaki Tuna (page 234) or Bowties with Pancetta & Tuna (page 75).

Make a double batch of the sauce and use it as a marinade and/or sauce for chicken, pork, or shrimp. Use half as a marinade and the other half as a sauce to drizzle over the top.

Warm Edamame–Rice Salad with Teriyaki Tuna

Edamame (fresh soybeans) are widely available and make a great addition to any meal. In this dish, I partner them with sweet carrots and scallions, tangy teriyaki sauce, ready-to-eat tuna, and fresh cilantro. Nestled into radicchio cups, the meal is as impressive as it is delicious.

Total Time: 15–20 minutes

Prep time: 10–15 minutes

Active cooking time: 5 minutes

Serves 4

2 teaspoons toasted sesame oil

One 10-ounce package fresh or thawed frozen shelled edamame

1/2 cup diced carrots

1/4 cup chopped scallions (white and green parts)

1 cup rice, regular or instant, cooked according to package directions

Two 7-ounce tuna fillet foil packs (sold next to the canned tuna) or two 6-ounce cans water-packed chunk light tuna, drained

2 tablespoons reduced-sodium teriyaki sauce

1 teaspoon hot Dijon-style or regular Dijon mustard

2 tablespoons chopped fresh cilantro

Salt and freshly ground black pepper to taste

4 large radicchio leaves or 4 large red-tipped lettuce leaves

1. Heat the oil in a large skillet over medium-high heat. Add the edamame, carrots, and scallions and cook, stirring, for 2 minutes. Add the cooked rice, tuna, teriyaki sauce, mustard, and cilantro, stir to combine, and cook for 1 to 2 minutes to heat through. Season with salt and pepper.

2. Arrange the radicchio leaves on individual plates or a serving platter. Spoon the edamame-rice salad inside the leaves and serve.

make it a meal kit Combine the edamame, carrots, and scallions; combine the tuna, teriyaki, mustard, and cilantro; make the rice and let cool. Store each component separately in sealable containers or plastic bags for up to 2 days in the refrigerator. When ready to finish the meal, follow the recipe as directed, using the already prepped ingredients.

morph it Instead of packaged tuna, make the dish with extra halibut from Chipotle–Lime Glazed Halibut (page 225).

Salmon & Chickpea Salad over Mirin Rice

This recipe calls for canned salmon, but it's a wonderful way to use up leftover salmon fillets or steaks from another meal (check out the other salmon recipes in this chapter and think about making twice the amount of salmon in those so that you can morph it into this salad later in the week). An excellent side dish is Garlic-Roasted Asparagus with Almonds (page 241).

Total Time: 15–20 minutes

Prep time: 15–20 minutes

Serves 4

1 cup rice, regular or instant

¼ cup mirin or rice wine

Salt and freshly ground black pepper to taste

⅓ cup mayonnaise

1 teaspoon finely grated lemon zest

½ teaspoon garlic powder

Two 6-ounce cans salmon, drained and picked over for skin and bones

One 15-ounce can chickpeas, rinsed and drained

1 stalk celery, diced

2 tablespoons chopped fresh cilantro

1. Cook the rice according to the package directions, substituting the mirin for an equal amount of the water called for. Season with salt and pepper.

2. Meanwhile, in a large bowl, whisk together the mayonnaise, lemon zest, and garlic powder. Fold in the salmon, chickpeas, and celery. Season with salt and pepper.

3. Serve the salmon mixture over the warm rice, sprinkled with the cilantro.

make it a meal kit Cook the rice and let cool. Combine the salad ingredients except for the cilantro. Store each separately in sealable containers or plastic bags for up to 3 days in the refrigerator. When ready to finish the meal, reheat the rice in the microwave for 1 to 2 minutes on HIGH, then serve the salad on top of the warm rice, sprinkled with the cilantro.

have it your way Make the dish with canned tuna or cubed or shredded chicken (such as a rotisserie chicken) instead.

5-Ingredient Lemon Pepper Salmon

This may become one of your weekly staples. It's simple and delicious, yet elegant enough for guests. I recommend making lots of this salmon so you can enjoy the leftovers in other recipes (see my Morph It note). I like to serve this with Sautéed Red Cabbage with Mandarins (page 247) and fluffy instant rice.

Total Time: 11 minutes
Prep time: 5 minutes
Active cooking time: 6 minutes

Serves 4

1 tablespoon olive oil

4 salmon fillets (about 5 ounces each)

Salt to taste

Lemon pepper seasoning to taste

¼ cup balsamic vinegar

Heat the oil in a large skillet over medium-high heat. Season both sides of the salmon with salt and lemon pepper. Add the salmon to the hot pan and cook until browned, about 2 minutes per side. Add the vinegar and cook until the fish is just cooked through and fork-tender and the liquid has evaporated, about another 2 minutes.

bank a batch Make a double batch of the entire meal and store the extra in a sealable container for up to 3 days in the refrigerator or up to 3 months in the freezer. Thaw overnight in the refrigerator or in the microwave for 3 to 4 minutes on LOW. Reheat in the microwave for 2 minutes on HIGH.

morph it Make a double batch of the salmon and morph the extra into Salmon & Chickpea Salad over Mirin Rice (page 235) or Smoked Salmon with Apple–Horseradish Cream & Black Bread (at right).

have it your way Make this with flounder, tuna, trout, or tilapia instead.

Smoked Salmon with Apple–Horseradish Cream & Black Bread

Smoked salmon is the ideal Quick Fix ingredient because it requires no cooking, just assembly. This not only makes a great dinner, it's also a nice lunch or brunch dish for guests. I like to serve it with 5-Ingredient Watercress Salad with Pears, Goat Cheese & Pine Nuts (page 283) or Fennel–Walnut Salad with Sweet Gorgonzola (page 277).

Total Time: 10–15 minutes

Prep time: 10–15 minutes

Serves 4

APPLE–HORSERADISH CREAM

¼ cup mayonnaise

¼ cup plain yogurt

¼ cup grated McIntosh apple

1 tablespoon prepared horseradish

1 teaspoon Dijon mustard

1 pound smoked salmon of your choice, sliced

Black bread, sliced into wedges

Lemon slices

Capers

1. In a medium bowl, combine the mayonnaise, yogurt, apple, horseradish, and mustard until well blended.

2. Arrange the salmon on a serving platter. Set the black bread slices alongside and garnish with lemon slices. Sprinkle capers over the salmon. Serve with the Apple-Horseradish Cream on the side.

make it a meal kit Make the horseradish cream and store in a sealable container for up to 3 days in the refrigerator.

morph it Make a double batch of the horseradish cream and serve it over roasted pork tenderloin, rotisserie chicken, or baked ham slices.

7

Side Dishes and Salads

I N THE QUICK FIX KITCHEN, my mantra is, "The side dish had better be faster than my main course!"

That's the case with most of my side dishes, and when it's not, I've given you Quick Fix strategies (such as prepping ahead) so that you can make mealtime a breeze. For example, Twice-Baked Potatoes with Cheddar & Bacon (page 253) take a long time because you have to cook the potatoes two times. But, if you cook the potatoes once earlier in the week, you can finish and enjoy them on a busy weeknight without spending any extra time.

Twice-baked potatoes aside, most of my side dishes are ready in a flash. To make sure it's worth the extra effort (versus microwaving a box of frozen spinach), I've given you ingredient combinations that turn simple side dishes into sensational showstoppers. Something as simple as a fresh herb, a spice, a quick zest of lime, or a splash of lemon can turn a boring side dish into a memorable one. You can quickly and easily transform ordinary vegetables (fresh, frozen, and canned) and starches like rice and couscous into something extraordinary any night of the week.

. . . I've given you ingredient combinations

that turn simple side dishes into

sensational showstoppers.

Garlic-Roasted Asparagus with Almonds

This is a simple and impressive way to prepare asparagus. I use garlic powder instead of fresh minced garlic so that the flavor coats every inch of the asparagus. This is great with steak, chicken, pork, and seafood.

Total Time: 25 minutes

Prep time: 10 minutes

Walk-away time: 15 minutes

Serves 4

Cooking spray

2 bunches asparagus (about 2 pounds), ends trimmed

1 teaspoon garlic powder

Salt and freshly ground black pepper to taste

¼ cup slivered almonds

1. Preheat the oven to 400°F. Coat a large baking sheet with cooking spray.

2. Arrange the asparagus on the prepared sheet in a single layer and coat with cooking spray. Season with the garlic powder and salt and pepper. Roast for 10 minutes, then sprinkle the almonds over them and continue to roast until the asparagus spears are tender and the almonds are golden brown, about 5 more minutes.

bank a batch Double the recipe and store the extra in a sealable container or plastic bag for up to 3 days in the refrigerator or up to 3 months in the freezer. Thaw overnight in the refrigerator or in the microwave for a few minutes on LOW. Reheat in the microwave for a few minutes on HIGH.

have it your way For added zing, sprinkle the top of the asparagus with grated Parmesan cheese just after seasoning with the garlic powder, salt, and pepper.

This recipe also works great with broccoli and cauliflower florets or Brussels sprouts (roast the sprouts whole).

Roasted Green Beans with Grape Tomatoes & Olives

Snap up grape and cherry tomatoes whenever you hit the produce aisle—they add color and a burst of flavor to all kinds of dishes. I love their sweetness with salty Greek olives and fresh green beans. In fact, in this dish, you need little else; the oven does the job of roasting and caramelizing, and the oregano ties everything together.

Total Time: 20–25 minutes

Prep time: 10 minutes

Walk-away time: 10–15 minutes

Serves 4

1 pound fresh green beans, ends trimmed, or thawed frozen green beans

1 cup halved grape or cherry tomatoes

1/2 cup diced pitted kalamata olives

1 tablespoon olive oil

1 teaspoon dried oregano

1/2 teaspoon salt

1/2 teaspoon freshly ground black pepper

1. Preheat the oven to 450°F.

2. In a large bowl, combine the green beans, tomatoes, olives, oil, oregano, salt, and pepper. Arrange on a large baking sheet in a single layer and roast until the beans are crisp-tender, 10 to 15 minutes.

make it a meal kit Toss all the ingredients together and store in a sealable container or plastic bag for up to 3 days in the refrigerator. Roast as directed just before serving.

morph it Double the recipe and use the extra as a savory base for a pasta sauce. Transfer the roasted vegetables to a medium saucepan, add 1 1/2 cups reduced-sodium chicken broth or canned tomato sauce or tomato puree, and bring to a simmer. Serve over your favorite pasta shape, sprinkled with grated Parmesan cheese.

have it your way Instead of green beans, make this with snap peas, snow peas, or broccoli or cauliflower florets (the smaller vegetables and florets will be ready in closer to 10 minutes). And, instead of kalamata olives, substitute pitted green or oil-cured olives.

Green Beans with Pineapple Vinaigrette

Think beyond fruit salad when you consider pineapple. I like to serve this warm with dinner or chilled for picnics and tailgate parties.

Total Time: 15 minutes
Prep time: 10 minutes
Active cooking time: 5 minutes

Serves 4

4 cups green beans, ends trimmed

2 medium shallots, minced

One 8-ounce can pineapple tidbits or pineapple chunks in juice, drained and juice reserved

1 tablespoon olive oil

1/2 teaspoon Dijon mustard

1/2 teaspoon onion powder

1/4 teaspoon salt

1/4 teaspoon freshly ground black pepper

1. Place the green beans in a colander set over simmering water, cover, and steam until crisp-tender, about 5 minutes (or steam in the microwave in a shallow dish with 1 tablespoon water, covered with plastic wrap or a paper towel, on HIGH for 2 to 3 minutes).

2. Transfer the beans to a large bowl, add the shallots and pineapple, and toss to combine.

3. In a small bowl, whisk together the reserved pineapple juice, oil, mustard, onion powder, salt, and pepper. Pour over the beans, toss to combine, and serve.

make it a meal kit Steam the green beans, make the vinaigrette, and store each separately in sealable containers or plastic bags for up to 3 days in the refrigerator. When ready to finish the dish, reheat the green beans in the microwave for 2 minutes on HIGH, then toss with the vinaigrette, shallots, and pineapple. This can also be served chilled.

morph it Double the recipe, dice the green beans, and fold the whole mixture into cooked white or brown rice for a more substantial side dish. Fold in diced rotisserie chicken, diced cooked pork, or cooked shrimp and you've got a complete meal.

have it your way This is also a nice way to prepare sugar snap peas and snow peas (same cooking time).

Balsamic Roasted Beets

If you don't enjoy beets regularly, you're truly missing out. Thanks to pre-cooked beets, this is a super-easy way to prepare them. Serve with pork, chicken, turkey, or a hearty fish like tuna or swordfish.

Total Time: 25 minutes
Prep time: 5 minutes
Walk-away time: 20 minutes

Serves 4

2 tablespoons balsamic vinegar

2 teaspoons olive oil

1 teaspoon Dijon mustard

Pinch of salt

Pinch of freshly ground black pepper

Two 16-ounce cans or jars whole beets (not pickled), drained

1. Preheat the oven to 400°F.

2. In a medium bowl, whisk together the vinegar, oil, mustard, salt, and pepper. Add the beets and toss to coat. Transfer to a large baking sheet and roast until heated through, about 20 minutes.

make it a meal kit Combine the vinegar, oil, mustard, salt, and pepper, add the beets, and store in a sealable container or plastic bag for up to 3 days in the refrigerator. Roast as directed just before serving.

bank a batch Double the recipe and store the extra for up to 3 months in the freezer. Thaw overnight in the refrigerator or in the microwave for a few minutes on LOW. Reheat in the microwave for a few minutes on HIGH.

morph it Make a double batch and morph the extra into Beet–Arugula Salad with Buttermilk–Blue Cheese Dressing (page 270).

have it your way Brussels sprouts work great prepared this way (reduce the roasting time to 10 to 15 minutes).

Roasted Brussels Sprouts with Sun-Dried Tomatoes

Oil-packed sun-dried tomatoes are like four ingredients in one when it comes to flavor. I often used the soaking oil as a base for sautéed dishes because it adds a sweet tomato flavor.

Total Time: 30–35 minutes

Prep time: 10 minutes

Walk-away time: 20–25 minutes

Serves 4

Cooking spray

3 cups fresh or thawed frozen Brussels sprouts, ends trimmed

1 cup diced oil-packed sun-dried tomatoes

1. Preheat the oven to 400°F. Coat a large baking sheet with cooking spray.

2. In a large bowl, combine the Brussels sprouts and sun-dried tomatoes. Toss to combine. Arrange the mixture on the prepared sheet in a single layer and roast until the sprouts are tender and golden, 20 to 25 minutes.

make it a meal kit Roast the Brussels sprouts and tomatoes and store in a sealable container or plastic bag for up to 2 days in the refrigerator. Reheat in the microwave for a few minutes on HIGH.

bank a batch Double the recipe and store the extra for up to 3 months in the freezer. Thaw overnight in the refrigerator or in the microwave for a few minutes on LOW. Reheat in the microwave for a few minutes on HIGH.

have it your way Instead of Brussels sprouts, try mixed broccoli and cauliflower florets, asparagus spears, or diced eggplant (reduce the cooking time for all of these to 10 to 15 minutes).

Roasted Broccoli with Red Onion & Walnuts

This dish was inspired by two great flavors from Greece—honey and walnuts.

Total Time: 30 minutes
Prep time: 10 minutes
Walk-away time: 20 minutes

Serves 4

6 cups broccoli florets

1 small red onion, cut into 2-inch wedges

1 tablespoon olive oil

1/2 teaspoon salt

1/2 teaspoon freshly ground black pepper

1/4 cup chopped walnuts

2 tablespoons balsamic vinegar

1 tablespoon honey

1 teaspoon dried thyme

1. Preheat the oven to 450°F.

2. In a large bowl, combine the broccoli, onion, oil, salt, and pepper. Toss to coat the vegetables with the oil. Arrange on a large baking sheet in a single layer and roast for 10 minutes.

3. Meanwhile, in a small bowl, combine the walnuts, vinegar, honey, and thyme. Remove the baking sheet from the oven and sprinkle the walnut mixture over the top. Return to the oven and roast until the broccoli is crisp-tender and the walnuts are golden brown, about 10 more minutes.

make it a meal kit Cut up the broccoli and onion and store in a sealable container or plastic bag for up to 5 days in the refrigerator. Or, pre-roast the vegetables for the first 10 minutes and, once cool, store as directed. When ready to finish, combine the pre-roasted broccoli and onion with the walnut mixture and finish roasting as directed.

morph it Double the recipe and create a vegetarian main course by serving the extra roasted broccoli and walnuts over rice, couscous, or orzo pasta.

have it your way Instead of broccoli, try Brussels sprouts, asparagus spears, cauliflower florets, snow peas, or string beans. Instead of walnuts, try pecans, pine nuts, or shelled sunflower or pumpkin seeds.

Sautéed Red Cabbage with Mandarins

This is a beautiful dish—ruby red cabbage with bright orange mandarins. Serve it alongside pork, lamb, beef, chicken, or turkey.

Total Time: 14 minutes

Prep time: 10 minutes

Active cooking time: 4 minutes

Serves 4

2 teaspoons olive oil

6 cups cored and shredded red cabbage

One 11-ounce can mandarin oranges, drained

2 tablespoons balsamic vinegar

1 tablespoon sugar

Salt and freshly ground black pepper to taste

Heat the oil in a large skillet over medium-high heat. Add the cabbage and cook until it wilts, about 3 minutes, stirring frequently. Add the mandarins, vinegar, and sugar and cook for 1 minute, until the liquid reduces and evaporates. Season with salt and pepper and serve.

bank a batch Double the recipe and store the extra in a sealable container for up to 3 days in the refrigerator or up to 3 months in the freezer. Thaw overnight in the refrigerator or in the microwave for a few minutes on LOW. Reheat in the microwave for a few minutes on HIGH.

have it your way I use pre-shredded red cabbage (sold in the produce aisle), but you can also use shredded green cabbage or cole slaw mix instead.

Saucy Roasted Eggplant with Toasted Polenta

Most of the work in this dish is done by the oven. Convenient packaged polenta is the last step, and, since it's already prepared, toasting is the only work required.

Total Time: 37 minutes

Prep time: 10 minutes

Active cooking time: 27 minutes

Serves 4 to 6

1 medium eggplant, peeled and diced

One 15-ounce can tomato sauce

2 tablespoons balsamic vinegar

4 to 6 anchovy fillets, minced

1 teaspoon sweet paprika

2 tablespoons chopped fresh parsley

Salt and freshly ground black pepper to taste

One 24-ounce log prepared corn polenta, plain or flavored, cut crosswise into ½-inch-thick slices

¼ cup freshly grated Parmesan cheese

1. Preheat the oven to 450°F. Coat a large baking sheet with cooking spray.

2. Arrange the eggplant on the sheet and roast until golden brown and tender, about 20 minutes.

3. Meanwhile, in a medium saucepan, combine the tomato sauce, vinegar, anchovies, and paprika. Set the pan over medium heat and bring to a simmer. Partially cover and let simmer for 10 minutes. Add the roasted eggplant and simmer for 5 more minutes.

4. Remove from the heat, stir in the parsley, and season with salt and pepper.

5. Preheat the broiler. Arrange the polenta slices on the same baking sheet you roasted the eggplant on and place under the broiler until golden brown, about 2 minutes.

6. Arrange the polenta slices on a serving platter, top with the eggplant mixture and Parmesan, and serve immediately.

make it a meal kit Roast the eggplant and make the tomato sauce mixture (the tomato sauce through the salt and pepper). Store together in a sealable container or plastic bag for up to 3 days in the refrigerator. When ready to finish the meal, reheat the eggplant mixture in a medium saucepan over medium heat or in the microwave for a few minutes on HIGH. Broil the polenta and finish as directed.

morph it Make a double batch of the roasted eggplant and tomato sauce and morph the extra into a topping for grilled or roasted chicken or fish or use as a sauce for pasta. It will keep for up to 3 months in the freezer. Thaw overnight in the refrigerator or in the microwave for 3 to 5 minutes on LOW. Reheat in a medium saucepan over medium heat or in the microwave for a few minutes on HIGH.

Most of the work in this

dish is done by the oven.

Mushrooms with Garlic, Parmesan & Bread Crumbs

This is an elegant, rich side dish worthy of your most sensational main course. Toasted bread crumbs and golden brown Parmesan cheese add unbelievable flavor to earthy sautéed mushrooms. Plus, you get the "crust" everyone loves without having to turn on the oven and bake!

Total Time: 17 minutes

Prep time: 10 minutes

Active cooking time:
7 minutes

Serves 4

2 teaspoons olive oil

2 cloves garlic, minced

1½ pounds button mushrooms, sliced

1 teaspoon dried thyme

¼ cup dry bread crumbs, plain or seasoned

¼ cup freshly grated Parmesan cheese

Salt and freshly ground black pepper to taste

Heat the oil in a large skillet over medium-high heat. Add the garlic and cook for 1 minute. Add the mushrooms and cook, stirring a few times, until softened, about 3 minutes. Add the thyme and cook for 1 minute, until it's fragrant. Add the bread crumbs and Parmesan and cook until the liquid evaporates and the bread crumbs are golden brown, about 2 minutes. Season with salt and pepper and serve.

make it a meal kit Slice the mushrooms and store in a sealable container or plastic bag for up to 3 days in the refrigerator. Or make the entire recipe and store for up to 3 days in the refrigerator.

bank a batch Double the recipe and store the extra in a sealable container for up to 3 months in the freezer. Thaw overnight in the refrigerator or in the microwave for a few minutes on LOW. Reheat in the microwave for a few minutes on HIGH.

morph it Transform this fabulous mushroom mixture into a hearty pasta sauce. Double the recipe and transfer the extra to a medium saucepan. Add 1 cup reduced-sodium chicken or beef broth and bring to a simmer over medium heat. Simmer for 5 to 10 minutes. Spoon the mixture over cooked pasta (any pasta shape that's quick and handy) and top with freshly grated Parmesan cheese and chopped fresh basil.

have it your way You may substitute any mushroom variety or combination of varieties, including wild mushrooms.

. . . a side dish worthy of your most

sensational main course.

Sautéed Carrots & Parsnips

Parsnips look like cream-colored carrots and they have a similar sweetness, but they also possess a surprising peppery note. I like to sauté the two together for a rustic side dish. This is an excellent side dish for chicken, turkey, beef, pork, veal, and seafood.

Total Time: 16 minutes

Prep time: 10 minutes

Active cooking time: 6 minutes

Serves 4

1 tablespoon olive oil

2 medium carrots, peeled and cut into 1-inch dice

2 medium parsnips, peeled and cut into 1-inch dice

2 scallions, chopped

1 teaspoon dried oregano

½ cup reduced-sodium chicken broth

Salt and freshly ground black pepper to taste

Heat the oil in a large skillet over medium-high heat. Add the carrots, parsnips, and scallions and cook, stirring, for 2 minutes. Add the oregano and cook for 1 minute, until fragrant. Add the broth and simmer until it is absorbed and the vegetables are fork-tender, about another 3 minutes. Season with salt and pepper and serve.

make it a meal kit Dice the carrots and parsnips and store in a sealable container or plastic bag for up to 3 days in the refrigerator. Or make the entire recipe and store for up to 3 days in the refrigerator.

bank a batch Double the recipe and store the extra for up to 3 months in the freezer. Thaw overnight in the refrigerator or in the microwave for a few minutes on LOW. Reheat in the microwave for a few minutes on HIGH.

have it your way This is a great way to prepare lots of vegetables. Try pairing Brussels sprouts with red onions; broccoli and/or cauliflower florets with chives; chopped bok choy (the stems and leaves) with canned baby corn and a little soy sauce; halved string beans with chopped leeks; and sugar snap peas or snow peas with shallots and a little lime juice.

Twice-Baked Potatoes with Cheddar & Bacon

This is an excellent use for leftover potatoes. In fact, they're so good, I often bake extra potatoes (when I'm serving plain baked potatoes) so I can whip these up anytime I want. They're great with steak, roasted chicken, or pork chops.

Total Time: 90 minutes

Prep time: 10 minutes

Walk-away time: 80 minutes

Serves 4

4 baking (Idaho or russet) potatoes

4 slices bacon, cooked until crisp and crumbled

1 cup sour cream

½ cup shredded Cheddar cheese

Salt and freshly ground black pepper to taste

2 tablespoons chopped fresh chives

1. Preheat the oven to 400°F.

2. Place the potatoes in the oven and bake until tender, about 1 hour. (Or, you can microwave them on HIGH for 10 minutes.) Leave the oven at 400°F.

3. When cool enough to handle, cut each potato in half lengthwise, scoop out the flesh, leaving a ¼-inch-thick shell, and transfer the flesh to a large bowl. Add the bacon, sour cream, and Cheddar and mix until blended. Season with salt and pepper. Spoon the mixture back into 4 of the shells and discard the remaining shells or save them for another use (you can store the shells in a plastic bag for up to 3 days in the refrigerator or up to 3 months in the freezer; thaw overnight in the refrigerator or in the microwave for a few minutes on LOW before using).

4. Arrange the stuffed potatoes on a baking sheet and bake until golden brown, about 20 minutes. Top with the chives before serving.

make it a meal kit Bake or microwave the potatoes and store in a plastic bag for up to 4 days in the refrigerator. When ready to finish, cut them in half and proceed as directed.

bank a batch Make a double batch and store the extra stuffed potatoes (before the second baking) for up to 3 months in the freezer (cover each one with plastic wrap, then aluminum foil). Thaw overnight in the refrigerator or in the microwave for 4 to 6 minutes on LOW before baking as instructed.

Braised Spinach with Pink Beans & Ham

Sautéed salty ham and fiber-rich pink beans take spinach over the top in this amazing side dish. This is a great use of leftover ham, or you can purchase a thick slice from the deli department or a ham steak from the meat department. It's excellent served with chicken, turkey, pork, or seafood.

Total Time: 10 minutes

Prep time: 5 minutes

Active cooking time: 5 minutes

Serves 4

2 teaspoons olive oil

½ cup diced baked ham

One 10-ounce bag fresh baby or regular spinach leaves, washed well (coarse stems removed if using larger spinach leaves)

One 15-ounce can pink beans, rinsed and drained

½ cup reduced-sodium chicken broth

Salt and freshly ground black pepper to taste

Heat the oil in a large skillet over medium heat. Add the ham and cook, stirring a few times, until golden brown, about 2 minutes. Add the spinach, beans, and broth, cover, and steam until the spinach wilts, about 3 minutes. Season with salt and pepper and serve.

bank a batch Double the recipe and store the extra in a sealable container or plastic bag for up to 3 days in the refrigerator or up to 3 months in the freezer. Thaw overnight in the refrigerator or in the microwave for a few minutes on LOW. Reheat in the microwave for a few minutes on HIGH.

morph it Turn a simple side dish into a stellar soup! Double the recipe and transfer the extra to a medium saucepan. Add 4 cups reduced-sodium chicken broth, bring to a simmer over medium heat, and let simmer for 10 minutes. Remove from the heat, ladle into bowls, and top with a little chopped fresh parsley and freshly grated Parmesan cheese.

have it your way You can make this with any type of green, such as kale, Swiss chard, or bok choy. Collards work too; just increase the cooking time to 6 minutes.

Roasted Butternut Squash with Cumin & Coriander

Roasting brings out the sweetness of all squash varieties, but I particularly love the taste of butternut. Because the squash is so sweet, lemony coriander is the perfect partner, as is smoky cumin. This is perfect with roasted chicken, pork chops, steaks, and burgers.

Total Time: 35 minutes
Prep time: 10 minutes
Walk-away time: 25 minutes

Serves 4

1 large butternut squash, peeled and cubed (about 4 cups)

1 tablespoon olive oil

1 teaspoon ground cumin

1 teaspoon ground coriander

½ teaspoon salt, plus more to taste

½ teaspoon freshly ground black pepper, plus more to taste

2 tablespoons chopped fresh cilantro

1 tablespoon fresh lime juice

1. Preheat the oven to 400°F.

2. In a large bowl, combine the squash, oil, cumin, coriander, salt, and pepper and stir to coat. Transfer the squash to a large baking sheet and roast until tender and browned, about 25 minutes.

3. Transfer to a serving bowl, add the cilantro and lime juice, season with salt and pepper, toss to combine, and serve.

make it a meal kit Cube the squash and toss with the oil and spices. Chop the cilantro and squeeze the lime juice. Store each of the components separately in sealable containers or plastic bags for up to 2 days in the refrigerator. When ready to finish, roast the squash as directed and toss with the cilantro and lime juice. Or, prepare the entire recipe and store for up to 3 days in the refrigerator.

bank a batch Double the recipe and store the extra for up to 3 months in the freezer. Thaw overnight in the refrigerator or in the microwave for a few minutes on LOW. Reheat in the microwave for a few minutes on HIGH.

have it your way You can substitute acorn squash for the butternut.

5-Ingredient Mashed Chipotle Sweet Potatoes with Lime

This is a great side dish with meatloaf, burgers, steaks, pork, and roasted chicken and turkey.

Total Time: 18 minutes
Prep time: 10 minutes
Active cooking time: 8 minutes

Serves 4

2 large sweet potatoes, peeled and cut into 2-inch chunks

¼ cup sour cream

2 teaspoons minced chipotle chiles in adobo sauce

2 tablespoons chopped fresh cilantro

Salt and freshly ground black pepper to taste

1 lime, cut into wedges

Place the sweet potatoes in a large saucepan and pour over enough water to cover. Set the pan over high heat, bring to a boil, and let boil until the potatoes are fork-tender, about 8 minutes. Drain and return to the pan. Mash the potatoes with the sour cream and chipotles until almost smooth (or smooth, if that's your preference). Stir in the cilantro and season with salt and pepper. Serve with the lime wedges on the side.

make it a meal kit Prepare the mashed potatoes and store in a sealable container or plastic bag for up to 3 days in the refrigerator. Reheat in the microwave for a few minutes on HIGH or in a medium saucepan over medium heat, adding more sour cream if necessary to prevent them from drying out.

morph it How about a fiery, rich soup? Double the recipe and transfer the extra sweet potatoes (before adding the cilantro) to a medium saucepan. Add 4 cups reduced-sodium chicken broth and bring to a simmer over medium heat. Using an immersion blender, puree until smooth (or puree in batches in a regular blender). Return the soup to the saucepan if necessary and bring to a simmer again over medium heat. Simmer for 5 to 10 minutes. Remove from the heat, ladle into bowls, and top with a little chopped fresh cilantro.

Black & Pink Beans with Rice

This side dish was inspired by the southwestern flavors of salsa, onion, cumin, oregano, garlic, cayenne, beans, and corn. It's a fiesta on your plate! You could easily make this a complete meal by adding a grilled chicken breast, grilled steak, or pan-seared pork chops.

Total Time: 20–25 minutes

Prep time: 10–15 minutes

Walk-away time: 10 minutes

Serves 4

2 cups instant brown rice

One 8-ounce can tomato sauce

1 cup prepared salsa

1 tablespoon onion flakes

1½ teaspoons ground cumin

1 teaspoon dried oregano

1 teaspoon dried thyme

½ teaspoon garlic powder

¼ teaspoon cayenne

One 11-ounce can black beans, rinsed and drained

One 11-ounce can pink beans, rinsed and drained

One 11-ounce can corn, drained

Salt and freshly ground black pepper to taste

In a large saucepan, combine all the ingredients except for the salt and pepper, and set the pan over medium-high heat. Bring to a simmer, reduce the heat to low, cover, and simmer until the rice is tender and the liquid absorbed, about 10 minutes. Fluff with a fork, season with salt and pepper, and serve.

bank a batch Double the recipe and store the extra in a sealable container or plastic bag for up to 3 days in the refrigerator or up to 3 months in the freezer. Thaw overnight in the refrigerator or in the microwave for a few minutes on LOW. Reheat in the microwave for a few minutes on HIGH.

morph it Make a double batch and morph the extra into a flavorful filling for burritos and enchiladas. Store for up to 3 days in the refrigerator.

have it your way Substitute any bean variety for the black and pink beans; white, red, kidney, and chickpeas all work great. You may also substitute fresh or frozen corn kernels (no need to thaw the corn first).

Vegetable Sauté with Black Bean Sauce

This side dish is nice with anything, not just Asian-inspired meals. Also, try substituting the black bean sauce with hoisin, ponzu, Asian barbecue, or spicy Sichuan sauce.

Total Time: 15–18 minutes

Prep time: 10 minutes

Active cooking time:
5–8 minutes

Serves 4

1 tablespoon olive oil

½ onion, sliced into half-moons

2 to 4 cloves garlic, minced

1 large green bell pepper, seeded and cut into thin strips

1 large red bell pepper, seeded and cut into thin strips

1 bunch asparagus, ends trimmed and cut into 3-inch lengths

1 cup baby carrots

½ cup Chinese black bean sauce

Heat the oil in a large skillet over medium-high heat. Add the onion, garlic, bell peppers, asparagus, and carrots and cook, stirring, until golden brown, 3 to 5 minutes. Stir in the black bean sauce and simmer until the vegetables are crisp-tender, 2 to 3 minutes.

make it a meal kit Cut up the vegetables and store in a sealable container or plastic bag for up to 3 days in the refrigerator or up to 3 months in the freezer. There's no need to thaw the vegetables before cooking. For a greater time-saver, grab fresh vegetables from the salad bar and skip the cutting step altogether! Or, make the entire recipe and store in the refrigerator for up to 3 days.

bank a batch Double the recipe and store the extra for up to 3 months in the freezer. Thaw overnight in the refrigerator or in the microwave for a few minutes on LOW. Reheat in the microwave for a few minutes on HIGH.

morph it For an Asian-inspired main dish, double the recipe and serve the extra over cooked jasmine or basmati rice or Asian noodles such as soba, somen, or rice noodles.

have it your way You may use any variety of canned, frozen, or fresh vegetables to change up this recipe. I recommend any combination of canned baby corn, sliced water chestnuts, fresh or frozen broccoli and cauliflower florets, snap peas and snow peas, fresh asparagus, zucchini, and yellow squash.

Rosemary-Roasted Vegetable Medley

In this refreshing dish, I combine summery vegetables (tomatoes and squash), but you can use any vegetable you want, such as asparagus, broccoli, cauliflower, and Brussels sprouts. That way, you can enjoy the dish year-round. It's *perfect with* beef, poultry, pork, and fish.

Total Time: 30 minutes

Prep time: 10 minutes

Walk-away time: 20 minutes

Serves 4

Cooking spray

2 medium ripe beefsteak tomatoes, cut into 8 wedges each

1 medium zucchini, cut into ¼-inch-thick rounds

1 medium yellow squash, cut into ¼-inch-thick rounds

1 cup sliced mushrooms (any variety or combination of varieties)

1 medium red onion, thinly sliced into half-moons

Salt and freshly ground black pepper to taste

2 tablespoons chopped fresh rosemary

1. Preheat the oven to 400°F. Coat a large baking sheet with cooking spray.

2. Arrange the vegetables on the sheet and spray with cooking spray. Season with salt and pepper and sprinkle with the rosemary. Roast until the squash are tender, about 20 minutes.

make it a meal kit Cut up all the vegetables and store in a sealable container or plastic bag for up to 3 days in the refrigerator. Roast as directed just before serving. You may also make the entire recipe and store for up to 3 days in the refrigerator. Reheat in the microwave for a few minutes on HIGH.

bank a batch Double the recipe and store the extra for up to 3 months in the freezer. Thaw overnight in the refrigerator or in the microwave for a few minutes on LOW. Reheat in the microwave for a few minutes on HIGH.

morph it Roast a double batch of vegetables and morph the extra into 5-Ingredient Pesto–Vegetable Strudel Bites (page 35).

Also, the vegetables make a terrific pasta topping. For a "sauce" for pasta, double the recipe and dice the extra vegetables into ½-inch pieces. Transfer to a medium saucepan and add 1 cup reduced-sodium chicken broth or tomato sauce. Simmer for 5 to 10 minutes. Spoon over your favorite pasta and top with freshly grated Parmesan cheese.

Vegetable Fricassée with Saffron Cream

Fricassée is a fancy word for a stew, one that's typically made with chicken or meat. In my vegetable version, saffron provides both color (golden yellow) and flavor. You can save on prep time by getting all your vegetables from the salad bar, pre-sliced and -diced.

Total Time: 20–25 minutes

Prep time: 10–15 minutes

Active cooking time: 10 minutes

Serves 4

2 teaspoons olive oil

2 to 3 cups sliced vegetables of your choice (any combination of bell peppers, onions, asparagus spears, zucchini, yellow squash, carrots, and mushrooms)

1 teaspoon saffron threads

1 teaspoon dried thyme

1/2 cup dry vermouth or dry white wine

1 cup milk (preferably 1% milk fat or higher)

1/2 cup sour cream

Salt and freshly ground black pepper to taste

1. Preheat the broiler.

2. Heat the oil in a large, high-sided, ovenproof skillet over medium-high heat. Add the vegetables and cook, stirring, for 3 minutes. Add the saffron and thyme and cook for 1 minute, until fragrant. Add the vermouth and cook for 2 minutes. Reduce the heat to low, stir in the milk and sour cream, bring to a simmer, and let simmer for 2 minutes. Season with salt and pepper.

3. Place the pan under the broiler and broil until the top is golden brown, about 2 minutes, then serve.

make it a meal kit Prepare the fricassée and, before broiling, let cool, then store in a sealable container or plastic bag for up to 3 days in the refrigerator. Reheat in the same pan over medium heat until heated through, then broil as directed.

morph it Make a double batch and serve the extra as a meat-free meal over rice or couscous.

have it your way You may substitute any vegetable you desire, and, for a more anise-like cream sauce, substitute 1 teaspoon dried tarragon for the saffron.

Toasted Coconut Rice

Toasting the coconut adds depth and a distinct nuttiness, while the coconut milk provides richness. This is the perfect side dish for Asian-inspired entrées.

Total Time: 13–15 minutes
Prep time: 5 minutes
Active cooking time:
8–10 minutes

Serves 4

¼ cup sweetened flaked coconut

1 cup instant white or jasmine rice

One 14-ounce can unsweetened light coconut milk

Place the coconut in a dry medium saucepan and set the pan over medium heat. Cook until the coconut is golden brown and toasted, 3 to 5 minutes, shaking the pan frequently to prevent burning. Add the rice and coconut milk. Increase the heat to medium high, bring to a simmer, cover, and let simmer for 5 minutes. Remove from the heat and let stand for 5 minutes before serving.

bank a batch Double the recipe and store the extra in a sealable container or plastic bag for up to 3 days in the refrigerator or up to 3 months in the freezer. Thaw overnight in the refrigerator or in the microwave for a few minutes on LOW. Reheat in the microwave for a few minutes on HIGH.

morph it Make a double batch and morph the extra into Asparagus–Wild Mushroom Risotto with Parmesan (page 76).

Garlic–Herb Couscous

This 5-minute side dish is a Quick Fix cook's "wingman," meaning it has your back on any crazy weeknight. I use garlic-and-herb seasoning for its one-stop-shop quality (lots of ingredients in one spice blend), but you can use whatever you have on hand. Plus, I've given you free rein in the fresh herb department.

Total Time: 10–15 minutes
Prep time: 5–10 minutes
Walk-away time: 5 minutes

Serves 4

1¼ cups water

1 cup couscous, regular or whole wheat

1 teaspoon garlic-and-herb seasoning (preferably salt free)

2 tablespoons chopped fresh herbs, such as cilantro, mint, parsley, or basil, or a combination of any of these herbs

½ teaspoon salt

¼ teaspoon freshly ground black pepper

1. Bring the water to a boil in a medium saucepan. Add the couscous, garlic-and-herb seasoning, fresh herbs, salt, and pepper and mix well.

2. Remove from the heat, cover, and let stand until the liquid is absorbed, about 5 minutes. Fluff with a fork before serving.

bank a batch Double the recipe and store the extra in a sealable container or plastic bag for up to 3 days in the refrigerator or up to 3 months in the freezer. Thaw overnight in the refrigerator or in the microwave for a few minutes on LOW. Reheat in the microwave for a few minutes on HIGH.

Parmesan-Crusted Rolls

Thanks to prepared bread dough, these are a snap to whip up on a busy weeknight. These are so quick, they'll be ready in the time it takes to reheat dinner or prepare a Quick Fix meal from scratch!

Total Time: 18–23 minutes
Prep time: 10–15 minutes
Walk-away time: 8 minutes

Makes 8 rolls

Cooking spray

1 pound fresh or thawed frozen bread dough

¼ cup freshly grated Parmesan cheese

1. Preheat the oven to 450°F. Coat a large baking sheet with cooking spray.

2. Break the dough into 8 equal pieces and roll each piece into a ball. Place the balls on the prepared sheet, coat with cooking spray, and sprinkle with the Parmesan. Bake until puffed up and golden brown, about 8 minutes.

bank a batch Double the recipe and store the extra baked rolls in a plastic bag for up to 3 days in the refrigerator or up to 3 months in the freezer. Reheat the rolls directly from the freezer (no need to thaw) in a 300°F oven until warm, 10 to 15 minutes.

have it your way Use your favorite cheese; I particularly like Asiago, pecorino romano, and finely shredded Cheddar.

. . . these are a snap to whip up . . .

Onion Knots

I love crescent rolls, but who says you have to shape them like the package photos? A simple knot and sprinkle of onion and you've got the perfect partner for soups, stews, salads, and pasta dishes.

Total Time: 20–22 minutes

Prep time: 10 minutes

Walk-away time:
10–12 minutes

Makes 8 knots

One 8-ounce package refrigerated crescent rolls

Olive oil cooking spray

2 tablespoons onion flakes

1. Preheat the oven to 375°F.

2. Unroll the crescent dough into 8 triangles. Tie each triangle into a knot by stretching two points out and then crossing them over and under, as if tying a shoe. Place the knots on a baking sheet. Coat them with cooking spray, then sprinkle with the onion flakes. Bake until puffed up and golden brown, 10 to 12 minutes.

bank a batch Double the recipe and store the extra baked knots in plastic bags for up to 3 days in the refrigerator or up to 3 months in the freezer. Reheat the knots directly from the freezer (no need to thaw) in a 300°F oven until warm, 10 to 15 minutes.

have it your way For garlic knots, use garlic flakes instead of onion flakes. For sesame knots, use sesame seeds and a little coarse salt instead of onion flakes.

. . . the perfect partner for soups, stews,

salads, and pasta dishes.

Bruschetta with Chipotle–Cilantro Butter

I call this "butter with a blast"! In this case I'm using it on bruschetta (a fancy word for toast), but you can slather it on sandwich bread, crackers, mashed potatoes, rice, pasta, or grilled or roasted chicken, steak, pork, or seafood.

Total Time: 11–13 minutes

Prep time: 5 minutes

Active cooking time:
6–8 minutes

Serves 4 to 6

1 French baguette, cut crosswise into 1-inch-thick slices

CHIPOTLE–CILANTRO BUTTER

¼ cup (½ stick) unsalted butter, softened

1 tablespoon chopped fresh cilantro

½ teaspoon salt-free southwestern chipotle seasoning (McCormick®)

1. Preheat the oven to 400°F.

2. Arrange the bread slices on a large baking sheet. Bake until golden brown, 6 to 8 minutes.

3. Meanwhile, in a small bowl, combine the butter, cilantro, and seasoning until well blended.

4. Spread the butter on the toasted bread and serve.

make it a meal kit Toast the bread and store in a plastic bag at room temperature for up to 3 days. Make the butter and store in a sealable container for up to 1 week in the refrigerator. Reheat the bread on a baking sheet in a 300°F oven until warm, about 10 minutes. Top the bread with the butter just before serving.

morph it Make a double batch of the butter and morph the extra into a topping for grilled or roasted chicken, fish, shellfish, or pork. Store the butter for up to 3 months in the freezer. To make frozen butter more spreadable, thaw in the microwave for 20 to 30 seconds on LOW.

have it your way Instead of cilantro and chipotle seasoning, try chopped fresh basil and salt-free garlic-and-herb seasoning (also a great topping for pasta and rice), or chopped fresh parsley and salt-free lemon-and-herb seasoning (also wonderful with fish).

Traditional Potato Salad

This mayo-based salad boasts pickle relish, fresh parsley, and hard-boiled eggs. That's what makes it traditional to me. It's perfect alongside burgers and hot dogs, but I also serve it with flank steak and roasted chicken. Make a big batch—you'll need it!

Total Time: 18–23 minutes
Prep time: 10–15 minutes
Active cooking time: 8 minutes

Serves 4 to 6

2 pounds small red potatoes (8 to 10), quartered

2 tablespoons cider vinegar

1/2 cup mayonnaise

1 stalk celery, chopped

1/4 cup minced red onion

3 tablespoons pickle relish

2 teaspoons Dijon mustard

2 tablespoons chopped fresh parsley

Salt and freshly ground black pepper to taste

2 large hard-boiled eggs, peeled and diced

1. Place the potatoes in a large pot and pour over enough water to cover. Set the pan over high heat, bring to a boil, and let boil until the potatoes are fork-tender, about 8 minutes. Drain and transfer to a large bowl. Add the vinegar and toss to coat the potatoes.

2. In a small bowl, combine the mayonnaise, celery, onion, relish, mustard, and parsley. Add to the potatoes and toss to combine well. Season with salt and pepper. Fold in the eggs and serve warm or chilled.

make it a meal kit Boil the potatoes and toss with the vinegar. Combine the mayonnaise mixture (the mayonnaise through the parsley). Store each separately in sealable containers or plastic bags for up to 3 days in the refrigerator. Finish as directed. For a warm salad, reheat the potatoes in the microwave for 2 minutes on HIGH before tossing with the mayonnaise mixture and eggs.

have it your way You can substitute an equal amount of Yukon Gold potatoes for the red potatoes.

To cut calories and fat, use light mayonnaise, light sour cream, or low-fat yogurt instead of full-fat mayo.

German Potato Salad

Cider vinegar, salty bacon, and scallions lend their flavors to not-too-starchy Yukon Gold potatoes (that means Yukons hold up well in salads *and* hold flavor when mixed with other ingredients). Since there's no mayonnaise, this is the perfect salad to take along to a picnic or tailgate party.

Total Time: 18 minutes

Prep time: 10 minutes

Active cooking time: 8 minutes

Serves 4

6 small to medium Yukon Gold potatoes, cut into 2-inch chunks

½ cup chopped scallions (white and green parts; about 6 scallions)

4 slices turkey bacon, cooked until crisp and crumbled

3 tablespoons cider vinegar

1 tablespoon olive oil

Salt and freshly ground black pepper to taste

1. Place the potatoes in a large saucepan and pour over enough water to cover. Set the pan over high heat, bring to a boil, and let boil until the potatoes are fork-tender, about 8 minutes. Drain and, while still warm, transfer to a large bowl.

2. Add the scallions, bacon, vinegar, and oil and toss to combine. Season with salt and pepper. Serve warm or chilled.

make it a meal kit Make the salad and store in a sealable container for up to 3 days in the refrigerator.

have it your way You may substitute red potatoes for the Yukon Golds if desired. You can also substitute red wine vinegar or sherry vinegar for the cider vinegar.

Southwest Cabbage Slaw

What makes this a Southwest slaw? The combination of sour cream, pickled chile peppers, salsa, cilantro, and cumin. With this flavor punch, you might not be able to enjoy regular slaw again! This is excellent with chicken, turkey, pork, and steak.

Total Time: 10 minutes

Prep time: 10 minutes

Serves 4

2 cups shredded cole slaw mix (cabbage and carrots)

½ cup sour cream

⅓ cup sliced pickled jalapeño chile peppers

¼ cup prepared salsa

2 tablespoons chopped fresh cilantro

1 teaspoon ground cumin

Combine all the ingredients in a large bowl and toss to combine.

make it a meal kit Slaws tend to get better with age (since the flavors have a chance to blend), so feel free to make this side dish in advance and store in a sealable container or plastic bag for up to 3 days in the refrigerator.

have it your way You can substitute an equal amount of broccoli slaw for the cole slaw if desired.

5-Ingredient Broccoli Ranch Slaw

Super-convenient broccoli slaw mix is sold in the produce aisle next to the other shredded ingredients. It's a nice change from regular cabbage-based slaw, and I love the fresh broccoli flavor it contributes to the salad. Choose your favorite ranch dressing and you'll have the best slaw on the block!

Total Time: 10 minutes

Prep time: 10 minutes

Serves 4

One 10-ounce bag shredded broccoli slaw mix

¾ cup ranch dressing

2 tablespoons chopped fresh chives

2 tablespoons red wine vinegar

1 teaspoon Dijon mustard

Combine all the ingredients in a large bowl and toss to combine.

make it a meal kit The flavor of this slaw improves with age, so feel free to make the salad in advance and store in a sealable container or plastic bag for up to 3 days in the refrigerator.

. . . you'll have the best

slaw on the block!

Beet–Arugula Salad With Buttermilk–Blue Cheese Dressing

Sweet beets, citrusy mandarins, and peppery arugula have fun together on this salad plate, that's for sure! Smooth buttermilk and tangy crumbled blue cheese come together in seconds for a delicious creamy dressing.

Total Time: 10 minutes

Prep time: 10 minutes

Serves 4

4 cups fresh arugula leaves

1 cup jarred or canned sliced beets

One 11-ounce can mandarin oranges, drained

BUTTERMILK–BLUE CHEESE DRESSING

⅔ cup buttermilk

¼ cup crumbled blue cheese

Salt and freshly ground black pepper to taste

1. Arrange the arugula on a serving platter. Top with the sliced beets and orange segments.

2. In a small bowl, whisk together the dressing ingredients. Pour over the salad and serve.

make it a meal kit Wash, then dry the arugula leaves and make the dressing. Store each separately in sealable containers or plastic bags for up to 3 days in the refrigerator. When ready to serve, finish as directed.

morph it Make the dish with extra beets from Balsamic Roasted Beets (page 244).

have it your way Instead of arugula, use a wedge of iceberg lettuce. Remove the outer leaves, then slice the head into 4 equal wedges. Set each wedge on its side, top with the beets and mandarin oranges, then pour the dressing over the top.

You can also substitute grapefruit sections for the mandarin oranges. To save prep time, use the grapefruit sections sold in jars in the refrigerated section of the produce aisle in your grocery store.

Black Bean & Corn Salad

Tex-Mex and Mexican flavors (cumin, lime, and cilantro) shine in this quick and easy salad. Add grilled chicken, fish, or steak—and a cold beer—and you've got a complete meal!

Total Time: 10 minutes
Prep time: 10 minutes

Serves 4 to 6

One 15-ounce can black beans, rinsed and drained

One 14-ounce can corn kernels, drained

1 medium red bell pepper, seeded and diced

2 tablespoons chopped fresh cilantro

1 tablespoon fresh lime juice

$\frac{1}{2}$ teaspoon ground cumin

Salt and cayenne to taste

In a large bowl, combine the beans, corn, bell pepper, cilantro, lime juice, and cumin, tossing to mix. Season with salt and cayenne.

make it a meal kit Prepare the salad and store in a sealable container or plastic bag for up to 3 days in the refrigerator. Serve chilled or at room temperature.

have it your way You may use 1 cup thawed frozen corn instead of canned. You can also substitute any color bell pepper (green, yellow, or orange) or use $\frac{1}{2}$ cup diced roasted red peppers instead.

Cucumber Salad with Oranges & Mint

Anything that comes together in one bowl is a winner in my book. This colorful salad boasts sweet oranges, tangy mint, and refreshing cucumber in a mild sherry vinegar dressing.

Total Time: 10 minutes

Prep time: 10 minutes

Serves 4

1 English (seedless) cucumber, sliced into ¼-inch-thick rounds

One 12-ounce can mandarin oranges, drained

¼ cup fresh mint leaves, finely chopped

1 tablespoon sherry vinegar

2 teaspoons olive oil

Salt and freshly ground black pepper to taste

In a large bowl, combine the cucumber, oranges, mint, vinegar, and oil. Toss to combine. Season with salt and pepper.

make it a meal kit Prepare the salad and store in a sealable container or plastic bag for up to 3 days in the refrigerator.

have it your way Instead of an English cucumber, substitute a regular cucumber. To remove the seeds from a regular cucumber, halve it lengthwise and use a small spoon to scoop them out. No cukes in the house or you're in the mood for a different flavor? Very thinly slice a fennel bulb—the flavors work incredibly well together.

Romaine Salad with Roasted Cherry Tomatoes & Blue Cheese

I grew up eating blue cheese, and my boys inherited those genes! In this dish, I partner the tangy crumbles with caramelized roasted tomatoes and lettuce, then I nestle everything under a delightful honey mustard–spiked dressing. This is excellent with pasta dishes, steak, and chicken.

Total Time: 35 minutes
Prep time: 10 minutes
Walk-away time: 25 minutes

Serves 4

Cooking spray

2 cups cherry or grape tomatoes, cut in half

1/2 teaspoon salt

6 cups chopped romaine lettuce

1/4 cup crumbled blue cheese

1/4 cup garlic-flavored or regular olive oil

2 tablespoons balsamic vinegar

2 teaspoons honey mustard

Salt and freshly ground black pepper to taste

1. Preheat the oven to 400°F. Coat a large baking sheet with cooking spray.

2. Spread the tomatoes out on the sheet, cut side up, and sprinkle with the salt. Roast until the tomatoes are browned and slightly shriveled, about 25 minutes.

3. Arrange the lettuce on a serving platter and top with the roasted tomatoes and blue cheese.

4. In a small bowl, whisk together the oil, vinegar, and mustard. Season with salt and pepper. Pour the dressing over the salad and serve.

make it a meal kit Roast the tomatoes and make the dressing (the olive oil through the salt and pepper). Store each separately in sealable containers or plastic bags for up to 3 days in the refrigerator. When ready to serve, arrange the tomatoes on top of the lettuce and drizzle the dressing over the top (for warm tomatoes, reheat them in the microwave for 1 to 2 minutes on HIGH).

morph it Roast a double batch of the tomatoes and morph the extras into Mixed Cherry Tomato Salad (page 281; the roasted tomatoes add a wonderful sweet flavor to the salad). The extra tomatoes also make a great addition to any pasta or rice dish.

Pear–Cucumber Salad with Balsamic & Shaved Romano Cheese

Pears and cucumbers partner so well that I just had to combine them in a salad. They're both mildly sweet, so I added tangy balsamic vinegar and distinct pecorino romano cheese to round out the flavors. This is an excellent side dish for steak, chicken, turkey, pork, and veal.

Total Time: 10–15 minutes

Prep time: 10–15 minutes

Serves 4

2 cups cored and diced pears (2 to 3 pears)

2 cups diced English (seedless) cucumber (about 1 cucumber)

2 tablespoons balsamic vinegar

2 tablespoons chopped fresh parsley

2 teaspoons olive oil

Salt and freshly ground black pepper to taste

One 4-ounce chunk pecorino romano cheese

In a large bowl, combine the pears, cucumber, vinegar, parsley, and oil, tossing to mix. Season with salt and pepper. Transfer the salad to a serving platter. Using a vegetable peeler, shave the cheese over the top and serve.

make it a meal kit Make the salad and store in a sealable container or plastic bag for up to 3 days in the refrigerator. Shave the cheese over the top just before serving.

have it your way Instead of pears, try the salad with Granny Smith or McIntosh apples. And instead of pecorino romano cheese, try Parmesan, smoked mozzarella, or sharp Cheddar.

Warm Spinach Salad with Pancetta, Gorgonzola & Pine Nuts

Salty smoked bacon, sweet red onion, fresh green spinach, and tangy blue cheese come together on one plate. The spinach wilts to perfection when topped with the warm ingredients and the crowning touch—crunchy toasted pine nuts.

Total Time: 17–21 minutes

Prep time: 10 minutes

Active cooking time: 7–11 minutes

Serves 4

2 tablespoons pine nuts

¼ cup diced pancetta or bacon

¼ cup minced red onion

⅔ cup reduced-sodium chicken broth

½ teaspoon salt

¼ teaspoon freshly ground black pepper

6 cups baby or regular spinach leaves, washed well

¼ cup crumbled Gorgonzola or other blue cheese

1. Place the pine nuts in a small dry skillet set over medium heat and toast them until golden brown, about 3 minutes, shaking the pan frequently to prevent burning. Remove from the heat.

2. Place a large skillet over medium-high heat. Add the pancetta and cook, stirring a few times, until browned, 3 to 5 minutes. Add the onion and cook, stirring, until softened, 3 to 5 minutes. Add the broth, salt, and pepper, bring to a simmer, and let simmer for 1 minute to heat through.

3. Place the spinach in a large bowl. Pour the warm pancetta sauce over it and sprinkle with the Gorgonzola just before serving.

make it a meal kit Toast the pine nuts, prepare the pancetta dressing (the pancetta through the salt and pepper), and wash and dry the spinach. Store each component separately in sealable containers or plastic bags for up to 3 days in the refrigerator. When ready to finish, reheat the dressing in a small saucepan over medium heat or in the microwave for 1 to 2 minutes on HIGH.

have it your way Feel free to substitute any leafy green for the spinach; romaine leaves, mustard greens, arugula, and red lettuce also work nicely.

Seared Goat Cheese over Greens

Why sear cheese? Because it creates a golden brown crust and creamy interior you won't get if you just slice the cheese and plop it on top of your salad. This is a great side dish for hearty pasta dishes.

Total Time: 11–16 minutes

Prep time: 10–15 minutes

Active cooking time: 1 minute

Serves 4

2 tablespoons seasoned dry bread crumbs

4 ounces goat cheese, cut crosswise into 4 equal rounds

1 tablespoon olive oil

4 cups mixed greens

¼ cup reduced-sodium vegetable or chicken broth

1 tablespoon fresh lime juice

1 teaspoon Dijon mustard

Salt and freshly ground black pepper to taste

1. Place the bread crumbs in a shallow dish, add the goat cheese slices, and turn to coat both sides. Heat the oil in a medium skillet over medium heat. Add the crumb-coated goat cheese to the hot pan and sear until golden brown, about 30 seconds per side.

2. Arrange the greens on individual salad plates and top with the seared goat cheese.

3. In a small bowl, whisk together the broth, lime juice, and mustard. Season with salt and pepper. Pour the dressing over the goat cheese and greens and serve.

make it a meal kit Coat the goat cheese with the bread crumbs. Whisk together the dressing (the broth through the pepper). Store each separately in sealable containers for up to 3 days in the refrigerator. Finish as directed.

have it your way Instead of goat cheese, try making this with regular or smoked mozzarella or any firm feta cheese.

Fennel–Walnut Salad with Sweet Gorgonzola

This is an elegant-looking salad that you can feel comfortable serving at your fanciest dinner party. I love the blast of tastes from licorice-like fennel, peppery watercress, and tangy blue cheese. I balance those flavors with an orange juice–based dressing that's kicked up with shallots and sage. Add crunchy toasted walnuts on top and you'll be the star of the table!

Total Time: 13–15 minutes
Prep time: 10–15 minutes
Active cooking time: 3 minutes

Serves 4

2 cups chopped fennel bulb

1 cup packed watercress leaves

½ cup walnuts, toasted in a dry skillet over medium heat until golden brown, 2 to 3 minutes

⅓ cup orange juice

1 tablespoon olive oil

1 teaspoon Dijon mustard

1 tablespoon minced shallot

1 tablespoon chopped fresh sage

Salt and freshly ground black pepper to taste

½ cup crumbled Gorgonzola cheese

1. In a large bowl, combine the fennel, watercress, and walnuts, tossing to mix.

2. In a small bowl, whisk together the orange juice, oil, mustard, shallot, and sage. Season with salt and pepper. Pour this over the fennel mixture and toss to combine. Transfer to a serving plate, top with the Gorgonzola, and serve.

make it a meal kit Toast the walnuts. Whisk together the dressing (the orange juice through the pepper). Store each separately in sealable containers for up to 3 days in the refrigerator. Finish as directed.

have it your way Instead of sage, try parsley or basil. Instead of Gorgonzola, try Stilton or any other crumbly blue-veined cheese. Instead of walnuts, try almonds or macadamia nuts. The possibilities and varieties are endless!

Radicchio Cups with Hearts of Palm, Yogurt & Dill

Ruby red radicchio leaves make perfect little "bowls" for all kinds of ingredient combinations: in this case, crisp-tender hearts of palm and a tangy dressing of yogurt, fresh dill, and pungent Dijon mustard.

Total Time: 10 minutes

Prep time: 10 minutes

Serves 4

4 radicchio leaves

One 15-ounce can hearts of palm, drained and cut crosswise into
1/2-inch-thick pieces

1 cup plain yogurt

1 tablespoon chopped fresh dill

1 teaspoon Dijon mustard

Salt and freshly ground black pepper to taste

1. Arrange the radicchio on a serving platter and fill each leaf with the hearts of palm pieces.

2. In a small bowl, whisk together the yogurt, dill, and mustard. Season with salt and pepper. Spoon the dressing over the hearts of palm and radicchio and serve.

make it a meal kit Slice the hearts of palm. Whisk together the dressing (the yogurt through the pepper). Store each separately in sealable containers or plastic bags for up to 3 days in the refrigerator. Finish as directed.

have it your way Try substituting artichoke hearts, sliced water chestnuts, or canned baby corn for the hearts of palm.

Baby Spinach Salad with Strawberry–Sherry Vinaigrette

You'll simply adore the combination of fresh spinach and strawberries in a strawberry preserves–based vinaigrette that's both sweet and tangy.

Total Time: 10 minutes

Prep time: 10 minutes

Serves 4

6 cups baby spinach leaves, washed well

1 cup hulled and sliced fresh strawberries

STRAWBERRY–SHERRY VINAIGRETTE

¼ cup strawberry preserves (preferably seedless)

3 tablespoons olive oil

3 tablespoons sherry vinegar

1 teaspoon Dijon mustard

Salt and freshly ground black pepper to taste

1. Arrange the spinach in a large serving bowl. Place the strawberry slices on top.

2. In a small bowl, whisk together the vinaigrette ingredients. Pour over the spinach and strawberries just before serving.

make it a meal kit Wash and dry the spinach. Whisk together the dressing. Store each separately in sealable containers or plastic bags for up to 3 days in the refrigerator. Finish as directed.

have it your way Instead of strawberries and strawberry preserves, try fresh raspberries and raspberry preserves or fresh blackberries and blackberry preserves.

To make this a more substantial and complete meal, add 1 sliced cooked chicken breast, 1 cup lump crabmeat, or 1½ cups cooked medium shrimp.

Mesclun Greens with Avocado & Corn in Citrus Vinaigrette

Mesclun, also called field greens or spring mix, is a classic salad mix that typically contains any combination of young leaves and shoots of endive, dandelion, arugula, radicchio, chervil, sorrel, frisée, purslane, and, sometimes, edible flowers. You'll find a greater variety of greens at a farmers' market; supermarket mesclun might have just 3 or 4 different greens in it. This salad is fantastic with leftover lobster or shrimp from a restaurant doggy bag.

Total Time: 10 minutes

Prep time: 10 minutes

Serves 4

6 cups mesclun or other salad green mix

1 ripe avocado, pitted, peeled, and diced

One 14-ounce can corn kernels, drained

¼ cup sliced pitted black olives

CITRUS VINAIGRETTE

⅓ cup orange juice

1 tablespoon fresh lime juice

2 tablespoons olive oil

2 teaspoons Dijon mustard

Salt and freshly ground black pepper to taste

1. Arrange the mesclun on a serving platter and top with the avocado, corn, and olives.

2. In a small bowl, whisk together the vinaigrette ingredients, then drizzle over the salad and serve.

make it a meal kit Prepare the vinaigrette and store in a sealable container for up to 3 days in the refrigerator. When ready to finish, arrange the mesclun, avocado, corn, and olives on the platter and pour the vinaigrette over them.

have it your way You can substitute fresh or thawed frozen corn for the canned. You may also use any combination of lettuce greens you have handy.

Mixed Cherry Tomato Salad

Cherry tomatoes are such fun to pop in your mouth. This easy and light salad gets a jolt of flavor from fresh basil, and it's the perfect partner for heavier dishes such as cream-based pasta dishes and hearty casseroles.

Total Time: 10 minutes

Prep time: 10 minutes

Serves 4 to 6

2 cups halved cherry or grape tomatoes

2 cups halved yellow cherry tomatoes

¼ cup chopped fresh basil

1 tablespoon red wine vinegar

2 teaspoons olive oil

Salt and coarsely ground black pepper to taste

In a medium bowl, combine the tomatoes, basil, vinegar, and oil, tossing to mix. Season with salt and pepper.

make it a meal kit Make the salad and store in a sealable container or plastic bag for up to 2 days in the refrigerator.

have it your way You may use any variety and combination of tomatoes for this salad, including diced beefsteak, plum (Roma), yellow, or heirloom.

. . . use any variety and

combination of tomatoes . . .

Red Lettuce with Honey–Maple Vinaigrette

I like to combine honey and maple syrup, not because I have an incredible sweet tooth, but because I like the different types of sweetness they provide. Add a little vinegar and thyme and you've got a sweet-tart dressing in less than 5 minutes.

Total Time: 10 minutes

Prep time: 10 minutes

Serves 4

HONEY–MAPLE VINAIGRETTE

¼ cup honey

2 tablespoons maple syrup

2 tablespoons olive oil

2 tablespoons white wine vinegar

1 tablespoon chopped fresh thyme or 1 teaspoon dried

Salt and freshly ground black pepper to taste

4 to 6 cups chopped red lettuce leaves, or any lettuce variety

1. In a small bowl, whisk together the vinaigrette ingredients.

2. Arrange the lettuce on individual salad plates and spoon the dressing over the top just before serving.

make it a meal kit Wash and dry the lettuce. Whisk together the vinaigrette. Store each separately in sealable containers or plastic bags, the lettuce for up to 3 days in the refrigerator, the vinaigrette for up to 1 week. Finish as directed.

morph it Make a double batch of the vinaigrette and morph the extra into a marinade and dipping sauce for chicken, turkey, salmon, or pork tenderloin. Use half as a marinade and the other half as a dipping sauce after cooking the protein.

5-Ingredient Watercress Salad with Pears, Goat Cheese & Pine Nuts

Watercress is somewhat "spicy," so I like to pair it with sweet ingredients like fruit (in this case, pears).

Total Time: 10 13 minutes

Prep time: 10 minutes

Active cooking time:
2–3 minutes

Serves 4

¼ cup pine nuts

4 cups loosely packed watercress leaves

2 ripe pears, cored and thinly sliced

4 ounces goat cheese, crumbled

1 to 2 tablespoons balsamic vinegar

1. Toast the pine nuts in a small dry skillet over medium heat until golden brown, 2 to 3 minutes, shaking the pan frequently to prevent burning.

2. Arrange the watercress on individual salad plates. Top with the pear slices, goat cheese, and pine nuts. Drizzle the vinegar over the top and serve.

make it a meal kit Wash and dry the watercress. Toast the pine nuts. Crumble the goat cheese. Store each of the components separately in sealable containers or plastic bags up to 3 days in the refrigerator. Finish as directed.

have it your way Instead of pine nuts, use pecans or slivered almonds. Instead of pears, use sliced apples such as McIntosh or Golden Delicious. Instead of watercress, use baby spinach leaves. And instead of goat cheese, try crumbled feta or blue cheese.

Desserts

Why put a dessert chapter in a Quick Fix cookbook?

Because my night's not complete unless I've eaten something sweet. But, it's not sweet to me if it's not ready fast. That's why I use my Quick Fix strategies to make dessert too. I either create desserts that are ready before my sweet tooth starts aching, or I prep ahead so that I can finish the treat in just minutes. Many of my desserts work well in my Bank a Batch strategy too. You can assemble them ahead and freeze them until you're ready to serve or bake.

You may notice that there's not a huge selection of desserts (compared, say, to the chicken and pasta chapters), but I've given you a variety to suit every sweet tooth—chocolate, fruit, cold, warm, crunchy, creamy, etc. For me, all those things on one plate would be the ultimate perfection! How sweet it is.

You can assemble them ahead and freeze them

until you're ready to serve or bake.

Pizza Cookie

Get the kids involved in this one—it's a blast. I roll out refrigerated cookie dough to the size and shape of a pizza and then bake it. Once it's golden brown, I top it with sweet things that look like they belong on a real pizza ("sauce," "cheese," "pepperoni," etc.). You'll have a ton of fun creating your own version!

Total Time: 20–27 minutes
Prep time: 10–15 minutes
Walk-away time: 10–12 minutes

Serves 8 to 12

One 11-ounce package refrigerated sugar cookie dough

½ cup strawberry preserves

½ cup shredded white chocolate, or more if desired

Fruit leather in various colors (red, green, yellow), cut into desired shapes and sizes (see below)

1. Preheat the oven to 375°F.

2. Roll the cookie dough into a ball. On a lightly floured work surface, roll the ball out into a 12- to 14-inch circle. Transfer the circle to a baking sheet (if the dough rips at all, don't worry, just press it back together once it's on the baking sheet) and bake until golden brown, 10 to 12 minutes.

3. Remove from the oven and, while it's still hot, spread the preserves over the top like you would tomato sauce over a pizza. Sprinkle over the chocolate (mozzarella cheese!), then top with red fruit leather cut out to look like pepperoni or green leather cut into strips to look like bell peppers, or whatever else you'd like on your "pizza"!

make it a meal kit Bake the cookie, shred the chocolate, and cut the fruit leather into shapes. When you're ready to finish, assemble the pizza as directed. (The chocolate won't melt when the cookie's not hot, but it still looks cool!)

Frozen Key Lime Pie

My grandmother used to make this pie every time we'd visit her in the Florida Keys. She had a Key lime tree, so it was easy for her to whip up this pie any day of the week. I don't expect you to walk out your back door for Key limes, so feel free to make this delectable pie with fresh lime juice.

Total Time: 40 minutes

Prep time: 10 minutes

Walk-away time: 30 minutes

Makes one 9-inch pie;
serves 6

One 8-ounce container nondairy whipped topping, thawed slightly

One 14-ounce can sweetened condensed milk

1/2 cup fresh lime juice

One 9-inch prepared graham cracker pie crust

Finely grated lime zest for sprinkling

1. In a medium bowl, whisk together the whipped topping, condensed milk, and lime juice until smooth. Spoon the mixture into the graham cracker crust and smooth the surface with a rubber spatula.

2. Set in the freezer until firm, about 30 minutes. Sprinkle the lime zest over the top before serving.

bank a batch Once the pie is frozen, cover it with plastic wrap, then aluminum foil. It will keep in the freezer for up to 1 month. Sprinkle the top with lime zest just before serving.

have it your way For variety, use fresh lemon or orange juice instead of lime juice.

Anita's Impossible Buttermilk Pie

My friend Anita calls this "Impossible Buttermilk Pie" because it's impossibly easy to make. There's no crust—it's simply a mix-and-bake dish. I like to dust the top with confectioners' sugar or cocoa.

Total Time: 50–60 minutes

Prep time: 10 minutes

Walk-away time:
30–40 minutes

Resting time: 10 minutes

Makes one 9-inch pie;
serves 8

Cooking spray

1⅓ cups sugar

1 cup buttermilk

½ cup Bisquick®

⅓ cup unsalted butter, melted

1 teaspoon vanilla extract

3 large eggs

Confectioners' sugar and/or unsweetened cocoa powder (optional)

1. Preheat the oven to 350°F. Coat a 9-inch pie plate with cooking spray.

2. Combine the sugar, buttermilk, Bisquick, melted butter, vanilla, and eggs in a blender and process until smooth. Pour into the prepared pie plate and bake until browned and still a little jiggly (the pie will set as it cools), 30 to 40 minutes.

3. Let cool for 10 minutes before slicing into wedges. If desired, sift confectioners' sugar or cocoa (or a combo) over the wedges before serving.

have it your way For a twist on Anita's original, add 1 teaspoon finely grated orange zest or ½ teaspoon almond extract.

Mixed Fruit Tart with Vanilla Cream

Thanks to refrigerated piecrusts and pre-sliced fruit in the produce aisle, you can put this together in no time. The creamy filling in the tart is a simple combination of cream cheese, confectioners' sugar, and vanilla. Wow your friends and family with this one and pat yourself on the back for giving it a try!

Total Time: 24–26 minutes

Prep time: 15 minutes

Active cooking time: 9–11 minutes

Makes one 9-inch tart; serves 6 to 8

One 9-inch refrigerated piecrust

One 8-ounce package cream cheese, softened

1 cup confectioners' sugar

1 teaspoon vanilla extract

2 cups assorted seasonal fruit, such as pitted and sliced peaches, plums, or nectarines; hulled and sliced strawberries; blueberries, blackberries, or raspberries; and/or peeled and sliced kiwis

½ cup apricot preserves

1. Preheat the oven to 450°F.

2. Press the piecrust into the bottom and up the sides of a 9-inch tart pan with a removable bottom. Bake until the crust is golden brown, 9 to 11 minutes.

3. Beat together the cream cheese, confectioners' sugar, and vanilla in a medium bowl until smooth. When the tart shell is cool, spread the cream cheese mixture over the bottom and smooth the surface with a rubber spatula. Top with the fruit.

4. Place the preserves in a small bowl and microwave on HIGH for 30 seconds, until warm and thin, then brush over the fruit. Serve at room temperature or chilled.

bank a batch Assemble the tart and store for up to 3 days in the refrigerator.

Blueberry–Nectarine Galette

A galette (or *crostata* in Italian) is a flat crust of pastry covered with sugar, pastry cream, or fruit. In this recipe, I top a refrigerated piecrust with a combination of peaches, blueberries, and cinnamon before folding the edges of the crust up slightly over the filling. Why add cornstarch? It helps thicken the fruit's juices as the galette cooks, creating a wonderfully thick filling.

Total Time: 30–35 minutes
Prep time: 10–15 minutes
Walk-away time: 20 minutes

Serves 6

One 9-inch refrigerated piecrust

2 medium ripe nectarines or peaches, peeled, pitted, and thinly sliced

1 cup fresh or frozen blueberries (keep frozen until ready to use)

2 tablespoons sugar

1 teaspoon ground cinnamon

1 teaspoon cornstarch

1. Preheat the oven to 375°F. Unroll the piecrust onto a large baking sheet.

2. In a large bowl, combine the nectarines, blueberries, sugar, cinnamon, and cornstarch and toss to combine. Arrange the fruit mixture in the center of the pie crust, leaving a 2-inch border around the edges. Pull up the sides of the crust slightly and fold over the filling, covering it somewhat, but leaving the center uncovered. Bake until the crust is golden brown, about 20 minutes.

make it a meal kit Assemble the galette, cover with plastic wrap, and refrigerate for up to 2 days. When ready to finish, bake as directed.

have it your way Instead of nectarines and blueberries, try apples and dried cranberries or pears and slivered almonds.

Strawberry Soup

Soup for dessert? Yes, when it's made from sweet strawberries. The berries are livened up with orange juice, then turned into a rich and creamy soup with the help of yogurt and vanilla. In this recipe, I serve the soup with whipped topping on top, but sometimes I swirl it into the soup just before serving.

Total Time: 10 minutes

Prep time: 10 minutes

Serves 4

2 cups hulled and sliced fresh or thawed frozen strawberries

1 cup orange juice

1 cup vanilla yogurt

½ teaspoon vanilla extract

Whipped topping as needed

Fresh mint sprigs (optional)

In a blender, combine all the ingredients except the whipped topping and mint and process until smooth. Ladle the soup into bowls and top with a dollop of whipped topping. Garnish with mint if desired.

make it a meal kit Make the soup and store in a sealable container for up to 3 days in the refrigerator. Garnish just before serving.

bank a batch Make a double batch of the soup and store the extra for up to 3 months in the freezer. Thaw overnight in the refrigerator (I don't recommend thawing in the microwave). Garnish just before serving.

have it your way You may substitute fresh or frozen raspberries or blackberries for the strawberries if desired.

Brown Sugar–Glazed Pineapple with Toasted Almonds & Coconut

Because pineapple is pretty tart, I love to add brown sugar to sweeten the flesh, then bake the sugar-topped fruit with nuts and coconut. The pineapple gets tender and caramelized, and the almonds and coconut are toasted to perfection.

Total Time: 20–25 minutes

Prep time: 10 minutes

Walk-away time:
10–15 minutes

Serves 4

Cooking spray

12 pineapple rings (fresh or canned in juice)

¼ cup firmly packed light brown sugar

¼ cup slivered almonds

¼ cup sweetened flaked coconut

1. Preheat the oven to 375°F. Coat a large baking sheet with cooking spray.

2. Arrange the pineapple rings on the prepared sheet and sprinkle the brown sugar, almonds, and coconut over the top. Bake until the almonds and coconut are golden brown and pineapple is tender, 10 to 15 minutes.

have it your way Fresh peach slices also work very well.

Orange-Poached Pears with Fudge Sauce

Most people relish the thought of slicing into a tender pear that's been simmering in a flavorful, sweet broth. What they don't like is taking the time to poach the pear first. In this recipe, you can poach the pears as instructed, *or* you can used canned pears (see Have It Your Way) and slash the cooking time.

Total Time: 45 minutes
Prep time: 10 minutes
Walk-away time: 35 minutes

Serves 4

1 cup orange juice

1 orange, left unpeeled and cut into ¼-inch-thick rounds

¼ cup sugar

5 whole cloves

1 teaspoon vanilla extract

4 pears, peeled with stems intact

1 cup prepared fudge topping or fudge sauce

1. In a medium saucepan, combine the orange juice, sliced orange, sugar, cloves, and vanilla. Set the pan over high heat and bring to a simmer. Add the pears, reduce the heat to low, cover, and simmer for 15 minutes. Uncover and simmer until the liquid thickens and reduces and the pears are tender, about another 20 minutes.

2. Warm the fudge topping in a small saucepan over low heat or in the microwave for 1 minute on HIGH, until warm.

3. Remove the pears from the liquid and transfer to shallow dessert bowls. Remove the cloves from the poaching liquid and spoon the liquid over the pears. Spoon the warm fudge sauce over the top and serve immediately.

make it a meal kit Combine the poaching liquid (the orange juice through the vanilla) and store for up to 3 days in the refrigerator. When ready to finish, transfer the liquid to a saucepan and finish as directed. Or, poach the pears and store them for up to 3 days in the refrigerator (in the poaching liquid). Reheat the pears in the liquid in a saucepan over medium heat or in the microwave for a few minutes on HIGH before topping with the fudge sauce.

have it your way To cut cooking time drastically, substitute canned pears. Instead of simmering covered for 15 minutes, simply prepare the poaching liquid as directed, add the canned pears, and simmer for 5 to 10 minutes to allow the flavors to permeate the pears.

Grilled Orange Slices with Frozen Yogurt & Raspberry–Nutella Sauce

Grilling fruit is a fantastic way to bring out its natural sweetness. If you don't have an outdoor grill (or don't want to fire it up just for dessert), you can easily grill the orange slices on a stovetop grill pan or griddle or in a large skillet over medium high heat.

Total Time: 15 minutes

Prep time: 10 minutes

Active cooking time: 5 minutes

Serves 4

Cooking spray

2 oranges, left unpeeled and sliced into ¼-inch-thick rounds

½ cup Nutella or chocolate syrup

¼ cup raspberry preserves

2 cups vanilla frozen yogurt

1. Coat an outdoor grill or stovetop grill pan with cooking spray and preheat to medium high.

2. Arrange the orange slices on the hot grill and grill until golden brown, about 2 minutes per side.

3. In a medium bowl, combine the Nutella and preserves. Cover and microwave on HIGH for 1 minute, until warm. Mix well to combine.

4. Arrange the orange slices on shallow dessert plates and spoon the frozen yogurt over the top. Top with the sauce and serve immediately.

make it a meal kit Grill the orange slices. Combine the Nutella and preserves. Store each separately for up to 3 days in the refrigerator. When ready to finish, warm the orange slices in the microwave for 30 seconds on HIGH. Heat the sauce in a small saucepan over medium heat or in the microwave for 1 minute on HIGH. Serve as directed.

have it your way Mix up the flavors in your sauce; instead of raspberry preserves, try strawberry, blackberry, or apricot preserves or orange marmalade. You may also choose any flavor of frozen yogurt or ice cream.

Quick Fix Fruit Crumble

Fruit crumbles are so easy to prepare from scratch, and, when you make your own, *you* choose the fruit and *you* create the topping, meaning you can add more nuts, different nuts, more sugar, less sugar, and so on.

Total Time: 25–30 minutes
Prep time: 10–15 minutes
Walk-away time: 15 minutes

Serves 4

4 cups pitted and sliced fresh peaches or thawed frozen peach slices

⅓ cup all-purpose flour

⅓ cup rolled oats

2 to 3 tablespoons vegetable oil

2 tablespoons light brown sugar

1 teaspoon ground cinnamon

½ cup chopped walnuts or pecans

1. Preheat the oven to 400°F.

2. Arrange the peaches in the bottom of a shallow 7x11-inch baking dish.

3. In a small bowl, combine the flour, oats, 2 tablespoons of the oil, the brown sugar, and cinnamon. Stir with a fork until the mixture is crumbly, adding more oil if necessary. Fold in the nuts. Sprinkle the topping over the peaches and bake until golden brown, about 15 minutes.

make it a meal kit Assemble the crumble in advance, cover with plastic wrap, and store for up to 2 days in the refrigerator. Remove the plastic and bake as directed just before serving (bake the crumble during dinner so it will be hot when you're finished eating).

have it your way You may substitute cored and sliced apples or pears or mixed berries for the peaches if desired. When using frozen berries, there's no need to thaw them before using.

5-Ingredient Sweet Rice Pudding with Mango

We love dried mango so much in my house that I have to get huge bags at the warehouse store to make sure I always have some in the pantry. In this Moroccan-inspired dessert, it's the star attraction in a creamy, super-sweet rice pudding that boasts the warm flavor of cinnamon.

Total Time: 10 minutes

Prep time: 5 minutes

Active cooking time: 5 minutes

Serves 4

1 cup instant white rice

One 12-ounce can sweetened condensed milk

½ cup diced dried mango

1 teaspoon ground cinnamon

Fresh mint sprigs (optional)

1. In a medium saucepan, combine the rice, condensed milk, mango, and cinnamon. Set the pan over medium-high heat and bring to a simmer. Reduce the heat to low, cover, and simmer until the liquid is absorbed, about 5 minutes.

2. Spoon the rice pudding into bowls and garnish with mint if desired.

make it a meal kit Make the pudding in advance and store in a sealable container for up to 4 days in the refrigerator. Serve chilled, or reheat in the microwave for a few minutes on HIGH.

have it your way Instead of dried mango, try dried papaya, dried currants, dried blueberries, dried cherries, or dried cranberries.

To make the pudding with regular rice, add 1 cup of milk when you add the condensed milk and simmer for 20 minutes, until the liquid is absorbed.

Anita's Blueberry Cobbler

You'll cherish this warm, wonderful dessert when you need a little comfort after a hard day. It's especially fantastic with vanilla ice cream.

Total Time: 50–65 minutes
Prep time: 15–20 minutes
Walk-away time: 35–45 minutes

Serves 8 to 10

Cooking spray

One 16-ounce bag (2 cups) frozen blueberries (keep frozen until ready to use)

1½ cups sugar, divided

1 cup all-purpose flour

1 teaspoon baking powder

½ cup (1 stick) unsalted butter, softened

¾ cup milk

1. Preheat the oven to 350°F. Coat a 9x12-inch baking pan with cooking spray.

2. In a large bowl, combine the blueberries and ½ cup of the sugar. Toss to combine and set aside.

3. In a medium bowl, combine the remaining 1 cup sugar, the flour, and the baking powder.

4. In a large bowl, beat the butter and milk together until smooth. Gradually beat the flour mixture into the butter mixture until smooth. Pour the batter into the prepared pan, then scatter the blueberries over the batter, letting them sink in, without mixing. Bake until the top is golden brown, 35 to 45 minutes. Let cool slightly before serving.

make it a meal kit Combine the blueberries and ½ cup of the sugar and store in a sealable container or plastic bag for up to 2 days in the freezer. Combine the remaining 1 cup sugar, the flour, and the baking powder and store at room temperature for up to 3 days. Finish as directed.

bank a batch Double the recipe and bake in 2 baking pans. When cool, cover the extra cobbler with plastic wrap, then aluminum foil, and freeze for up to 3 months. Thaw overnight at room temperature. To warm the thawed cobbler, place in a preheated 300°F oven for 15 minutes before serving.

have it your way Instead of blueberries, try frozen raspberries, fresh or frozen blackberries or strawberries (or a combination), or frozen sliced peaches.

Chocolate-Covered Pretzels

I love making huge batches of these chocolate-dunked pretzel rods and then giving them as gifts. I adorn the chocolate (I often use both white and dark) with a variety of toppings and, when dry, I assemble the rods in pretty vases with a bow. It's simple, but it makes a striking presentation and gift.

Total Time: 15–20 minutes

Cook time: 5 minutes

Prep time: 10–15 minutes

Serves 6 to 12

One 12-ounce bag semisweet chocolate morsels

1 cup finely chopped walnuts

24 pretzel rods

1. Melt the chocolate in a double boiler or in a large bowl set over simmering water or in the microwave for a few minutes on HIGH (stirring every minute). Spread the nuts over a large plate.

2. Dip each pretzel rod halfway into the chocolate and turn to coat. Transfer the chocolate-covered pretzel to the walnuts and turn to coat. Place on a sheet of waxed paper to cool. Repeat with the remaining pretzels.

bank a batch Make a double batch and store the extra in freezer bags for up to 3 months in the freezer. No need to thaw before serving.

have it your way Additional fun toppings for the pretzels (in addition to or instead of walnuts) include colored sprinkles, chopped peanuts and almonds, shredded coconut, and crushed peppermint candy.

Chocolate–Caramel Fondue

When I was growing up, fondue pots were the rage. This is my version of chocolate fondue, a caramel-spiked chocolate dipping sauce that's truly amazing.

Total Time: 15 minutes
Cook time: 5 minutes
Prep time: 10 minutes

Serves 8 (with extra sauce for the fridge or freezer!)

One 16-ounce bag semisweet chocolate morsels

1 cup store-bought caramel sauce

½ cup milk (preferably 1% milk-fat or higher)

ASSORTED INGREDIENTS FOR DUNKING

Sliced bananas

Sliced apples

Sliced peaches

Angel food cake, cut into cubes

Marshmallows

Graham crackers

1. Melt the chocolate in a double boiler or in a large bowl set over simmering water or in the microwave for a few minutes on HIGH (stirring every minute). Stir in the caramel sauce and milk until blended and smooth.

2. Remove from the heat and transfer to a serving bowl. Arrange the fruit, cake, and other goodies around the chocolate mixture and start dunking!

make it a meal kit Make the chocolate fondue and store in a sealable container for up to 1 week in the refrigerator or up to 3 months in the freezer. Thaw overnight in the refrigerator or in the microwave for a few minutes on LOW. Reheat in a medium saucepan over low heat or in the microwave for a few minutes on HIGH.

Banana Cream Pie Parfaits

Banana cream pie most certainly isn't a Quick Fix dessert. But making a parfait that tastes like the real pie is a Quick Fix delight. You can crush the vanilla wafer cookies by putting them in a plastic bag, then mashing them with a rolling pin, meat mallet, or heavy skillet.

Total Time: 15 minutes

Prep time: 15 minutes

Serves 4

2 cups vanilla yogurt

2 large ripe bananas, peeled and sliced

1 teaspoon vanilla extract

32 vanilla wafer cookies, crushed

One 16-ounce container nondairy whipped topping

Unsweetened cocoa powder

1. In a blender, combine the yogurt, bananas, and vanilla and process until smooth.

2. Arrange half of the crushed cookies in the bottom of 4 tall glasses. Top with half of the banana mixture. Top with the remaining crushed cookies and remaining banana mixture. Top with the whipped topping, sift cocoa over the top, and serve.

make it a meal kit Assemble the parfaits, cover with plastic wrap, and store for up to 2 days in the refrigerator. Sift the cocoa over the parfaits just before serving.

have it your way Instead of bananas, try raspberries, blackberries, blueberries, or sliced peaches and strawberries. You can also substitute any flavored yogurt variety or use low-fat sour cream.

Quick Fix Recipe Index

5 INGREDIENT OR LESS RECIPES

Grilled Orange Slices with Frozen
Yogurt & Raspberry–Nutella Sauce
(page 295)
5-Ingredient Sweet Rice Pudding with
Mango (page 297)
Chocolate-Covered Pretzels (page 299)

MARINADES AND GLAZES

*(Marinate chicken breasts, turkey tender-
loin, pork tenderloin, pork chops, and lean
steak for up to 24 hours. Marinate fish and
shellfish for up to 30 minutes. Drain, then
roast, bake, or grill as desired.)*

Honey–Sesame Dressing (page 128) with
shrimp, salmon, or chicken breasts
Strawberry Glaze (page 142) with scallops,
tilapia, halibut, or chicken breasts
Orange–Hoisin Glaze (page 151) with
shrimp, salmon, or chicken breasts
Garlic–Rosemary Marinade (page 179)
with pork tenderloin or chicken breasts
Wasabi–Mustard Dressing (page 188) with
tuna steaks or chicken breasts
Chile–Lime Marinade (page 193) with
pork tenderloin or chicken breasts
Ginger–Hoisin Glaze (page 217) with
pork tenderloin or chicken breasts
Pineapple Vinaigrette (page 243) with
shrimp or scallops
Strawberry–Sherry Vinaigrette (page 279)
with pork tenderloin, chicken breasts,
or turkey tenderloin
Citrus Vinaigrette (page 280) with tilapia,
halibut, or chicken breasts
Honey–Maple Vinaigrette (page 282) with
pork tenderloin or turkey tenderloin

SIMMER SAUCES

*(With simmer sauces, you can either sim-
mer the sauce and serve it over the suggested
protein, or actually cook the protein in the
simmering sauce for a quick one-pot meal.)*

Béchamel Sauce (page 66) with turkey
tenderloin or salmon
Pesto Cream (page 68) with chicken
breasts or sliced grilled flank steak

Spicy Raisin Ketchup (page 98) with
meatballs, roast beef, or pork
tenderloin
Orange–Ginger Sauce (page 102) with
salmon, shrimp, or turkey tenderloin
Merlot & Raspberry Sauce (page 103)
with sliced grilled flank steak, pork
tenderloin, or tilapia
Apricot Sauce (page 127) with pork chops
or shrimp
Raisin–Cognac Sauce (page 141) with
any sliced grilled lean steak or turkey
tenderloin
Cherry–Port Sauce (page 148) with any
sliced grilled lean steak or chicken
breasts
Mustard–Sage Sauce (page 150) with
chicken breasts or salmon
Maple–Mustard Sauce (page 153) with
salmon, scallops, or chicken breasts
Root Beer BBQ Sauce (page 164) with
chicken breasts or turkey tenderloin
Thai Peanut Sauce (page 182) with
shrimp or chicken breasts
Tomato Soup French Dressing (page 194)
with pasta, chicken sausage, or
chicken breasts
Tangy Tomato Dipping Sauce (page 210)
with chicken meatballs or pork
tenderloin
Mango–Ginger Sauce (page 228) with
pork tenderloin or shrimp
Chipotle–Citrus Sauce (page 233) with
sliced grilled flank steak or chicken
breasts

SIDE SAUCES, SALSAS, PESTOS,
AND OTHER TOPPINGS

Curry Cream (page 92) with turkey
tenderloin, flank steak, salmon, tilapia,
or halibut
Pistachio–Parsley Pesto (page 104) with
flank steak, pork chops, or shrimp
Green Spinach–Horseradish Sauce
(page 112) with salmon or pork chops
Artichoke–Basil Pesto (page 114) with
pasta, pork chops, shrimp, or salmon

Rhubarb Chutney (page 136) with
chicken breasts, turkey tenderloin,
or chicken sausage
Cranberry–Horseradish Sauce (page 137)
with flank steak or turkey tenderloin
Apricot Mayonnaise (page 138) with
chicken breasts, shrimp, or salmon
Avocado–Mango Salsa (page 143) with
shrimp or chicken breasts
Jalapeño–Apple Chutney (page 156)
with pork chops, chicken breasts, or
flank steak
Spicy Rémoulade (page 178) with chicken
breasts, pork tenderloin, salmon, or tuna
Buttermilk–Horseradish Sauce (page 181)
with salmon, tuna, or pork tenderloin
Ancho–Honey Mayo (page 187) with
chicken breasts, turkey tenderloin, or
pork chops
Mint–Cilantro Mojo (page 190) with pork
tenderloin, lamb, shrimp, or scallops
Parsley–Basil Chimichurri (page 192)
with tilapia, halibut, salmon, shrimp,
lamb, or chicken breasts
Jalapeño–Papaya Salsa (page 206) with
flank steak or pork tenderloin
Salsa Verde (page 211) with any lean steak
or chicken breasts
Lime & Roasted Garlic Coulis (page 214)
with chicken breasts, tilapia, halibut,
or salmon
Pico de Gallo–Black Bean Aïoli (page 218)
with pork chops or turkey tenderloin
Shallot–Lemon Butter (page 224) with
chicken breasts, shrimp, or pasta
Chipotle Aïoli (page 226) with flank steak
or pork tenderloin
Cucumber–Mint Relish (page 230) with
lamb, salmon, or chicken breasts
Apple–Horseradish Cream (page 237)
with shrimp, chicken breasts, or pork
chops
Chipotle–Cilantro Butter (page 265) with
tuna steaks, chicken breasts, or pasta
Buttermilk–Blue Cheese Dressing
(page 270) with chicken breasts,
salmon, or pasta

Index

Equivalency Charts

LIQUID/DRY MEASURES	
U.S.	**METRIC**
¼ teaspoon	1.25 milliliters
½ teaspoon	2.5 milliliters
1 teaspoon	5 milliliters
1 tablespoon (3 teaspoons)	15 milliliters
1 fluid ounce (2 tablespoons)	30 milliliters
¼ cup	60 milliliters
⅓ cup	80 milliliters
½ cup	120 milliliters
1 cup	240 milliliters
1 pint (2 cups)	480 milliliters
1 quart (4 cups; 32 ounces)	960 milliliters
1 gallon (4 quarts)	3.84 liters
1 ounce (by weight)	28 grams
1 pound	454 grams
2.2 pounds	1 kilogram

OVEN TEMPERATURES		
°F	**GAS MARK**	**°C**
250	½	120
275	1	140
300	2	150
325	3	165
350	4	180
375	5	190
400	6	200
425	7	220
450	8	230
475	9	240
500	10	260
550	Broil	290